RENAISSANCE MAN AND CREATIVE THINKING

A History of Concepts of Harmony
1400-1700

HARVESTER STUDIES IN PHILOSOPHY

General Editor: Margaret A. Boden
Reader in Philosophy and Psychology, University of Sussex

Harvester Studies in Philosophy is a new series which aims to stress the wider implications of philosophical discussion. Many books are cross-disciplinary in emphasis, and problems of general concern predominate.

The philosophy of mind and of psychology are prominently featured in the series. So too are the philosophy of science, particularly the human and biological sciences.

Other titles in preparation

Renaissance Man and Creative Thinking

A History of Concepts of Harmony 1400-1700

DOROTHY KOENIGSBERGER

Senior Lecturer in the History of Ideas, School of Humanities,
The Hatfield Polytechnic

THE HARVESTER PRESS

First published in Great Britain in 1979 by
THE HARVESTER PRESS LIMITED
Publisher: John Spiers
2 Stanford Terrace, Hassocks, Sussex

© Dorothy Koenigsberger, 1979

British Library Cataloguing in Publication Data
Koenigsberger, Dorothy
  Renaissance Man and creative thinking.
  1. Renaissance   2. Analogy   3. Europe–Intellectual life
  I. Title
169'.094   AZ331

ISBN 0-85527-554 5

Printed in England by Redwood Burn Limited
Trowbridge & Esher

to
Madeline Robinton
and
Ron Fryer

CONTENTS

ACKNOWLEDGEMENTS

For their suggestions, criticism and advice I am most grateful to: Herbert Butterfield, Terrence Cave, W.R. Fryer, Joan Kelly-Gadol, Dietrich Gerhard, Henry Guerlac, Bernard Hamilton, Denys Hay, Ivor Keys, H.G. Koenigsberger, Fred Marcham and D.P. Walker.

I would also like to thank: my parents, Margaret and Henry Romano, and The Society for Italian Historical Studies for their prize for an earlier version of this essay in 1969, and also Margaret and Jim Jacob and Madeline Robinton for splendid encouragement and support.

PREFACE

The goal of this essay is to help historians to form clearer impressions of some of the roles of a highly evocative image, the notion of harmony. The interpretation is of selected examples of the thinking of creative persons living between the fifteenth and the seventeenth century. Analogy here is not primarily considered as an intellectual process and/or method of reasoning, but rather as a suggestive area of reference for the framing of assumptions about nature and art. These frequently appear to be important in the examples and in the cultural atmosphere of this period.

> '...Nor must we withdraw from the analogy of nature, since that is commonly simple and always in harmony with itself.'
>
> Isaac Newton

Pythagoras is said to have discovered that nature was harmonious by drawing an analogy between numbers and sounds. Ratios between low numbers appeared in the rates of string vibration of consonant tones. From this inspiration a long historical tradition developed wherein thinkers assumed that the universe was harmonious.

During the Middle Ages harmony had also been associated with other assumptions. These emphasized the divisions between the ideal and the real, between the heavens and the earth. The universe was, of course, harmonious; but ideal harmony was only seen to be dimly reflected in life on earth.

In *Renaissance Man and Creative Thinking* the history of the assumption of natural harmony is the story of a shift from the traditional vision of harmony, that which was only vaguely reflected in the region of human experience, to a modern and dynamic vision. Natural harmony can be recognized directly from experience. Consequently men's knowledge of nature is infinitely perfectible and scientific progress is possible.

In several important instances the assumption of an analogy between the whole and the parts of nature provided the image and inspiration of progressive attitudes in the learned world. Some Renaissance versions of this analogy tended to minimize the hierarchical divisions between the whole and the parts. Thus the experience of the examples in nature could be seen to lead directly to recognition of its first principles, of its order, harmony or laws. This did not happen all at once, for men only experience parts and that only over a period of time. However, instead of seeing through a glass darkly they saw what was actual and real.

True to this modern position, many Renaissance and seventeenth century thinkers tended to see the arts and all human works as having value in so far as they expressed the analogies in nature. This expression could be physical; for instance, Pythagorean proportions imitated in architecture. And it could also be psychological, for instance, Renaissance music recreating the passions of the soul. In either case the creation and experience of works was not wholly social or subjective. Men designed in imitation of nature. The mind recognized and re-expressed true harmony.

As they saw it, divine ideas were implicit in the creation. In some mysterious way God's order, or his providence, was immanent in the whole and all the parts of the universe all at once. However, the divine order was also accessible and was partly recognizable within human experience. Bit by bit men could perfect their knowledge of nature and imitate it in their works.

Renaissance Man and Creative Thinking explores a rational tradition of *imitazione* in some detail. By rational I mean the Renaissance tendency in theory of knowledge to eliminate hierarchical divisions and characterize the human mind as the agent that could seize the essence of the images and discover the laws of nature. The value of this dynamic vision of progress is unquestionable.

History, however, is not an exercise in logic and so I have had to admit the unusual combination of this sort of rational theory of knowledge with magical theories. I am not, of course, speaking of witchcraft.

Far from eliminating the hierarchies, magical traditions tended to multiply them. The order of the universe and the realm of human experience were seen to be separated by an incredible variety of agencies and spirits, all having powers beyond those of the human mind. It was, however, held that the human mind could summon them, or at least that some human minds could summon them. With Giordano Bruno, for instance, we get a marriage of total contradictions when he combines the philosophy of Nicholas of Cusa, who eliminated the hierarchies and believed in the mind's recognition of the harmony of nature, with occult mysticism and magic, in which the hierarchies were both acknowledged and elaborated. But in historical terms this contradiction is not entirely real.

The essential characteristic of a modern theory of knowledge is not so much its method as its ability to confirm and fortify the human capacity to recognize, understand and even, to some extent, to control the reality of nature. Thus, following along from Cusa, some fifteenth century inventors of linear perspective tended to obscure the hierarchies and emphasize human capacities of recognition and understanding. The proponents of magic called upon and used spiritual agencies in order to achieve these capacities and to accomplish related works. Thus, in the sixteenth and seventeenth centuries, both these contradictory partners confirmed the efficacy of human understanding and the idea of progress.

The association of God, the creator, with man, the maker, and macrocosm directly with microcosm also generally advanced the phenomenon called universality. Historically the *uomo universale* should be associated with beliefs in universal principles or axioms of nature and even with the universal system of knowledge advanced in the French Encyclopaedia of 1751. All of these ideas developed within modern formulations of the assumption of natural harmony, of its imitation in works, and of harmony as the basis of associations between the disciplines.

INTRODUCTION

In his notes on acoustics, Leonardo da Vinci writes:

> Although the voices penetrating the air spread in circular motion from their sources, there is no impediment when the circles from different centres meet, and they penetrate and pass into one another, keeping the centres from which they spring. Because in all cases of motion there is great likeness between water and air.

Leonardo continues with an example. He writes that if two small stones are simultaneously thrown, while at some distance apart, on a sheet of motionless water, you will observe circles formed around the separate percussions. The circles will meet as they increase in size and penetrate and intersect each other. At the same time, however, they will maintain their original centres, the spots hit by the stones. Leonardo says this is because the water only appears to move and, in fact, it does not leave its original position. The reason for this is that the opening made by the stones is closed again immediately. The opening and closing of the water has produced only a shock which may be described as *tremor*, rather than movement. He continues:

> In order to understand better what I mean, watch the blades of straw that . . . are floating in the water, and observe how they do not depart from their original position in spite of the waves underneath them caused by the arrival of the circles.

Then he concludes that since the impression on the water is only tremor and not movement, the circles cannot break one another on meeting. And since the water is of the same quality throughout, its parts transmit the tremor to one another without change of position. Thus, the water which remains in the same position transmits the tremor to its adjacent parts with gradually diminishing force.[1]

On first view this analogy shows itself to be a concise

description of the proposed action of sound waves in the air by a description of the behaviour of tremors on the water. Leonardo's style is persuasive as well as illustrative. For when he introduced the blades of straw floating on the water, he devised a test for confirming that the wavelets did not represent the moving of the water.

Thus, we can see that analogies drawn between different processes, events, and objects can be useful indicators of the ways in which people think. When men use the real or seeming similarities, or the identical likenesses, between one thing and another, when they attempt to describe what is less known from that which they feel they already know, their description by analogy provides a miniature picture of their associations, of what they assume as the important relationship between different things. I think that the pictures drawn from the content of analogies used in the past can provide valuable material for historians of ideas. By discussing a selection of such pictures, I hope to be able to depict the role and the importance of the analogy between the whole and the parts of nature from the Renaissance through the seventeenth century.

At first reading, the analogy that I have been quoting from Leonardo seems to be used simply as a means of description. However, I believe that I can suggest a fuller picture of what Leonardo was doing with this analogy and make the possibly wider implications of his use of it plausible. The key phrase is, '... because in all cases of motion there is great likeness between water and air.' The phrase implies a more general analogy, one between motion in water and motion in air, and this general statement involves a greater number of possible similarities than did the analogy between tremors and sound waves. Was this more general analogy real for Leonardo? Did he use anything similar at any other time or was it just a convenient way of making this one point? Confirmation of the fact that it was important and that Leonardo generally believed in, and used, motion in water in an analogous relationship to motion in air, is suggested by many of the analogies that he drew in the context of his studies of the flight of birds. In one of these he compares the control of the movement of a ship in water with that of a bird in the air. An almost imperceptible movement of the rudder, Leonardo says, can turn a ship, in spite of its large size, heavy cargo, and all the water which presses on it from all directions, and in spite of the winds which fill its sails. Leonardo continues:

> Therefore, we may be certain, in the case of those birds which can support themselves above the course of the winds without beating their wings, that the slight movement of the wing or tail which will

serve them to enter either below or above the wind will suffice to prevent the fall of the said bird.[2]

Other related analogies appear in his writings. Also Leonardo put it in a nutshell: 'Swimming on the water teaches men what birds do in the air.'[3]

It is generally recognized that the study of flight fascinated Leonardo. He was trying to find out how men could fly, and the analogies that I have mentioned here show that one of the important ways that he did this was by watching activities on the water. Not only does swimming describe what birds do, it teaches men about both phenomena. In some ways these events, the swimming and the flying, are analogous, and it is implied that they are likely to be analogous because nature itself is a harmonious order in which many analogies are expressed between the parts. The operations of all of the parts compromise harmony of the whole.

This example shows Leonardo observing nature closely. Yet, at the same time he is also drawing upon a grand body of assumptions that were popular both before and during the Renaissance. These involved nature and the universe and what were thought to be the essentially harmonious principles of nature and the universe. Leonardo is assuming that there is an analogy between the whole and the parts of nature. The whole expresses an order in which the parts, in this instance the mediums of air and water, bear analogies to each other. In this example the analogies were close. The objective behaviour of bodies moving through a medium of water can give scientific information about bodies moving through air. But this analogy is not only a useful learning device, it is also the expression of a point of view, of Leonardo's view of likelihood in nature. And in this instance his objective conclusion was sound. However, Leonardo's more general, or wider, assumptions about nature involve many different conditions of likeness. In the second chapter his parallel between man and the earth where he says that the bones are like the rocks is cited. Nicholas of Cusa also used this ancient analogy. Certainly bones and rocks can be seen to perform some common functions but, all in all, this is a metaphorical parallel. It is important to realize, however, that metaphorical analogues like this one are the close relations of scientific analogies, like those in the first example. When a Renaissance thinker expresses some form of the analogy between the whole and the parts of nature he is never doing less than confirming the harmony or orderliness of nature and the reality of the world, but he is not necessarily being scientific or even correct in his idea about that order.

Frequently, the analogy between the whole and the parts of nature was involved with a group of interrelated assumptions that all form the subject matter of this work. These are, that one or another of the arts or that human works, can imitate nature when they are designed so that they embody principles that are natural. Such principles would be expressed in the parts and in the whole of nature. So men can imitate the harmonious relationship between the whole and the parts in various but limited ways so that, for example, a picture can be made to express real beauty, or an invention true mechanical laws. The human mind is clearly implied in the analogy between art and nature because no work can be designed without a designer who, in some way, comprehends the harmony of nature. Another way of expressing this version of the analogy is that, as God creates, man comprehends. Human knowledge is seen as a partial and limited analogue of divine creativity. In this philosophical way, man is made in the image of God.

At the same time we know that man cannot wholly be the image of God: for, man himself is created whereas God is uncreated and eternal. Like all things in the universe, man is limited and finite. Thus, in these finite ways man can be seen to be also the image of the universe, a microcosm. This microcosmic assumption was expressed in many forms ranging from strict astrological analogies to looser parallels between man and nature. It is not my point here to codify all the possible forms of expression of this group of interrelated analogies; instead, I am identifying my subject. I am concerned with this group of analogies in the precise ways that they were assumed and/or expressed by a selection of early modern thinkers and I am hopeful that the examples will provide a way to see the historical role and the character of this body of assumptions.

I begin with a picture of these assumptions from the thoughts of Nicholas of Cusa, Leon Battista Alberti, and Leonardo da Vinci. This is because these three have a relation to both the arts and the sciences and also because I think they were involved with each other's assumptions. By this I mean that Alberti and Leonardo were influenced by Cusa's view of knowledge and reality.

The group of basic assumptions was certainly not exclusive to them and, from the beginning, I also identify past traditions and different forms of the expression of these assumptions. A central chapter, dealing with the antithesis of harmony, begins to describe the wider historical field in which I attempt to see this group of assumptions at work. Vincenzo Galilei, Descartes, Francis Bacon and others provide examples in the ways that they saw harmony. General attitudes such as optimism, the desire for

efficacy and the expression of universality are brought out of
this material.

The historical role of assumptions of natural harmony certainly cannot be drawn from a narrow view, nor can it be wholly
abstracted from the examples of its use. Harmony is always
pleasant to generally contemplate. However, its historical significance is elusive. Like the unfailing smile on the lips of Brown-
ing's 'My Last Duchess', it can look like everything and nothing
at the same time.

While acknowledging this, the elusiveness of the historical
significance of the notion of harmony, I still point to the fact that
there is nothing terribly elusive about the above examples from
Leonardo. Likewise, it is possible to develop a series of examples
that can illustrate the role of the analogy between the whole and
the parts of nature, or one of its participant similarities or parallels.[4] The interpretation of such a series would go a long way
towards delineating the historical role of assumptions of harmony. My approach is to develop my argument from a number
of examples that are generally seen to be important in the history of thought. For this I choose leading figures and works that
are known and accessible.[5] Although sometimes I unearth the
examples myself and also show how they contribute to the
historian's developing picture of the role of the assumption of
harmony, sometimes I also use examples that have been provided by others and that are generally known. However, I interpret these and try to show how the examples dramatize the
shifting vision and role of the analogy.

I am not really aiming at any codification of analogy as a
method of reasoning at all. I want primarily to discover the
significance of the analogy between the whole and the parts of
nature in the mentalities of the individuals who evoke it, and to
discover something of the relation between their thinking in this
vein and the surrounding European culture.

This forces me to use ideas that sometimes arouse deep scholarly suspicions. A long dualist tradition makes all of us more at
ease with reasoning than with imagination. It seems clearer to
speak of more thought than of thinking, and more of the argument than of the mentality of the one who argues and of his
cultural biases. Despite this, many cultural historians now acknowledge the value of trying to uncover imaginative assumptions as well as tracing out the internal logic of arguments in
treatises. One can go about this in a conscientious way with the
understanding that an imperfect analogy, expressed by a past
thinker, does not indicate an ill-considered argument in the
mind of the historian concerned with the role of that analogy.
Yes, it must go this far: not only will I use similarities of struc-

ture and/or function between parts as real analogies, or joint
participants in a greater whole, I will even use a thinker's
assumption that he is, in fact, drawing some sort of analogy,
whether his parallel has any objective validity or not, or even
whether it is, in the logical sense, a true analogy or not.

The shifts within the frame of reference of the thinkers in the
examples is the thing that really interests me. And so my attempt
is to make my examples decisive rather than comprehensive. In
no way do I see myself writing an intellectual history of the west
from the fifteenth to the seventeenth century, nor a Renaissance
history, nor a conceptual monograph about analogy, or time, or
any of the other germinal concepts that appear in this work. My
aim is far more modest. The points I have to make, through
selected cases, are, I think, relevant to and throw some real light
upon the creative imagination in the period of cultural history
between the fifteenth and the end of the seventeenth century.

Notes to Introduction

1. Leonardo da Vinci, *Literary Works,* ed. J.P. Richter (Oxford
   1939) (1130 A)
2. *Ibid.* (1114 A)
3. *Ibid.* (1114 B)
4. As this is not a monograph, I make no claim to be covering all
   the literature on all of the figures or themes of the essay. My
   points rest largely upon their relevance to the primary material
   cited and also upon the comparative relations that I draw between the selected cases.
5. These are not all the possible works either. The theme is so huge
   that it might involve a discussion of all the important works of
   over two hundred years. This would hardly be the point in
   attempting to get at a general notion. The essay is developed
   from selected cases and these are thought to be sufficiently
   important to be able to disclose something of the real importance of harmony.

1
LEON BATTISTA ALBERTI: AESTHETICS AND SCIENCE

> ... Nay all the analogy of nature is in favour ...
> Samuel Taylor Coleridge

Natural harmony

The dominant analogy, which is indeed the dominant philosophical idea in the works of Leon Battista Alberti (1404-1472), is one that was very old and that was revived and held by many of the men whose ideas are considered part of the positive fruits of Renaissance thought.[1] Essentially, Alberti's version of the idea is summarized in his belief that the different parts of nature are related to each other by means of an analogy based on numbers. The features of this analogy can and must be extended to works of art to make them aesthetically satisfying to men. He expresses it concisely in *De Re Aedificatoria* when he writes:

> I am every day more and more convinced of the truth of Pythagoras's saying, that nature is sure to act consistently, and with a constant analogy in all her operations: from which I conclude that the same numbers by means of which the agreement of sounds affects our ears with delight, are the very same which please our eyes and our mind.[2]

Alberti's version of this analogy and the methods by which he translated it into theories of art are of interest because the implications of his ideas extend far beyond purely aesthetic questions and because he personally embodied many of the characteristics that are associated with the description Renaissance Man. Therefore he is interesting in his own right, but he can also serve as an example which we might compare and contrast with others for whom this particular analogy was a dominant theme. The result of these comparisons may indicate many subtle changes in the imaginative framework of thinkers in general during the early modern period.

Before beginning to describe Alberti's belief in an analogy of universal form we must note that he discussed all the details of his ideology with reference to particular problems, both practical and theoretical. Alberti did not write a philosophy of nature. He never gave a complete description of the manner of operation, or even of the total structure, of his harmonious universe. However, he talked about such a structure or used ideas which referred to it while he examined the particular questions that interested him. So Alberti's idea of harmony appears in the form of an assumption rather than of a hypothesis, and certainly never in the form of a completely argued philosophy and cosmology.

The fact that Alberti's views of nature and art were based on a universal analogy, but presented only in this practical manner, certainly leaves interpretative problems. Principally, Alberti expresses his concept of natural harmony indirectly, in the course of arguments that concentrate mainly on artistic problems. Nevertheless it is possible to form a picture of his assumptions about nature from these arguments. If this picture is compared with both past and Renaissance ideas of harmony, Alberti's view often appears to be rather more sophisticated and modern. For instance, medieval analogies between parts and the whole of creation had often been symbolic in a purely literary or contemplative sense. The parallels that they had expressed pertained to a world of archetypal ideas that was only thought to be very dimly reflected in the actual physical world and in human experience. Nonetheless these vague analogies had expressed matters of great metaphysical importance. In the same spirit, Alberti's mathematical and harmonic analogies also had great metaphysical importance for him, but his conceptions show a vision based on a more integrated analogy between actual nature and the divine ideas. He saw a graspable and consistent natural order that was stimulating to men first in their desire to comprehend it, and then in their complimentary desire to reproduce natural harmony in works, in the human arts and sciences. By contrast, earlier mystical Neo-Platonists had been far more concerned with philosophical realizations than they had been with helping men to embody ideal forms in mere human works. This is the attitude that comes across in the classical *Consolation of Philosophy* of Boethius, a work that profoundly influenced medieval Neo-Platonists. Here God puts eternal ideas in nature, and men look towards them in order to comfort their spirits; but they have to gaze through a mass of obscuring material that philosophy can only partially uncloud. Hence Boethius' Lady Philosophy will use the arts of rhetoric and music to preface her teachings; but the precepts that she teaches can only be attained through serious philosophical contemplation. In this tradition, no art form could convey these precepts by means of aesthetic impressions. Such directness, straight from the eye to the ideas could only be seen to come about in the Renaissance, in one of Alberti's buildings for example. Music, the high art which had traditionally been seen to represent divine harmony, even exalted music, had to be understood intellectually. The music of the mind was the true music. So in the Neo-Platonic tradition, aesthetic experiences, at their best, had represented a preface or an awakening to the arguments of philosophy and the inspirations of the spirit. But later, for Alberti, the aesthetic experience had the moving force of philosophy itself. The work, for instance a building, both as a whole unit and in the proportions between the parts, represented an actual example of divine harmony in experience. This is a conception that raises the value of human works and of human sensibilities in that these actually contribute to knowledge. In the more traditional views even precise mathematical analogies were often intended to allude to or to commemorate higher truths rather than to contain them, or embody them. For a building, such an allusive analogy would be one in which twelve columns might stand for symbols of the apostles, another twelve for the prophets, and so on.[3] The allusions in such an analogy were not of slight importance for the formulators. These parallels had had great mystical significance; but the symbols expressed an accumulation of references to the real blazing truths of archetypes that existed on an entirely different plane of spiritual reality. By contrast, Alberti's analogies were based on a direct recognition and representation of ideal proportions in a work of art. Alberti's formulation of the analogy between the whole and the parts of nature and between the precepts of nature and those of the arts is a truly modern concept because it places actions and works on the same level as thought.

It would be a mistake entirely to separate Alberti from the ancient and medieval Neo-Platonists despite this important and stark difference of values. He took over a great deal from traditional Neo-Platonism and combined it with inspirations from Florentine life in the fifteenth century. Because Alberti never undertook to explain directly about his assumption of harmony of the whole and the parts of nature, he implicitly invites us to fill in many facts from a general knowledge of the traditional views.

Congruity exists in the mind and in nature

Alberti believed that there was an order, involving mutually analogous relations between all parts of nature, and that the structure of this natural form was demonstrated by the mathematical nature of the relationship between the whole and all of its parts, and also by the relationships of the parts to each other. Believing, as he did, that it was not only 'real', but 'right', he called this relationship between the whole and the parts *congruity;* thus he writes:

> The business and office of congruity is to put together members differing from each other in their natures, in such a manner that they may conspire to form a beautiful whole . . . [and he continues]: Nor does this congruity arise so much from the body in which it is found, or any of its members, as from itself, and from nature, so that its true seat is in the mind and in reason . . . [congruity] runs through every part and action of man's life, and every production of nature herself, which are all directed by the law of congruity, nor does nature study anything more than to make all her works absolute and perfect . . .[4]

Congruity was most readily expressed in ratios, and some of these ratios existed in the form of traditionally prescribed proportions.[5] Thus, sometimes Alberti relied on past authorities to tell him what the ideal relationships or proportions were, and sometimes, when authorities were scant, he devised other means of finding out natural proportions. In the case of architecture and building he adopted a system of measuring and proportion that had been recommended by Vitruvius (Pollio Vitruvius was a Roman architect and military engineer of the first century B.C.). The proportions were more generally part of the Pythagorean and Platonic tradition of ideas. These proportions were derived from the numerical relationships of musical concords, from the roots and powers of numbers, or from the means: arithmetical, geometrical or harmonic.[6] The proportions derived from these things were not just workable and good. They were natural proportions that had been placed both in nature and in the mind of man by God. The authorities, the learned men, provided one source for knowing nature's favourite numbers. 'But among these numbers, whether even or uneven, there are some which seem to be greater favourites with nature than others, and more celebrated among learned men.'[7] However, neither learned men, nor ancient works of art in themselves could be seen to be exclusive sources of information about proportions or about the congruity expressed in the natural order. Alberti shows a

very modern cast of mind precisely because he thought that
men's direct experience of nature formed the most important
source of their ability to recognize harmony and goodness, or
indeed, disproportion and badness.

Nature is a book written in God's hand. We identify statements like this with the more progressive sorts of Renaissance
thinking. However, even the more mystical fifteenth-century
philosophy and theology was not entirely empty of such sentiment. I am now thinking specifically of a philosopher known to
Alberti and esteemed by him, of Nicholas of Cusa (1401-
1464).[8] In Cusa's writings, especially in the dialogues entitled
Idiota (1450), the truly wise man is a Socrates-type of figure
who sits in the market place and observes things. He reflects
about all that goes on there, about weight and measure, and
also about ultimate questions of knowledge. From these observations and, even more significantly, from the thought processes
that they inspire, the Idiot, or the unlearned man, teaches both
the scholar and the philosopher. I will speak extensively about
Cusa and about Alberti and Leonardo da Vinci in later chapters;
for, I believe that the Cusan's outlook was highly attractive to
Renaissance minds that were bent on the scientific examination of
phenomena without wanting to abstract this examination from a
more universal context, i.e. from the whole of nature and God.

Alberti can then be seen as one of the originators of this sort
of modern but reverent attitude insofar as he continually
praised the directly inspiring power of Nature in practical
treatises about human arts, actions, and works. Alberti generally praises the first-hand observation of nature, and praises
past authorities in the light of their individual insights. Clearly, it is possible to learn from respected authorities, but it is also
possible to learn from one's contemporaries. Alberti himself
went around to learn from the workmen of the market place.
Perhaps he and the Cusan had had similar motivations?
Everyone knows about this behaviour in Galileo Galilei and in
the natural philosophers of the early seventeenth century, but
this kind of modern attitude to work, and to discovering scientific principles in human works had already begun with some
thinkers in the early fifteenth century. However, the social and
cultural field that could receive and reflect this modern
attitude towards work was far more limited in the early Renaissance than it was one hundred and fifty years later.

Alberti valued insight and understanding for its own sake.
All such knowledge, past or contemporary, learned or
observed, all of it confirmed the important divine gifts to men,
the gift of a capacity to recognize and also of the power to
employ harmonious principles, themselves gained from the

clear and accessible sources in nature and in human experience.

Even at this early stage we should become aware that two
very general sorts of assumptions are involved in Alberti's view
of the analogy-based harmony. The natural harmony that men
found necessary for good design in all of their own constructs,
artistic or institutional, that harmony had to be both immanent
in the world and accessible to the human mind. Therefore
Alberti makes assumptions about the structure of nature and
he also makes assumptions about perception and knowledge.
When reading Alberti one quickly finds out his view of nature,
and also, that he praises human reason and perception to the
point of almost seeming to take these powers for granted. But
he does not quite take them for granted. Even though he
refuses to discuss the problem of how knowing takes place, he
does imply a specific view of this. Eventually I hope to clarify
what his opinions about thinking and knowing might have been
from the context of his more obvious discussions of beauty,
social harmony, and the problems of representation. We start
by being aware that, like many before him, Alberti believed
that the natural order was divinely conceived.[9] What is really
immediately interesting is his advance on the earlier view so
that he included an assumption relating to questions of perception and knowledge. Somehow he saw the presence of the
divine ideas in nature in a way that excluded interference from
hierarchical categories. In other words, instead of men
apprehending the divine forms of nature as reflected through
a glass darkly, they were in some way supposed to be able to
perceive them directly. Naturally, this does not mean that men
were gifted with the capacities to visualize the total harmony of
the universe all at once. But what they could easily see was an
unclouded series of examples before them. This unclouding of
examples removes the physical stigma from base matter, matter
that was supposed to muddle and obscure its own essential
forms, and it also removes the stigma that had been attached to
the senses. The senses can be reliable when the faculty of
reason is ready; so there is no need to resort to introverted
processes for comprehension. From these clear examples
derived from nature and from beautiful works, men can continually sharpen their apprehension of the actual principles of
harmony. Both Alberti and Leonardo advised such a sharpen-
ing process for those who wanted to represent or to use harmonious forms.

Now this sort of a view of knowledge and of representation is
certainly similar to some of the views of Nicholas Cusanus. I
hope to develop the significance of this association in terms of

examples of Alberti's mode of analogy-making, and afterwards
in the thought of Leonardo da Vinci. For now, let it suffice to
say that at one point Alberti allowed a spokesman for his own
views in *I Libri della Famiglia* to express the opinion that men
had been created by God precisely so that they would be able to
recognize the essential harmony of creation. Alberti writes:

> Man was created for the pleasure of God, *to recognize* the primary
> and original source of things amid all the variety, dissimilarity,
> beauty, and multiplicity of animal life, amid all the forms,
> structures, coverings, and colours that characterize the animals.
> He was made to praise God together with universal nature, *seeing*
> in every living thing such great and perfectly matched harmonies
> of variegated voice and verse and music combined in concord and
> loveliness.[10]

We see that man's powers of apprehension are of the greatest
importance to Alberti and this is true even though he tends to
express himself in an oblique manner when it comes to filling
in any details pertaining to methods of knowing.

Alberti refers to man's awareness of the goodness of natural
proportions and of harmony itself in a number of different
ways. For example:

> The most expert artists among the ancients . . . were of the
> opinion that an edifice was like an animal, so that in the formation
> of it we ought to imitate nature . . .

And he continues by inquiring why things are more or less
beautiful and concludes:

> Without question, there is a certain excellence and natural
> beauty in the figures and forms of buildings, which immediately
> strike the mind with pleasure and admiration.[11]

We can perceive natural proportions separately from matter
and materials. Alberti writes:

> We can in our thought and imagination contrive perfect forms
> of buildings entirely separate from matter, by settling and reg-
> ulating in a certain order, the disposition and conjunction of the
> lines and angles. Which being granted we shall call the design a
> firm and graceful pre-ordering of the lines and angles conceived
> in the mind, and contrived by an ingenious artist.[12]

So the congruity which you will remember results from a
naturally harmonious relationship between all the parts and the

whole, is implicit in all nature but the perception of congruity is situated specifically in man's mind. Whenever a harmonious composition is presented to the 'mind', either by sight or by hearing or by any of the senses, men immediately perceive its congruity.[13]

Historians like Erwin Panofsky and Joan Gadol have appreciated the wider significance of Alberti's view that the recognition of forms proceeds directly from nature. But at the same time, we all have to contend with the other much greater puzzlement about the process of recognition. Historians of art, of ideas, and of culture in general are all left with an incomplete picture of the very processes of mind that facilitated a condition that we all acknowledge to be of outstanding historical importance, namely, the Renaissance predilection to look outward in order to make generalizations from nature. This dilemma arises partly because Alberti did not see it as his purpose to write a full discussion about the process of recognition that he so readily commended. How did he and certain other Renaissance artists and thinkers come to trust experience more than ever; and how was the information of experience supposed to be processed in the mind? It is not possible to find direct answers to these questions; but Alberti's works do contain many assumptions relating to epistemological and psychological matters.

A strong point of view about these matters has been expressed by Professor Panofsky. He thought that both Alberti and Leonardo da Vinci did not believe in ideas of forms existing in the mind itself unless these ideas were gained exclusively from first-hand experience.[14] Gradually, I hope to show that stating the case in this way can lead to historical distortions. Alberti may even have believed in innate ideas, and Leonardo had such a mystical vision of the searching intellect of man that his views should not be equated with our contemporary understanding of a human mind abstracting principles from experience. Panofsky did make a valuable distinction between Alberti and Leonardo, and the Neo-Platonists of the Ficino type. Certainly, all of their preoccupations and their metaphors were different. Historians have often categorized Alberti and Leonardo as belonging within a technical, scientific, and mechanical stream of Renaissance thinking, in contrast to humanist and magical streams. Such descriptions do characterize the mainstream of the disciplinary commitments of many individual thinkers, but in an age that valued universality, the lines between these preoccupations must be seen to be almost infinitely flexible. Certainly Alberti started out as a humanist, and he did not rub all of this out in the later part of his career. While it is clear that neither Alberti nor Leonardo was sympathetic to Neo-Platonism in the style of the Florentine Academy, I do not feel secure with the idea that they were not advancing their own sorts of Neo-Platonism. They may have developed this from medieval thought with some aspects of humanism, and more tangibly, from a view of reality that had been expressed in the philosophy and the theology of Nicholas of Cusa. I feel strongly that we must begin to view their mental processes with greater subtlety. Alberti's and Leonardo's self-conscious commitment to representing beauty and to knowing truth suggest that these absolute norms were not immediately available to human minds that were devoid of some internal gifts of vision, and that were without some method of application. Naturally, neither thinker expressed a complete Baconian reliance on methods, and yet strong views about methods are certainly evident in their works. So, too, are assumptions about mental abilities and gifts which are not even expressed as clearly as their procedures and methods are, but these sorts of assumptions are still present in the thoughts of Alberti and Leonardo. In the long run it would be foolish for us to assume that they did not have strong opinions about the vital matter of recognition when so much of their own activity depended upon the validity of a recognition process.

Historians have to struggle in any case with this question about recognition because groups of Platonists and Neo-Platonists from classical times onward had not visualized the process in a uniform sort of way.[15] Alberti's general conclusion, that recognition was direct, that it took place from the immediate stimulation of experience, belongs specifically to the Renaissance - in contrast to the thoughts of medieval Neo-Platonists and in contrast even to rather more orthodox modern Neo-Platonists. Very often thinkers of a Platonic persuasion held a conception of the recognition process that I like to speak of as an inward-looking process. This involved a conscious reflection on ideas that were assumed to have been implanted in the mind by God. In general, those who tended to look inward still thought it was possible for men to apply their innate gift of ideas to sensuous experience. However, the impressions received from the world by the senses and ultimately by reason did not convey real ideas or the archetypal forms to men in a pure state. Because of great qualitative gaps between pure spirit and bodies, or matter, analogies between archetypal forms and the forms expressed on different planes of reality, did not represent full likenesses except within the confines and limitations of the stuff that harboured the forms. Hence the harmony exhibited and observed in physical nature

held a debased sort of analogy with the idea of harmony in the
artist's mind. Aristotelian physics that were popular in the early
Renaissance supported this view insofar as all earthly matter
was seen to be changeable and impure. The forms that Neo-
Platonists believed were the essence of material things in nature
would necessarily be obscured. It is interesting to note here
that Cusanus' cosmology rejected this Aristotelian distinction
between matter here on earth and matter above the moon and
that, practically simultaneously, Alberti side-stepped this issue
by maintaining that divine harmony was perceived directly
from nature, that is, earthly nature. However, the inward-
looking Platonists maintained hierarchical notions other than
those derived from Aristotle's physical ideas, and these notions
did definitely support contemplation as opposed to observation. For example, if we consider a typically Neo-Platonic sort
of schema that we find in the literature throughout the Middle
Ages, we see that specific physical examples embodying ideal
forms in earthly nature are strictly limited both by space and in
time. Thus, these examples are going to express the truth of
the forms in a very limited way, especially when these examples
are compared with analogous examples of the ideas expressed
in the form of concepts in the minds of men. The mind has the
power to range reflectively; it can perfect notions by accumulat-
ing examples, it can distinguish and generalize; and most
important, its content of thought is non-material. For most
Neo-Platonists the mind also contains spiritualized notions of
the ideas at the outset. These are the innate ideas. Historians
debate about whether Alberti believed in these innate ideas,
and I hope to demonstrate that he did believe in, and rely
upon, an innate ideational potential of the mind in the expression of his own view of the process of recognition. Such a
potential is expressed but not philosophically demonstrated in
Alberti's writings. What looks like a similar potential of the
human mind is elaborately described in the thought of
Nicholas of Cusa.

If we continue on this Platonic type of step ladder, the ideas
as they are held in the mind are still subject to consecutive
realization. At this level of expression then, the ideas are not as
clear and full as they are in the world soul, where they exist
concurrently. They are more fully realized still, as eternal
archetypes, completely above the created world. And their pristine context is in God where they exist in unity both simultaneously and eternally. Clearly such a tradition generally moved
men in the direction of looking inward for truer impressions of
harmony, truth, beauty, and goodness. And yet, this same tradition preserved an image of reality in which all things were

harmoniously interrelated, and in which the human mind occupied a special place because it was endowed with the power to perfect its understanding of nature's divinely arranged harmony. Alberti belongs in this tradition even though he does not climb its stairs in the manner of St Augustine, or make the dramatic spiritual ascent of a Pico della Mirandola. Alberti makes his own contribution when he gives the mind the unique power to recognize immediately the forms. At the same time he side-steps the view of the physical world as mutable and impure and aligns himself with a mathematical sort of Platonism. He concerns himself with a harmony seen in terms of mathematical relationships and numbers and diverges from those Neo-Platonists who were primarily occupied with the physical and elemental qualities of things. Possibly this divergence can explain how he views the recognition process in a new and not completely inward-looking manner.

In Alberti sense impressions go directly to reasoning faculties. As I have already quoted him as saying, he writes: 'For without question there is a certain excellence and natural beauty in the figures and forms of buildings, which immediately strike the mind with pleasure and admiration.'[16] This might seem almost mechanical, but it is not, for it does not only apply to single sense impressions but to experience in general. Also the recognition of goodness is viewed in the same way as the recognition of beauty, and the recognition of evil in the same way as of ugliness. Compare the above quotation from the treatise on architecture with the following one in which a spokesman for Alberti's views expresses himself in the treatise on the family.

> Now it is true of man, that as if guided by some innate power everyone who is not extremely stupid dislikes and condemns every sort of wickedness and dishonourable behaviour in others. There is no one who does not see something wrong about a wicked man.[17]

This recognition of beauty and goodness or of ugliness and badness in the world seems to be related to a sense of harmony that somehow is incorporated in the highest faculties of the mind. Then recognition might be a process of confirmation and of exchange between reasonably considered sensuous experiences on the one hand, and some innate power that the mind has been given on the other. This power enables the mind immediately to single out the essence from any experience. It should be clear that Alberti did not see this essence as being derived from a plodding induction. The sense of goodness is not simply eventually distilled from a huge batch of comparisons, it is first based on an instantaneous insight in the case of each experience that comes before the mind. Thus, the mind is gifted with a mysterious quality that enables it to single out and to recognize the truth of forms when it is stimulated by all of the diverse patterns in human experience.

Both the inward-looking and the Albertian outward-looking styles of recognition are matching processes. They are combinations of reflective and sense experiences. However, in the more orthodox Platonic recognition process the stress is definitely laid upon man's primary concentration on higher imprinted ideas, while in Alberti there is a contrasting acknowledgement of the needful stimulus of sense impressions for the mind. The world is the field in which the ideas are impressed and the mind has a recognizing power. So then man may not have strict archetypes of the good implanted in his mind like a map, but he certainly has a discriminating power that is expressed by an innate quality of mind. This power accounts for man's inspired seeing of causes, of the forms of things, and of the essential interrelationships between all things.

> But the judgement which you make that a thing is beautiful, does not proceed from mere opinion, but from a secret argument and discourse implanted in the mind itself; which plainly appears to be so from this, that no man beholds anything ugly or deformed, without an immediate hatred and abhorrence. Whence this sensation of the mind arises, and how it is formed, would be a question too subtle for this place.[18]

Despite Alberti's refusal to examine, it is possible to describe something of his version of the recognition process from the information written in Book IX of the treatise on architecture and from parts of his *Della Famiglia*. In the book on architecture we are told that the potential for awareness of harmony and beauty is innate in the mind, and that recognition of these truths occurs from the quick and direct stimulation of the senses. It seems that impressions of the senses go directly to the mind and that there, in the mind, are lodged some incorporated sensibilities. The specific character of these sensibilities is not clear. But they are apparently not so much whole archetypes stored in the mind, as they are a remembered story immediately awakened to consciousness by the necessary process of stimulation that starts with the senses. If Alberti had not assumed that the impressions of the senses were directly matched with innate sensibilities, I think he would have said so. By this I mean that if he was assuming some intermediate pattern of psychological steps in the mind, some pattern rather more expressive of the psychology of the early Renaissance, he would have indicated this. On the other hand, if he thought that innate sensibilities were mere mystic fantasy and superfluous to the all-important process of recognition, I do not think that he would have expressed himself as he did on a number of occasions. The theoretical points he makes in Book IX do not appear to me to be loosely formulated. *'Ut vero de pulchritudine iudices, non opinio, verum animis innata quaedam ratio efficiet.'* ('In order to judge truly of beauty it is not opinion which matters but rather a kind of reason which is innate in the mind.') Even considering antiquated styles in expression, this is a strange way to talk about beauty, if beauty is to be understood simply as a vision resulting from the impressions of a series of examples.[19] Shortly, we will see that inductive processes are involved in Alberti's reasoning, but that these processes always depend upon a prior step, and that this step involves a mental activity that is best described as insight. Alberti never moves far from his vision of beauty, truth, and goodness as absolutely fixed principles in man, in nature, and in the whole of reality. He cannot fit these principles in the mind by faith in the powers of reason alone. Later, Francis Bacon displayed such a faith, believing that inevitably true conceptions could only be arrived at by an inductive process; but Alberti in his time, believed in preordained limits and capacities; these were impressed in things and innate in all creatures and in man. Alberti's type of belief can only be illustrated by the rather lengthy quotations which follow. The first of these quotations certainly seems to seal the case for his visualization of some kind of innate intellectual faculty:

> Nature herself also seems to have bonded and incorporated in things, from the first day that they see the light, clear indications and manifest signs by which they fully declare their character. Men are able, therefore, to recognize and use them according to the uses for which they were created. In the mind and intellect of mortal man, nature has placed the seed and kindled the light of a knowledge, an insight into the remotest, most secret reasons for the clear and present causes of things. He knows whence and for what end things were born. To this nature added a divine and marvellous capacity for distinguishing and discriminating between what is good and what is harmful, between injurious and salutary, useful and useless.[20]

The insight that Alberti speaks about here corresponds to the intellectual gift of immediate recognition that I have been discussing at length. This is among the highest capacities of the human mind and it belongs to the spiritual part of the mind and soul. The distinguishing power that Alberti also mentions in this passage corresponds to the faculty of reason, as that faculty was generally characterized in Renaissance thought pertaining to psychology. The reasoning capacity generally works in an inductive manner but it is also subject to the initial insight, the vision sparked in the superior intellectual faculty. The metaphor of a seed in connection with the intellect is very important and I will return to it later, when bringing Cusa's influence into this picture.

The following thought has been given to a spokesman of Alberti's views:

> It is easier for me to believe Anaxagoras the philosopher, who when he was asked why God had created man, replied: 'He was made to contemplate the heavens, the stars, and the sun, and all the marvellous works of God.' This is a most plausible idea, especially when we observe that there is no animal but is bent and bowed with its head close to pasture and earth. Man alone stands erect with brow and countenance raised up, as though made by nature herself to gaze upon and know the paths and bodies in the heavens.[21]

We have already had the view that man was created to recognize divine harmony in nature. Here it is again in poetic form; Man was created to gaze upon the cosmos and to know. His knowledge follows upon the stimulus of seeing the works of God in natural events. This example is part of a larger passage in which Alberti appreciates certain of the ancients and disagrees with others, especially with Epicurus. Again he exhibits the habit I have mentioned earlier, that of selecting thoughts on an individual basis. His reverence for ancient philosophers is certainly not blind and the first source for human knowledge is clearly in created nature. In approving Anaxagoras he approves a philosopher who thought in terms of analogy, between the whole and the parts of nature, and between the creator and his unique creation, man.

The following thought is Alberti's:

> Nature, that is God, made man a composite of two parts, one celestial and divine, the other most beautiful and noble among mortal things. He provided him with a form and a body suited to every sort of movement, so as to enable him to perceive and flee from that which threatened to harm and oppose him. He gave him speech and judgement so that he would be able to seek after and to find what he needed and could use. He gave him movement and sentiment, desire and the power of excitement, so that he might clearly appreciate and pursue useful things and shun those harmful and dangerous to him. *He gave him intelligence, teachability, memory and reason, qualities divine in themselves*

and which enable man to investigate, to distinguish, to know
what to avoid and what to desire in order best to preserve himself. To these great gifts, admirable beyond measure, *God added
still another power of the spirit and mind of man, namely
moderation.* As a curb on greed and on excessive lusts, *he gave
him modesty and the desire for honour. Further, God established in the
human mind a strong tie to bind together human beings in society,
namely justice, equity, liberality, and love.*[22]

Let us associate this quotation with the one to follow shortly,
for together they develop a fuller view of Alberti's vision of
how all things are made, especially how man is made, and ultimately of what nature is.

First we must understand that Alberti is not a pantheist when
he writes 'Nature, that is God'; but that Alberti sees God as
thoroughly immanent in nature, but, of course, not complete in
nature. This is as many thinkers of his day would have seen it
but most of them would have placed nature down from God
because they would have had the debasement of spirit in matter in their minds. Although Alberti is aware that nature is not
perfect in the way that God is perfect, he conceives of nature as
continually perfecting itself: nature works to make every being
'complete' in its 'members' and 'capacities'. For our part we
already know that this is the exact advice that Alberti gives to
the architect, and to the painter, and to the sculptor in the
interest of creating real beauty. He gives it to man in general
for the perfection of human institutions. Alberti continues:

Nature tries to keep it [any being] free of any lack or defect, so
that it may preserve itself in its time and be in many ways helpful to other procreated things. They [scholars] further demonstrate that every animate being has from its beginning as much
strength, reason, and virtue as it will require to seek its neces-
sities and its rest . . . Everything by its *first complete nature* strives
towards its own greatest possible perfection, it certainly seems to
me we may say this much - all mortals are by nature sufficiently
able to love and preserve some honourable excellence. *Excellence,
indeed, is nothing but nature itself, complete and well formed.*[23]

This point of view stands firmly in the line of Christian Neo-
Platonism, but once again, stress is important. The whole way
that Alberti visualizes divine harmony in nature distinguishes
his views from many sophisticated but rather more orthodox-
Neo-Platonists. If man has been given divine qualities and physical qualities but the physical parts are so arranged that they
are pre-ordained to contribute to the working out of the insight
of the divine intellectual parts, if all of these things are true,

then the divine immanence in man is unique. Nature and
creatures can embody divine principles. The philosopher
Cusanus would have called things and creatures part of the divine
explication. Man embodies divine principles as a creature, and he
also possesses qualities of mind that are analogous to divine
qualities. Cusanus and other Christian Neo-Platonists would have
said man is indeed the image of God. Alberti centres this unique
mental and spiritual quality of man on two qualities that are
inevitably interrelated: the capacity to recognize and the capacity
to make. He can order and design, and work actively and
knowingly to facilitate the perfectible character of reality. If man
is corrupted it is because he fails to heed that which it has been
given him to recognize and know. When man is seen to be
endowed with such divine intellectual qualities, and when the
divine explication in nature takes a mathematical form, and we
know from Alberti's architectural writings, and from his
measurements for statues, and his work on perspective, that it did
take a mathematical form in his mind, then the immanence of
God has been so visualized that human knowledge can be seen to
be almost infinitely perfectible and clear. The spiritual and
mental limits of mortal man are the irrevocable ones of being
partial, of being limited in space and in time. These are the limits
of mortality and corporeality viewed in entirely mathematical and
metaphysical terms, in the terms of finite and infinite, in the
terms of parts, and of wholes, and of totality. But this is quite
different from seeing man with a muddled mind continually
swimming around in muddy waters. This shift in stress within the
Christian Platonic tradition, turning from murky reflections to
mathematical models, and turning away from orthodox Aristotelian physics to mathematical metaphysics - this shift forms the
very ground that Alberti walks on when he thinks that the
harmony of nature is analogous to divine harmony, and that man
has been gifted with a divine capacity to see causes immediately.
Perhaps what is most interesting about Alberti's manner of
thinking is that he not only sees all creatures perfecting
themselves towards the fullness of their innate gifts, and then
decaying, and finally resting, but that he sees in the human
intellectual process another whole level of fruition in and above
the capacities given to all other things and creatures. Not only is
man born to mature, and to die, and to strive for moral and
spiritual excellence in this process, man is born to see, to
recognize, to perfect his works, and to share his knowledge,
through love, with the human community. Hence, the innate
perfectibility of man and of human works is cumulative. It goes
through generations of human beings. Men can always become
more excellent, and the dynamics of this Albertian vision of

human perfectibility is almost as radical as Pico della Mirandola's vision of human spiritual transmutation. But the channel of expression in Alberti's view of progress is intellectual, albeit we must understand that this is a spiritualized intellectual process. This kind of view points us towards a dynamic of progress that later was to be much more self-consciously formulated in the natural philosophy of the seventeenth century.

Alberti is a theoretician, an artist and thinker, and not primarily a philosopher, so these philosophical shifts that he expresses are always stated within basically practical contexts, like the treatise on the family, or the books on architecture. There is only one Christian Platonic philosopher who exhibits remarkably similar shifts in formulation, shifts that occur in a contemporary lifetime; this is Nicholas of Cusa. Cusa saw divine immanence in man in terms that were both spiritual and very mental. Cusa directed the eye of man outward to the world so that man could understand both the workings of things, and then the limits of intellectual explanations. His visions of the spirit were first stimulated by the questions that faced men when they found that certain concepts could not be explained in worldly terms. And lastly, Cusa's idea of reality was described in mathematical terms, and even his idea of divinity could only be intimated through a series of geometrical metaphors.[24] Alberti had contact with Cusa's thought and he had a close friendship with Cusa's own friend, the mathematician, Paolo Toscanelli (1397-1482). Surely there is direct or indirect influence here in Florence, if not of the whole of Cusa's theology, then certainly of Cusa's style of visualizing reality.

Then when these men shift the emphasis of their Platonism from almost totally introspective processes to processes involving a high degree of observation and to seeing the stimulation of man's higher mental faculties as starting from nature and experience, they are undoubtedly reacting to tremendous social and intellectual forces that are at work in the advanced cities in Europe, and to some extent, in Rome in the quattrocento. No historian will deny the existence of such cultural pressures. The new mathematical emphasis is there, as is the shift from scholastic logic and physics to humanism and to new forms of expression in Neo-Platonism. The unique character of Padua, the new social and economic life in some cities, the intensified preoccupation with secular achievements in such cities, and the attempts at modernization and reform within the Church are all radically affecting the ways that some men live and think. The intellectual Florentine is particularly in the midst of all of these changes. However, when historians talk about precise formulations of ideas in the wake of rather amorphous forces they run the danger of courting some highly improbable notions. For example, if we think that Alberti side-stepped Aristotelian physical ideas, and that he was not attracted to them because he was a humanist and a Platonist, and, most of all, because he wanted to express a newly conceived power for created works of art, we can fairly say that Florentine cultural life had prepared the way of such an evasion. But the problem becomes much more complicated for the historian when we get down to the precise way that Alberti expresses himself. For instance, when he talks about an innate argument in the mind, or a seed of recognition in the mind, Alberti is modifying the Platonic concept of innate ideas to make it function as an innate ideational potential, a potential that is highly receptive, that is, indeed, needful of stimulation from nature and experience. The mind-soul of man and the senses and body of man are close and highly interdependent here. Alberti talks about nature and man perfecting themselves in time, and this perfectibility is viewed in an analogy to the mathematical terms of a partially infinite progression rather than in the more orthodox Christian terms of personal spiritual refinement. In other words, man's conceptions of beauty or truth or excellence can improve cumulatively through the lifetimes of successive individuals and societies, from generation to generation, while total and absolute beauty, or truth, or excellence is qualitatively out of man's grasp in finite existence. Man can become more and more excellent but Alberti says that the quality of excellence is nature complete and well formed; in other words, at rest. This kind of completion takes us out of a temporal series, out of the progressive continuity of motion, and into a spiritual and psychic area containing the infinite and absolute beauty, or truth, or excellence. Alberti has made the leap from a temporal and partially infinite series to a spiritual region of absolutely infinite qualities.

When historians consider Alberti's application of specific analogies like these to problems connected with human works, they would be foolish to imagine that his assumptions all arose on the crest of a wave of Renaissance social changes. Although the assumptions are not disconnected from the changes, we can be reasonably certain that Alberti is relying on some rather precise formulations for his imaginative views. If we do not want to see it in this way, then we have to imagine Alberti by himself, synthesizing from a vast body of Neo-Platonic literature, combining that synthesis with new mathematical and artistic concepts, and then not writing any of this out directly, but simply assuming it all and alluding to it in his practical treatises. The other Florentine synthesists, like Ficino, were not hiding their philosophical tasks: why should we imagine that Alberti would? If Alberti is unlikely to have been doing all of this gigantic but rather hidden assimilation and adaptation of philosophical and especially epistemological ideas, and I do think that it is unlikely, then he must have been adopting some things from an existing body of expression. I do not want to dampen Alberti's originality by remarking about this, but simply to state that even the originality of his views, for instance his idea of recognition, even that kind of originality has to have some specific formulation in its background. This could have been a verbal tradition in Florentine artistic circles, but these circles must have leaned on something for the specific epistemological assumptions that they apparently absorbed. The most plausible source of images and analogies is suggested by Alberti's personal contact with Toscanelli and by the mutual respect that they shared for the ideas of Cusanus. This suggestion will be amplified in chapters 2 and 3. Here are explanations of philosophical areas that these practical men did not explore too deeply themselves. Instead they needed to rely upon this body of formulation for spiritual and intellectual support. This is how they could attribute great meaning even to purely secular works, and this is where they found the full expression of a reality that they could honestly and honourably work within.

Looking carefully at the quotations cited above, leads me to suggest that even some of the innate content of the human intellect is listed there. When Alberti talks about 'powers of the spirit and mind' or qualities put 'in the mind' by God, he tells us that a sense of moderation and of modesty, the desire for honour, justice, equity, liberality and love, are all given to men at the outset. Notice that all of these qualities can be seen within a context of harmony. They all require the interplay of a sense of balance, a personal decorum, the feeling for more or less or an inner knowledge of propriety. It is very unlikely that Alberti viewed these qualities as living in the mind like a vast collection of statues, all formal and fixed there. Instead he saw a body of innate sensitivity living there, one that was purely intellectual and that was pretuned by God. *Men have been gifted with an awareness of the temporal possibilities for the expression of ideal qualities.* Thus, those who are attuned can respond with harmony in all of their decisions and acts.

The essentials of Alberti's assumed picture of reality look something like this. Nature has been arranged harmoniously by God in accordance with a divinely conceived pattern that is best described in mathematical terms. Men were created to recognize and know nature's harmony within the limits of their own

partial and temporal experience. Part of man's mental equipment is spiritual and intellectual and this part holds the ideational potential that is an innate gift. The gift is from God and
so it is something from beyond the limits of time and experience. The senses generally spark the human process of recognition by stimulating the mind to react to conditions in experience. All individuals are able to, and should react in terms of
their innate sense of harmony. And men's conscious awareness
of innate qualities, for example, the awareness of beauty, can
be increasingly magnified from an accumulation of good
examples.

Finally, before looking at how Alberti worked out his
assumptions in writings about the arts, I am quoting one of his
analogies where he shows how the innate desire for honour
can be seen to act like a kind of conscience informing the mind
of its best course. What he writes about honour here, can be
equally applied to equity, to justice, in fact, to any of the innate
qualities:

> Here is an analogy quite proper to the case: consider this holy
> and sacred source of honour as our very shadow, always beside
> us, always comprehending, weighing and judging whatever we
> do and the manner and purpose of all our actions. This sense of
> honour sees, distinguishes, examines everything. It concentrates
> full attention on whatever concerns us. It praises you affection-
> ately for the good you do, thanks you abundantly, gives you con-
> fidence and abundant strength. For evil it reprimands you
> angrily, casts harsh blame, laughs in a troubled way at you, tells
> the world your vice and disgrace. Be sure you consult your hon-
> our and that it behaves like this. . . .The man who scorns to hear
> or to obey that sense of honour which seeks to advise and to
> command him grows full of vice and will never be contented
> even if he is rich.[26]

This illustrates Alberti's outward-looking relationship between
the mind and experience. The Platonic ideas, if we can now call
them this, are evoked from and applied to nature and experience. But, at the same time we must remember that these ideas
do not entirely originate in the mind from experience.

Beauty is rare

As it is compared with the more orthodox Christian Platonists'
view of recognition where, you will remember, the major stress
was laid upon the superior directive force of imprinted ideas,
Alberti's view elevates and integrates the senses and nature

with the mind and the divine plan. The senses, and the whole
experience of society and nature both form a source and a field
of play for the expression of ideal principles in a temporal and
material context. The beauty that God put in nature, the gifts
that God put in man, and the recognition process, as Alberti
saw these things, all add up to man's real experience of real
beauty.[27] Nature does not exhibit shadow beauty to man and
man need not flee inward to see clearly. In fact, for Alberti, if
he does flee inward he is most likely to see his own imaginings,
his fantasies, hence to elaborate his ignorance. Alberti is Baconian in this one point. In Alberti's own more spiritual vision of
knowledge the eye will strike the mind and the mind will
yield its ideas and also describe with its rational powers, but
within the directive force of the innate gifts. Thus, we see how
Alberti's view diminished the orthodox feeling of a tremendous
gap between impressions of the senses and the high ideas that
were the exclusive property of the intellect and soul.

We must be aware that Alberti did not mean that everything
in nature was itself ideal or beautiful in form, but only that
beauty was essentially present in all nature. It is never entirely
clear whether he considers any specific natural unit as an ultimate exemplar of form. However, he talks generally about the
forms of animals and never about the forms of atoms. Naturally, artists and architects are most likely to be involved with visible forms rather than with a discussion of the primary units of
form. Even though all individual natural things are apparently
not beautiful, Alberti still understands beauty to be absolute
and operating within the whole and all of the parts of nature.
If you will remember the prior example of honour this vision is
much the same. Not all men are honourable but the desire for
honour is universal in man. Alberti's conception of how beauty
worked can be more easily understood if we keep in mind that
he saw man's formulation of a concept of beauty as continu-
ously being perfected from the recognition of beauty in the
experience of the artist. In his search for truly good forms in
nature, the artist continually shops for good examples, for
instance, for examples of human bodies, in *De Statua*. From the
proportions of these examples he gradually develops and
refines a clearer conception of a most beautiful expression of
that particular form. Eventually, in the course of many similar
pursuits, the artist perfects his awareness of a general idea of
beauty. Later we shall see by example something we can anticipate already, viz. that the choices the artist makes in the process
of selection are not simply based on matters of taste. The artist
depends on the ideational potential in the mind to recognize
the essential character of the beauty of each example. Men are

all gifted to recognize beauty, but the artist practises to perfect
his gift, and to represent his concept for men. He becomes our
teacher of beauty by the quality of the artistic examples that he
places before our eyes. In this way all of nature and art can be
understood to be subject to the universal quality of beauty. The
recognition of beauty centres on the divine gifts to the human
intellect. Men can make a mental distillation of the essence of
beauty from all of the variety represented in nature. Hence,
beauty is expressed directly in nature, and yet individual forms
in almost all cases will certainly not be perfect.[28]

> . . . *Complete beauties are never found in a single body, but are rare and
> dispersed in many bodies.* Therefore we ought to give our every
> care to discovering and learning beauty. . . .
>   In order not to waste his study and care the painter should
> avoid the custom of some simpletons. Presumptuous of their
> own intellect and *without any example from nature to follow with their
> eyes or minds, they study by themselves* to acquire fame in painting.
> They do not learn how to paint well, but become accustomed to
> their own errors. *This idea of beauty, which the well trained barely
> discern, flees from the intellect of the inexpert.*[29]

Alberti did not think the fact that certain gifts existed in the
mind accounted for all the details of men's opinions about
beautiful forms. This is because he was aware that he was dealing with a philosophical generalization, not a uniform
psychological experience, and so he purposefully pushed questions about people's personal variations in taste into a special
category which he did not elaborate. He describes this situation
by an amusing example, writing that some men admire women
for being slender, and others for being plump. He continues:

> You, perhaps, are for a medium between these two extremes,
> and would neither have her so thin as to seem wasted with sick-
> ness, nor so strong and robust as if she were a ploughman in
> disguise, and were fit for boxing: in short, you would have her
> such a beauty as might be formed by taking from the first what
> the second might spare. . . .[30]

Alberti says, however, that because you preferred one of these
women, it does not necessarily follow that you would despair
about the others having any claims to handsomeness or grace.
There is probably some 'hidden cause' why one pleases you
more than the others, a cause, he continues, ' . . . into which I
will not now pretend to inquire.' He leaves his metaphor by
saying once again that there is some natural ideal which makes
our judgement that something is beautiful extend beyond

'mere opinion' to some discourse implanted in the mind.[31]

By using the analogous harmony shared between parts and existing throughout the whole of nature, the artist can create beautiful works. And these works will harmonize with nature, if their proportions are analogous to ideal proportions. In the light of this conclusion Alberti advises the architect:

> Let your building therefore be such, that it may not want any members which it has not, and that those which it has, may not in any respect deserve to be condemned. . . .

Alberti cautions him against lack of variety, as long as he avoids the errors of excess:

> . . . for as in music, when the bass answers the treble, and the tenor agrees with both, there arises from that variety of sounds an harmonious and wonderful union of proportions which delights and enchants our senses. . . .

This is how it is with all things that please men.[32]

Alberti was aware that his criterion of natural harmony was not universally accepted as an aesthetic ideal, and he was consciously and purposefully incorporating this material into aesthetic theory.[33] Like all fervent enthusiasts he attributed the lack of general acceptance of his ideals to ignorance.[34]

The idea that an analogy existed between parts of nature was of course restated, rather than invented, by Alberti; and even the notion that this analogy especially consisted of prescribed mathematical relationships was not original but had its origins in Pythagoras and Plato. What was new was his general re-advocacy of these ideas together with the ways in which he incorporated them in his works. Of primary historical interest is the fact that his ways became possible in the fifteenth century, that the cultural environment was so that these ideas could be formed. How Alberti used these ideas, and the material with which they were incorporated, I will discuss immediately. However, their ultimate significance can only be gradually appreciated.[35]

Proportion and measurement

From Alberti's works there developed an entrely original combination of concepts of beauty and utility. Reality is perfectible in intellectual and moral terms, and also in aesthetic and

utilitarian terms. Refinements in utility are in no sense inferior
to refinements in beauty or in ethics. Alberti's readings of the
Romans, especially of Cicero, led him to reject the low Aristotelian view of the arts, and Alberti extended his exultation in
the perfection of taste into the area of function. There is a
congruity of function, as well as one of beauty. Hence, Alberti
incorporated many purely functional ideas and quantitative
expressions into philosophy and theory of art in such a way
that the practical content suffered no lapse in dignity in comparison with the idealistic content. It was all part of the same
exalted human work.

It is impossible to rely on a theory of good proportion without also writing about the subject of measurement; and equally
impossible to discuss measurement without attempting to prescribe methods. The greater part of his writings on architecture, painting, and sculpture are devoted to the concepts and
techniques of his methods. He is concerned with inventing
easy, clear, and reliable methods to help the artist with his
measuring tasks. In the invention of methods Alberti shows a
true Renaissance universality and preoccupation with crafts.
He uses philosophy and mathematics, but he also uses the
techniques and crafts of workmen, of the studio, of land surveying, and of map making in order to invent systems of measurement and techniques of representation for his naturalistic
conception of art. Joan Gadol's study of Alberti fills in the
details of his highly original and eclectic mind in these matters.
The area of his assumptions is still the one that I am most concerned to bring into sharper focus, and there is an interesting
example relating to his assumptions in the treatise on statues.
Here we will be able to see that Alberti was flexible in hunting
out his sources for specific good proportions. The flexibility I am
mentioning is to be seen in contrast to the more general habit of
relying on canons that that were already established and
expressed in classical and medieval philosophy. Alberti did not
always rely on canons, especially if there were blank spaces
within the authorities, spaces where the necessary proportions
were simply not to be found. But if he did adopt a canon, as
with his application of Boethian musical harmonies to architecture, then we can be certain that he saw those harmonies as
representing the reality of the harmony in nature. When he
invented proportions instead of borrowing them, we can also
be certain that he saw his newly formulated proportions as
analogous to the same natural harmony. One of Alberti's major
guides and sources, Vitruvius, had written comparatively little
about the subject of human proportions. Therefore Alberti
undertook to describe a new manner of determining the best

proportions of a man.[36] He had literary inspirations here, for it became a literary convention in the Renaissance to think of comparing examples and making a composite beauty.[37] Alberti took his proportions for statues from nature. He writes:

> ... Having taken the draught from those bodies, that of diverse others were judged by the most sagacious in this inquiry to be the most exactly built and composed with all their several measures and proportions, amd comparing them exactly together, to. observe wherein they excelled, or were excelled each by the other, (we) have made choice ...

From the selection of models and examples Alberti and his company then chose '...those middle proportions which seemed ... most agreeable, and which we have here set down by the lengths, the bignesses and the thicknesses of all the principal and most noted parts. ...'[38] Alberti prescribes the measurements in a chart where they are designated in feet, degrees and minutes. He concludes saying that 'by means of these measures it may easily be computed what proportion all the parts and members of the body have one by one to the whole length of the body; and what agreement and symmetry they have among themselves, as also how they vary and differ from one another....'[39] In his procedure the *pede* is equal to one-sixth of the total length of the body, so that the body is divided into 6 *pedes,* 60 *unceolae* and 600 *minuta.* These subdivisions enabled Alberti to express any length in terms of the proportion of the whole.[40] This method of measurement is similar to the one used in the perspectival picture where all magnitudes were measured with reference to the *braccio* (arm length).

Alberti's practical purpose in the *Aedificatoria* also seems to have been similar to that in the *De Statua.* Namely, he wanted to invent and describe easy ways that artists could use to incorporate natural and beautiful proportions in their works. Sometimes the similarity of the methods that he devised and recommended provide the best illustration of his singleness of purpose. For instance, we can compare the scale that he used in the *De Statua* and one that he recommends for use in finding the harmonic mean proportion in the *Aedificatoria.* The means, arithmetic, geometric and harmonic, were one kind of ideal standard that Alberti applied to determine good proportions in building.[41] The harmonic mean is that point which exceeds one extreme and is exceeded by the other by the same fraction of the extreme. In practice, Alberti's method is arithmetical. He says simply that in the case of any given length for which you want to find the harmonic mean, let 30 stand for the lesser extreme and 60 for the greater (cf. Fig. 2).

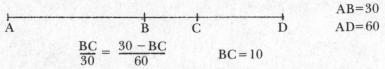

$$\frac{BC}{30} = \frac{30 - BC}{60} \qquad BC = 10$$

The lesser length stands in proportion to the greater as 1:2 which is the ratio of the frequency of vibrations of the octave. The aim is to divide the line BD at that point which will divide it also into a 1:2 proportion. All that this amounts to, by Alberti's method, is the addition of a third more, or 10, to 30.[42] A line of any given length, no matter what the standard measurement was, could be divided proportionally by this method, and this is a similar method to the one that Alberti used in the *De Statua* when he divided a body of any given length into 6 *pedes*. Any desired proportions could be incorporated along the line by using simple arithmetic. The use of 60 in the *Aedificatoria* is convenient because 60 is divisible by more factors than other possible choices, and it is comparable to the use of 6, 60, 600 in the *De Statua*. Both methods are directed to the end of the easy use of the desired proportions, either in a figure of any given length, or along a line of any given length.

The comparison of these two scales in this instance actually relates to an important historical point. Historians have noted that the proportions in the *De Statua* were taken from nature and experience. It has even been implied that the naturalism of the *Statua* moves Alberti away from Neo-Platonic idealism.[43] But this is only true of the more inward-looking Platonism which never attracted him, anyway. Actually his idealistic view of beauty is similar in the *Statua* and the *Aedificatoria*, and his naturalism does not arise as a consequence of his shedding of Platonic ideals. In fact, Alberti's naturalism was formulated as a complement to his own version of these ideals. The real difference between the selection of proportions in the *De Statua*, and that recommended in the *Aedificatoria*, arose from the fact that for architecture there already existed a detailed body of prescribed proportions. But, for the human figure no such body of detail existed. However, a tradition of human proportions was assumed to have existed in the past and was thought to have been part of the lost knowledge of the ancients.[44] Since Vitruvius only made some very general recommendations, Alberti, who was convinced that ideal human proportions were real, had to rely on another proposition of his personal Platonic philosophy to support his method of prescribing human proportions. His proposition was that a human capacity to recognize the harmony of nature in specific examples was somehow imprinted in the mind. When Alberti and his company chose by comparison the proportions that were seen to be most beautiful, and therefore naturally good, they were most certainly acting on this proposition. They were matching outer forms with inner concepts. They worked close to their examples, but Alberti made clear that this process was not akin to the judging of a beauty contest.[45] Instead, the judges were in quest of proportions that seemed to conform to a basic pattern which exists in all parts of nature. Therefore, the inspiration of this selection from nature is as much a part of Alberti's belief in an analogy between parts and the whole of nature as his total take-over of ideal numbers and musical proportions for architecture. Of course, the proportions of the *De Statua* were based on a real practice of direct observation.[46] Alberti's true originality lies in his stressing that a true apprehension of the naturally good proportions must be gained by man's use of judgement in the comparison of concrete instances as opposed to constructing them strictly by some kind of inner divination.

Sir Anthony Blunt has suggested that Alberti must have believed in a kind of faculty of artistic judgement.[47] He made this suggestion even though he himself tended to view Alberti's practice of natural observation as a significant move away from his Platonic idealism. However, historians must not cast away vital and necessary supports for theoretical and practical innovations involving the initiation of important scientific procedures. Contrary to Blunt's impression, Alberti was probably thinking of himself as adding to the ancient canons of perfection in the *De Statua*.

Now that some of Alberti's social ideas have been compared with his artistic ideas, it should become clearer that this so-called faculty of artistic judgement is, in fact, Alberti's much more general faculty of an innate intellectual capacity for the recognition of the good in all fields of experience. It was this gift that Alberti had in mind when he constantly reminded the artist to study nature. Undoubtedly, this is given as practical advice, but it is practical advice conceived of in Renaissance terms. 'He who dares take everything he fashions from nature will make his hands so skilled that whatever he does will always appear to be drawn from nature.'[48] Couple this statement with the following one: 'Trismegistus, an ancient writer, judged that painting and sculpture were born at the same time as religion, for thus he answered Aesclepius: mankind portrays the gods in his own image from his memories of nature and his own origins.'[49] And: 'The *istoria* [the story portrayed in the painting] will move the soul of the beholder when each man painted there clearly shows the movement of his own soul.'[50] Evidently, some form of communication is taking place involving actual physical nature, what is expressed in the naturalistic scene in the picture, and some common sensibilities of the human soul.

Thus, the widest meaning implied in Alberti's constant reminder to the artist to study nature can go far beyond the most obvious and straightforward communication contained in this advice. Certainly, it is clear that if an artist wants to achieve resemblance with nature in his works, he must learn to observe. Currently, however, we have seen Sir E.H. Gombrich demonstrate in *Art and Illusion* that the far more usual tendency for artists of almost any age has been primarily to yield to the influence of other artistic works, rather than to the impressions of nature at first hand.[51] Both Alberti and, later, Leonardo da Vinci had shown themselves to be sensitive to this common tendency among their own contemporary artists. They advocated the study of nature in strong terms because they were extremely aware of the traps of tradition and convention for those who were trying to create in a naturalistic style. But even more to the point, they were most acutely aware of precisely these traps in terms of the aesthetic and philosophical ideals that they themselves had attached to the achievement of a true naturalistic representation.

In the light of their own values, Alberti and Leonardo not only had to contradict the normal psychological tendencies of artists in general, but they also had to oppose something far more definite. This was an earlier medieval tradition of representation and of values attached to the acts of representing things or to devising works. As we recall, in this past tradition the artist had referred primarily to his own inner ideas of things, rather than to the actual things themselves.

The historian Paolo Rossi has shown us that an essentially Aristotelian estimation of the low value of human works had contributed to this negative medieval qualification of the possibility of embodying a high spiritual content in human works.[52] In this estimation works were only the most mundane comments on nature in a strict hierarchy of being. Nature had been praised. She was man's true mentor, while the human arts just copied nature, usually rather badly too. But later, by the early Renaissance, artists both expanded the very productive characterization of nature as man's teacher, and at the same time, they contradicted the orthodox low estimation of the value of human works. The views advanced by these artists were fantastically complementary to the arts, as we have already seen in Alberti's examples. Human works could affect the mind and soul profoundly, as indeed the experience of nature did have these effects. The arts almost perfected nature by bringing her various beauties together in a permanent image. And for the Pythagoreans, the arts could actually be seen to embody mathematical analogies to the essential forms and operations in the universe. This is quite different from the medieval view where men had imposed distinctions both of kind and of degree between the arts and nature. For, it had not been difficult for artists and thinkers who were influenced by medieval theology and Neo-Platonism to combine Aristotle's view of the arts, as the poor relations of nature, with the Platonic view of the arts, as representing shadows of a reflection. An Aristotelian hierarchy, or ladder of physical existence and being, which had started with the lowest existence and had extended up through all physical levels of sensibility, up to spirit or soul, this had been combined with Platonic distinctions in kind, distinctions between spirit and matter. Clearly, the direct representation of the harmony of nature was not easily conceivable from this conventional medieval framework, no matter where you look. On the other hand, when men saw fit not only to evoke geometry and music as arts that actually contained direct information about nature's harmony, but also to embody the information in their works, then the hierarchical aspects of the traditional idea of the harmony of nature could give way to more fluid views. These were Renaissance views, where the existence of ideal harmonies could still be called upon and be acknowledged; but neither nature nor human works nor the initial impressions of the senses could ever be cast down quite as far as they had been before.

There are complex reasons for the accentuated stress on man's power of direct imitation using the principles of geometry and music and on the potency of man's experience of nature. These reasons extend far out of the area of ideas. Historians have to look to many aspects of early modern civilization in order to find a full explanation of the pressures on at least some thinkers and artists to elevate their own estimation of the value of worldly experience. After all, Masaccio had not read Alberti. But, leaving the larger explanations aside for a while precisely because they are so difficult, this shift in men's estimation of the value of experience and of their own works was surely one of the most radical and significant changes that historians can connect with the term Renaissance. Because the causes for this shift are so varied, and because we generally tend to associate them with the more advanced elements in

western economy, politics and society, historians have sometimes been very surprised to find that some of the first formulations of these newly-triumphant values came from sources
that contained highly mystical and other-worldly inspirations.
Perhaps this is why some historians have liked to think that
Alberti left his Platonism behind when he went out into the
market place to observe, and to compare real operations and
things. But he didn't.

Alberti's search for good proportion in building itself, and in
the arts in general, shared similar historical roots. It was from
Vitruvius that Alberti developed the inspirations, both for the
incorporation of musical harmonies into architectural theory,
and for the belief in the ideal nature of the proportions of the
human body.[53] Kenneth Clark makes this important point general
in *The Nude*. He explains that, while Vitruvius was giving the
rules for the building of sacred edifices, he wrote that these
should have the proportions of a man. Vitruvius gave some
indications of what these proportions were, and said that man's
body was a model because, with arms and legs extended, it fitted into the perfect geometrical forms of the circle and the
square. Clark concludes by describing the importance of this
proposition to men of the Renaissance as the foundation of a
philosophy. This idea together with the musical scale of
Pythagoras relates human sensations to the existence of natural
order in the cosmos. This is because, put together, these ideals
describe both a state of reality (the existence of orderly principles of harmony in nature) and the cause of our positive rational and emotional reactions to that reality. The relationship
between ideal proportion in the human body and the proportions of the Pythagorean scale linked together geometric and
organic bases of beauty.[54] The ideal shapes, the circle, the
square and others, were taken over by Alberti from Vitruvius
as well, and with these shapes were associated the microcosmic
quality of the proportions of the human figure.[55] Vitruvius also
recommended, and Alberti adopted, the idea that classical columns should simulate the proportions, but not the size, of the
human body.[56] Thus Alberti's background affirms again that
what he was really after, in both the *De Re Aedificatoria* and the
De Statua, was an easy method for using good proportion in
objects of any size, and that this evolved out of his own
interpretation of basic Neo-Platonic notions, and involved no
subsequent rejection of any part of his philosophy.[57]

Proportion and continuity

The relationship between the analogy between parts and the whole and the methods proposed by Alberti in *Della Pittura* is not so obvious as it was in the *De Re Aedificatoria* or the *De Statua*; nonetheless, this relationship is subtly present and is interesting. It is not seen easily because some understanding of Alberti's method of perspective is necessary in order to comprehend it, and because in *Della Pittura* he stressed his practice rather than the philosophical relevance of the art.[58] Still, we can detect the same motifs that have appeared in other instances when Alberti used the analogy between parts and the whole of nature.

The first motif that appears is the now familiar one of proportion. Alberti writes, that an important concern of the student of painting should be about proportion or the correspondence of parts. He explains the term proportional, by making a simile between proportion in triangles and proportion in men. Just as in proportional triangles the corresponding sides are proportional to each other, so a small man is in proportion to a large man if they share the same proportions between the foot and the other parts of the body.[59]

Very often we hear the Renaissance painting referred to as a microcosm. This belief in ideal proportions had always been an important feature of the analogy between microcosm and macrocosm. In fact, Rudolf Allers' definition of a structural microcosm is one in which the microcosm and the macrocosm are seen as having corresponding parts as well as an overall correspondent structure.[60] The concept of correspondence between parts and wholes means that microcosm and macrocosm do not necessarily share identical likenesses but are analogous in terms of qualities seen as being parallel to each other. In this instance Alberti's use of the term correspondence, however, always involves an analogy based on mathematically proportional relationships and not a purely metaphorical analogy. Metaphorical correspondence is most easily illustrated by a typical analogy drawn between psychic and physical properties. For instance, knowledge in the mind of God has an analogy of correspondence with knowledge imprinted in the mind of man and in the earth's structure this quality of knowledge is deemed correspondent to the physical property of light.[61]

Now in the context of all three of Alberti's principal works we have seen that he revived the ancient notion of the correspondence of parts in connection with technical problems of proportion in art. However, his use of that ancient notion was restricted to one kind of analogy: that between the proportion-

ate character of reality and the directly corresponding character of physical nature and of art. He conceived of man's access
to that ultimate aesthetic reality and man's ability to perfect his
concept of reality through the direct observation of nature.
That is why he enjoins painters to 'put as much study and work
into remembering what (they take) from nature as (they do) in
discovering it.'[62]

The next motif found throughout the *Della Pittura* is that
of continuity. Continuity and proportion must be understood
together. The concept of continuity of space, together with the
objects in it arranged in true proportion, was developed in the
context of the problem of representation in perspective.[63]
Alberti advised the painter to think of the frame of his painting
as an open window. Through it, the arrangement of objects in
space could be imagined in true perspective. The contemporary theory of vision maintained that objects were seen along a
cone of lines, the apex of which was in the eye of the observer,
and extending to the farthest object or objects in focus. Alberti
recommended that the artist imagine a plane intersecting a
pyramid, instead of a cone. This plane should lie between the
artist's eyes and the objects he wishes to portray. On the plane
the picture could be traced in perspective. It is just as if you
were to trace what you saw through a window on the glass
pane. On this pane each surface, line, and point, even a point
of space, would be part of one continuous relationship. Further, on the pane each object would correspond to a real object
that was being viewed from a specific point in actual space. The
correspondence between the represented arrangements of
objects and spaces in the scene and the vision of the real ones is
based on proportion. The dimensions of any represented
objects, and of the spaces between them, are fixed by a rule of
construction. This rule depends upon the theoretical placement of the eye of the beholder at a specific point in space.
The distance between the eye and the section of the perspective
plane (like the window pane) is kept constant, but the artist
then changes the impression of distance between the eye and
the various parts of the scene being viewed.[64] Thus, the beholder must always be imagined as remaining at the same distance
from the window. Then the images traced on the window pane
will represent the same proportioned diminution of objects and
spaces, from the viewpoint of the beholder, as does the actual
scene he sees out of the window.

As window panes were not easily available for Renaissance
painters to place between themselves and their models, Alberti
suggested several similar methods as an aid to achieving the
effect of perspective. One of the most practical of these was the

velo, or net. It works rather like the window pane but with the additional advantage of a grid pattern which enables the painter to measure the degree of diminution of objects as against the unchanging size of the squares of the grid. Looking through a net the painter sees all the objects and spaces to be depicted through the parallels of its grid (like the grid on a map.)[65] By describing the proportional grid on a panel or wall the painter can reduce or enlarge his whole picture as he transfers it.[66] The spaces in the picture were treated in the same way as the objects. Both spaces and objects required the same kind of planning.[67] Thus, the concept of space as an absence of objects taking value from the objects it contained was not meaningful in the context of perspective representation. Space was conceived of and described purely geometrically just as if it were tangible.[68]

Just because geometrical perspective had developed as a theory and practice of painting that arose from earlier theories of vision, the application of perspective to the science of vision did not cease.[69] This is why perspective was seen to be a theory of the presentation of reality. It was not regarded only as a method just a device or trick for imitation. Picture space was ordered geometrically, and consequently, it was assumed that the structure of nature was geometrical as well. Then the analogy between painting and nature shows, once more, how Alberti had a vision of the direct portrayal of natural harmony in art. The geometrical symbols of the painting represent the patterns and organization of nature itself. Renaissance paintings also contained other symbols as well; these were referential symbols of a literary and often metaphysical nature. Now we have seen that, as a result of his theory of perspective, Alberti added to these symbols, or superimposed upon them, a direct mathematical embodiment of the harmony of nature.

Out of this practical problem of how to paint a picture in perspective new ideas developed which affected men's views about cosmology and perception. In the mixture of Aristotelian physics and Ptolemaic cosmology which was still prevalent in the fifteenth century, space had been accorded a relatively unimportant status as compared with objects or things. Man's immediate concern was with the objects and with the supposed tendency of the elements (earth, water, air and fire) to move toward their proper places in the universe. First, Cusanus rejected this theory of the elements and maintained that the elements were mixed in all places in the cosmos. Then Alberti and theorists of art and artists worked out the details of a nonphysical but geometric view of the relations between space and objects. The result was not a rival view of space, in the sense of its having developed directly out of a new physics. However, at the same time, in the sense of its having such a completely different orientation from Aristotelian physics, the geometrical view was truly a rival. The theory had the effect of an ideological rivalry mainly because the solution to problems of representation actually involved the formulation of a new description of reality. Out of Alberti's perspective, then, there eventually developed a new and important concept of space. In it space became wholly accessible to the methods of mathematics. Thus, there arose as well further stimulation for thought and experiment about visual perception. Alberti's desire for naturalistic representation once again provided specific material which was carried over into scientific questions.

Why did Alberti and the other inventors of perspective begin to look at the world in this particular and not very obvious way? It is impossible to offer more than a few suggestions about this here since I do not treat the history of styles systematically. However, the stylistic development of naturalism, including representation in perspective, appears to have occurred independently of the philosophy that was later to form the basis of its theory. Motifs like continuity appear independently, both as part of an artistic style and as part of Renaissance Neo-Platonism (for example in the work of Nicholas of Cusa). The philosophy of the continuous and infinite nature of the universe, and the stylistic concerns with proportion, continuity and infinity were brought together in the artistic theories of Alberti and Leonardo da Vinci.[70] However, the appearance of these concepts as part of artistic practice precedes their appearance in theory. Thus the historical links between the simultaneous appearances of these themes remain as yet unclear.

We can ask a much less ambitious question here; how is the concept of continuity developed by Alberti with relation to his general analogy between parts of nature? For this, a brief description of the background of the concept is useful. Aristotle maintained that there must be continuity in all quantities, lines, surfaces, solids, motions, and generally in time and space.[71] Things are continuous if either they retain relative samenesses through a series of positions, stages or changes, or if they simply share a limit in common. In the case of immaterial things, like time, each possible division or unit of time has the characteristic of sharing a limit with the same unit before it, and again with the one after it, and so on. Continuity operated in natural life and extended to inanimate things.

The Neo-Platonists combined natural continuity with the Platonic idea of the necessary fullness of nature, or plenitude. This idea of plenitude easily complemented that of continuity.

Belief in it, explained briefly, is that if between two species there is a theoretically possible intermediate type, that type must be realized.[72] Continuity and plenitude together formed the basis of an idea that the universe was a *great chain of being*. The chain was formed in an infinite number of links arranged in a hierarchical order.[73] Microcosmism, and the analogy between parts, related to the chain idea when the chain was thought of as an order within which all the links on the chain were constructed according to the same essential pattern. Thus, the acceptance of the idea of the great chain of being did not necessarily always include microcosmism. It is, of course, possible to believe in nature as an ordered whole without drawing a structural analogy between the parts. Placing Alberti's ideas against this general background we can surmise that his world view involved applications of the concept of continuity including the application of a continuous principle to the general structure of society and the natural order. His view of society was microcosmic because structural similarities were repeated in the parts; and we see in the *Libri della Famiglia* it was hierarchical as well.[74] Alberti hardly ever put these things quite as economically as he did in the following metaphor of the dirty feet:

> The old, then, should be common fathers to all the young. Indeed they are mind and soul to the whole body of the family. And just as having dirty naked feet brings dishonour on the face and on the whole man and is a disgrace, so the old, any of the elders, should realize that neglecting the least member of the house brings justified blame on them.[75]

The analogies should be clear, and these are heartfelt words from Alberti, for he himself was a neglected lesser member of the Alberti family. Thus general principles of form were found in inanimate nature and in living things, but also in the state, in the family and in man, and the products of man's mind when these were conceived of in accordance with the principles of harmony.

Alberti believed that the organization of society should be based on principles of natural harmony.[76] He imagined that social units were microcosmic, hierarchical and that they demonstrated continuity within the unit, be it a family, a city or a state. In the *Della Famiglia* Alberti talks of man in society as the occupier of both an active and a passive place.[77] He is active in his own particular and personal role, but passive insofar as he lets common interests take precedence over purely personal ones. The balance between these active and passive qualities in any individual is arranged in a continuous descending or

ascending scale of order throughout society. Thus, man subjects himself to leadership for his own good and for the good
of the whole, and he leads others for the same good.[78] Alberti
sees the relationship of each individual to the whole unit, the
family, in a similar way. Inside the units either of the family or
of the state continuity exists because the characteristics of the
role of any given individual's proper place in that unit are
defined with precise reference to the roles of individuals
occupying places directly above and below the given individuals
within this hierarchically constructed unit. The same idea of an
unbroken continuity is applied to the interrelationship between
social units. For example, the proper participation of each
family within the functions of the state is described partly by
the roles of families in a higher social position than that of the
given family, as well as by the limits of the roles of families
whose social position is one degree lower. Finally this hierarchical application of the concept of continuity was not unrelated to
continuity as it appeared in the relationships between space
and objects, and between the functions of the different figures
in the *istoria* of the painting. For, 'Bodies ought to harmonize
together in the *istoria* in both size and function.'[79] This is
analogy-making on two levels. First, the harmony of size in a
picture with perspective is conceived of in naturalistic imitation
of nature and happens according to a mathematical formula.[80]
Thus the appropriateness of the proportions of two separate
figures in different places in the picture is determined by the
correct perspective representation of the relation between these
figures in space. But the picture also represents another kind of
harmony of size and function. This has to do with the proper
and decorous representation of the figures according to the
theme of the *istoria*. This means that a giant or a king should
not appear small and insignificant next to more ordinary mortals. This type of decorum is also very much in evidence in
Alberti's *Della Famiglia*. However, the two analogies, the
naturalistic and the decorous, are both visualized as kindred
expressions of the same harmony. 'It would be absurd for one
who paints the centaurs fighting after the banquet to leave a
vase of wine still standing in such tumult. (We would call) it a
weakness if in the same distance one person should appear
larger than another, or if dogs should be equal to horses, or
better, as I frequently see, if a man is placed in a building as in
a closed casket where there is scarcely room to sit down. For these
reasons, all bodies should harmonize in size and in function to
what is happening in the *istoria*.'[81] Alberti envisaged that his
current day life in the family and in society was a kind of contemporary *istoria*. Nature and art took care of the harmony and

proportion of objects and spaces, but it was up to man to use rational means to institute the social decorum that would complement natural harmony.[82]

Infinity

The last major concept that appears in the *Della Pittura* is, like the others I have already mentioned, a motif of Neo-Platonic thinking in general. It is the concept of infinity. Infinity was thought to exist absolutely in God but also partially in nature, because the number of possible natural forms was imagined as infinite; and again, since infinity and continuity were conceived of as inter-related, infinity appeared in the idea that there was an infinite number of possibilities between any two points on the chain of being.[83] In a picture, however, infinity could only be symbolized, or implied, and its symbol in the perspective picture was the vanishing point. In a picture drawn in perspective all sets of parallel lines converge towards this point. Because of this point you feel the landscape in the background goes on; the road or stream does the same; beyond the wall, at the end of the passage, you feel the world continues. By this method a painting is a microcosm of the implied chain of being. It is both a compact unity of continuous and harmonious relationships and also one part of an implied greater whole.

Turning for a moment from Alberti and aesthetics we can reflect about an opinion of Lovejoy's that I think bears a relationship to many of the ideas brought into consideration here. Lovejoy considered the more general historical significance of ideas that combined concepts of 'plenitude', 'continuity' and 'infinity', to be of the greatest importance in promoting the development of the concept of an infinite universe. He goes so far as to suggest that these ideas might have been even more effective in breaking down the old Ptolemaic cosmology than the dramatic Copernican change over from geocentricity to heliocentricity.[84] I agree with Lovejoy, and I think that further study of the influence of analogies on the imaginations of a number of thinkers whose thoughts somehow involved these concepts will eventually lend support to his view. It seems to me that the development of the concepts of proportion, continuity, and infinity, in the philosophy of Nicholas of Cusa, and in artistic theories of representation, and, to some extent, in mathematics may have provided the most important elements contributing to the historical development of the idea of rational and comprehensible order in a vast infinite universe.

Therefore, with reference to some of the most sophisticated thinkers of the Renaissance, I place the psychological importance of these theories of representation perhaps even above that of Copernicanism, and of the impact of man's wider exploration of the globe. This is very unusual because the popularity of the latter two things was undoubtedly greater than that of the subtle view of an infinite universe launched by Cusanus in a very abstract theology, or than the geometrical handling of space described by Alberti and practised by artists. However, before the heavens fell and the whole Ptolemaic cosmos gave way, and before men had to relinquish the view that society and human experience reflected a neat and contained hierarchical type of harmony, some few men had already laid the foundations of an immeasurable harmony that still did not completely fly above men's heads. It was, in some way, seen to be accessible both in nature and in the arts. Thus, there was a basket ready in waiting for the thoughtful who presumably were shaken by Renaissance contradictions to the orthodox medieval cosmic order. All those who could place the human mind into some kind of contact with the infinite mind, and all those who believed that no matter how partial it was, experience held real keys to eternity, all these could afford not to mind whether the earth turned or whether it did not turn, or whether the order of society was upside down and inside out in Estotilant.[85] Harmony was preserved essentially in the mind and also in experience. And when men could not see clear evidence of this harmony, they mostly tended to refine their views of experience rather than to topple their gods completely.[86] So before the new star in 1577 had tainted the supposedly immutable heavens, and even before the Portuguese and Spanish explorers had brought back news of new lands and customs extending far beyond the imaginations of most Europeans, there was already flourishing in the minds of a few important thinkers an idea of a harmony of nature that contained within itself a real awareness of some of the possible implications of the notion of infinity in its application to the universe. This idea of the harmony of nature was to some extent a descendant of medieval ideas of the harmony between the microcosm of the earth and the macrocosm of the heavens, but it was already stripped of Aristotelian physical principles. The inspirations for the Renaissance idea of natural harmony came primarily from the humanist's readings of the classics, especially of the writings of some of the Romans on rhetoric, and it also was given its essential formulation in the Platonic mysticism of Nicholas of Cusa and was inspired by geometric models. The varied influence of these somewhat diverse sources will have to be described gradually as I proceed with examining shifts in men's analogies based on nature or on processes that were seen as being natural. Without doubt, the Renaissance idea of natural harmony inspired many outstanding minds to cultivate the study and practice of various types of mysticism and magic. The capacities of the mind had somehow to be able to stretch themselves in order to reach out to understand the infinite. However the most rational forms and applications of the newer Renaissance theory of harmony brought that harmony near to men directly in their experience in the world.[87] The origin of this very rational expression of harmony is to be found principally in the theories and practices of architecture, engineering, and of artistic representation that were formulated in and around Florence in the fifteenth century. If such dramatic historical consequences can be proposed as one primary effect of a combination of concepts (of proportion, of continuity, and of infinity), what then is the relationship of these ideas as they appear in theory of art, with these ideas in cosmology? An analysis of some of the analogies of Leonardo will shortly shed more light on this problem, as this is a very difficult question to even begin to answer at this point. However, we know that the concepts of continuity and infinity became popular in the theory of a style of art which really attempted to imitate nature. Both concepts had already been given a more general philosophical formulation by Cusanus in the 1430s. The same concepts also became popular afterwards in the actual fields of astronomy and cosmology. At the very least this indicates that leading concepts like infinity may have formed the associative threads that enabled men to interrelate nature and art and the different disciplines during the Renaissance.[88] So at this early point it is possible to make the suggestion that important themes, inspired from mathematical analogies and involving the concepts of proportion, continuity, and infinity, link natural science and artistic theory in the Renaissance. If we now place Alberti's implication of infinity within the picture frame into this much more general context, some awareness of its historical importance may begin to dawn. Certainly, we can begin to detect something of the atmosphere within which the wider (not just visual) revolution of man's ideas about nature and the universe occurred in the Renaissance.

One of the more precise effects of this dual appearance of concepts of continuity and infinity, both in aesthetics and in cosmology, might be described as their having yielded positive psychological value for thinkers of that age. We know that at least some thinkers and artists became intimate, certainly not with the infinite itself, but with some kind of notion or idea of it. When, for instance, such an artist was aware that each represented *istoria* was but one of an infinite number of other possible stories; and furthermore, when he knew that each physical position of each thing in the representation might have been constructed as having been viewed from an infinite number of other possible points, what then was the significance of his one particular selection in any single representation? Was it purposeless, purely personal, generally decorative? Did it only typify a bird's eye view of man and nature? No, we have seen the contrary. The psychological power of the representation was deemed to be great, and the depictive powers of the artists enabled them to contain in all their works real elements of the beautiful, the good, and the true. This is all in the highest philosophical sense of these qualities, as we have already seen from Alberti's attitudes. So then the idea of the harmony of nature and the rational design of the universe could only really be shattered for the many thinkers who relied primarily on Aristotelian physics for the explanation of natural harmony. These were the majority of minds. But there was a significant group of others, some educated in the north Italian studios and academies as much as in the universities, and some of these had been exposed to an altered view of natural harmony. This view, born of a kind of mathematical mysticism, influenced the Ficino type of Neo-Platonist, as well as rational mathematical and artist types, men such as Paolo Toscanelli, Alberti, and Leonardo. The person of Michelangelo seems to me to combine both offshoots of Renaissance Neo-Platonism, the psychological and mystical with the perceptual and rational. In other personalities, these things did not knit so well. However both sorts of Neo-Platonist shared something important in common. Neither branch of the tree would break when the full storm of the new cosmology burst upon men's heads. Natural harmony was secure. It was all in the mind of God. It was both born in men's minds first, and later recognized by men, in its parts from the examples of nature. It manifested itself in a vast universe perceived and recognized by the almost equally vast powers of mind that were seen to be given to men. From the most general inspiration of this sort of idea of harmony, men as diverse as Leonardo, Galileo, Campanella, Bruno, Mersenne, and Bacon will all visualize the mind as holding the keys to the order and organization of nature. This general inspiration began to find its first voice in the work of Neo-Platonists, mathematicians and artistic theorists and practitioners during the early fifteenth century; and this was because, at least for a time, these sorts of men had established a believable connection between the existing natural order and the divine idea or plan of the universe.

There is yet another important and original aspect to Alberti; as noted, he was one of the first, if not the first, theoretician of architecture and town planning who incorporated both functional and aesthetic considerations in his theories.[89] He invented a kind of harmonistic utilitarianism by combining his ideas of congruity in appearance with ideas of congruity in operation. He thereby elevated the general concepts of utility and function that were naturally the concern of all architects and planners into something grander, into ideals.

Another aspect of Alberti's harmonistic thinking is found in his handling of the then popular concept of vocation. Humanists had adopted the Platonic notion of imprinted abilities and developed it into an idea which approximated to the later Protestant idea of a calling.[90] Alberti adopted this idea and carried it somewhat further than most because he thought it was the duty of the state to guarantee each citizen's pursuit of his vocation, in the same way as it was the duty of the state to guarantee the social position of the family.[91] In this we see another example of Alberti's characteristic desire to prescribe what he sees as a natural harmony, and tell men how to arrange things according to it. By the seventeenth century Alberti is still referred to with reverence as the founder of the modern school of architecture. Thus Fréart de Chambray (died 1676) writes: '...Leon Battista Alberti, the most ancient of all the moderns and ... the most knowing in the art of building, as may be easily collected by a large and excellent volume which he has published, wherein he fundamentally shows whatever is necessary for an architect to know.'[92] The fame of Alberti is also witnessed by John Evelyn who praises him in *An Account of Architects and Architecture*.[93]

So Alberti's ideas influenced theorists and practitioners for two centuries afterwards, but it still is possible for us to question the importance of that influence. After all, were not his choices of proportions, in the end, completely arbitrary? Claude Perrault was certainly questioning them by the end of the seventeenth century, and in the eighteenth, Tommaso Temanza broke with the tradition of ideal proportion altogether. Therefore, was not the practical effect of Alberti's theory simply a change of style? It was, of course, partly this, and is therefore for this reason alone important, as setting down the precepts of that style of architecture. A style that (as we have seen) was accepted as beautiful by Europeans for over two centuries, and one that has produced some of the buildings we still consider as most beautiful. In terms of aesthetic questions, and in terms of questions about the importance of

Alberti himself in the history of art, the fact that Alberti's idea of proportion may not have embodied a single scientific truth is irrelevant.

However, I have already suggested that Alberti's handling of his philosophy of natural harmony has relevance with regard to historical developments outside theories of aesthetics or the history of style.

Alberti has been continually recommended to us as the man who put into theory the rules of the naturalism that was developing in contemporary artistic practice - naturalism was more than a style. It subsequently influenced man's whole way of looking at the world.

Observation was the key to the painter's practice of naturalism. But observation is also a fundamental practice of natural science. The nature-like images could be used for wholly aesthetic purposes or for illustration, education, and also for a record of phenomena. They were immediately used for all of these purposes. And no one questions the value for science in the development of a coherent practice of natural observation. But what about those important conclusions of science that appear to contradict the impressions of the senses? A typical question of the seventeenth century comes to mind; if indeed the earth moves, then why doesn't an object tossed into the air from the deck of a ship fall behind the ship? Were the Renaissance naturalists not impeding some kinds of science when they placed such great value on examples and on the eye? A possible answer to this lies deep within Alberti's sort of assumptions about knowledge and reality. We must recall the point that complete beauties were hardly ever seen in nature in any one example, but that the mind surmised from many examples and formed thoughts that evoked an inner sense of beauty. The same can be said for truth. If you will allow my characterizing it in this way, this belief in an inner dialogue can be seen to provide great security for the conclusions of the mind. It makes plausible the idea that the mind can perfect concepts that need not look like the examples that inspired the process, but that the concepts can really express something essential about the examples instead. Real beauty is in the mind, and so is truth. Alberti did not pursue his assumptions in quite this way but his sort of idea of knowledge does leave the opening for this aspect of science. Later, the Platonist Galileo used just this sort of an opening.

Because some historians tend to classify imprinted ideas as some of the medieval refuse to be displaced by modern science, I want to make this point clearer still. It is possible that, for a time, the notion of innate gifts or ideas existing in the mind

actually preserved the place and precedence of valuable characteristics of thought that were not clearly seen to develop as conclusions based upon the evidence of the senses. The development
of early modern science required both, first the confirmation of observation as a valid method, and then the recognition
that the mind had capacities that stretched its thoughts far
beyond what could be easily seen to be gleaned from examples.
In the early fifteenth century there existed a Neo-Platonic epistemology that could accommodate both of these needs without
clashing them. It is almost a pity that it could not have been
bottled like a divine elixir and then later fed to Bacon and
Descartes, and to others who could not quite regulate the question of stress, be it on the eyes or in the mind.

In terms of specific contributions to science, we have seen
that Alberti's setting down of the theory of perspective had the
effect of raising questions about visual perception, and of establishing a geometric conception of space. That conception, in its
turn, had important implications in the formulation of the new
cosmology.[94] Yet, Alberti's theory of perspective itself, as we
have also seen, is filled with harmonistic philosophy. Once
again, the issue of the correctness of the philosophy as a true
description of reality does not diminish the significance of its
role within this historical context.

The final and most important suggestion, which will be explored further on, is that the principal concepts in the analogy
between parts, concepts like proportion, continuity, and infinity, were vital concepts in the process of bringing together disciplines. The continuity between space and object in Alberti's
perspective was, we have seen, also applied by him to things as
unrelated as social philosophy and human relations. We will see
later on that the idea of continuity was applied by Leonardo da
Vinci within studies of human movement. Therefore I feel that
it is not impossible to say that out of Alberti's very personal use
of an ideology which eventually became in itself obsolete there
arose ideas, questions, and practices which appear to have been
important in the evolution of a more scientific or modern
ideology. This suggestion is to some extent borne out by the
observation that the humanist conviction about the harmony of
the external world, a harmony that was immanent in every
part, was expressed better by art than by philosophy:
'Mathematics and painting founded on the new geometrical
perspective had in common a power of exposition, a demon-
strability in advance of philosophical treatment.'[95]

Since I have described Alberti as having both scientific and
aesthetic interests, it may be well to point out why such
emphasis is here laid on his aesthetic theories. Alberti was not a

philosopher nor was he a natural scientist like those working in the Italian universities. His own choice of role was that of the teacher of practices and of practical things. He wrote primarily to instruct younger painters, architects and sculptors. In his works it is clear that his overwhelming commitment is to the production or reproduction of beauty, in and above the exploration of nature for its own sake. Beauty, the result of the congruity between parts and the whole, is something imprinted as a law in the organization of matter, and in the mind of man. Of the emotional effect that beauty can have Alberti writes: 'I will be bold to say, there can be no greater security to any work against violence and injury, than beauty and dignity.' And again: '. . .When we lift our eyes to heaven, and view the wonderful works of God, we admire him more for the beauties which we see, than for the conveniences which we feel and derive from them. . . .'[96] I do not believe we can wish for a clearer commitment than that to aesthetic views and aims.

Notes to Chapter One

1. Principal works: *Della Pittura* (1436), *Della Famiglia* (written during the 1430s), *De Re Aedificatoria* (1452, first edition 1485), *Della Statua* (written about 1464).
2. L.B. Alberti, *Ten Books on Architecture*, trans. J. Leoni (1st edn. 1726, London, 1955), Bk. IX, ch. v (243).
3. For an analysis of Alberti's analogies in contrast to medieval analogies see Joan Gadol, *Leon Battista Alberti: Universal Man of the Early Renaissance* (Chicago and London, 1969) pp. 102, 103, 151.
4. Alberti, *Architecture*, Bk. IX, ch. v (240).
5. Prescribed proportions were clearly known instances of ratios accepted as expressing natural harmony. These were accepted mainly from Pythagorean and Platonic sources.
6. Alberti, *Architecture*, Bk. IX (243-247).
7. *Ibid.* Bk. IX (242).
8. Eugenio Garin, *Portraits from the Quattrocento*, 'Paolo Toscanelli' (New York, 1963), pp. 119-21 Giuseppe Saitta, *Nicolo Cusano e l'Umanesino Italano* (Bologna, 1957), pp. 145-74.
9. For some of the historical background relating to ideas imprinted in nature and natural sensibilities in man, cf. A.O. Lovejoy, *The Great Chain of Being* (New York, 1960; first publ. 1936), *passim*. Also cf. R. Allers, "Microcosmos", *Traditio*, Vol. II, 1944, p.319-407. Cf. also C.G. Jung and W. Pauli, *The Interpretation of Nature and the Psyche* (New York, 1955), p.152.
10. Alberti, *I Libri della Famiglia*, trans. R.N. Watkins (Columbia, South Carolina, 1969), Bk. II, p.134, my italics.

11. Alberti, *Architecture,* Bk. IX (239, 240).
12. *Ibid.* Bk. I, ch. i (16)
13. *Ibid.* Bk. IX, ch. v (240).
14. Erwin Panofsky, *Idea* (Columbia, South Carolina, 1968), pp. 57-9.
15. Panofsky, *Idea, passim.*
16. Alberti, *Architecture,* Bk. IX (240).
17. Alberti, *Della Famiglia,* Bk. I, p. 75.
18. Alberti, *Architecture,* Bk. IX (239, 240).
19. Carroll W. Westfall, 'Society, beauty and the humanist architect in Alberti's *De Re Aedificatoria', Studies in the Renaissance,* vol. XVI, 1969.
20. Alberti, *Della Famiglia,* Bk. I, p. 60.
21. Alberti, *Della Famiglia,* Bk. II, p. 133.
22. Alberti, *Della Famiglia,* Bk. II, p. 135, my italics.
23. Alberti, *Della Famiglia,* Bk. I, p. 75, my italics.
24. Ernst Cassirer, *The Individual and The Cosmos in Renaissance Philosophy,* tr. M. Domandi, New York, 1963 (first pub. 1927), pp. 7-72, and also, Don Parry Norford, 'Microcosm and Macrocosm in Seventeenth Century Literature', *J. Hist. Ideas* v. XXXVIII, n. 3, July-Sept. 1977, pp. 409-422.
25. Eugenio Garin supports the influence of Cusa's mathematics in Florence, but he does not admit that Cusa's philosophical ideas had any significant reception there. While it is true that no Florentine took up Cusa's works and treated them systematically, I think that his highly original metaphors, and his supernatural visions with practical roots were undoubtedly attractive to some thinkers in the Florentine artistic and mathematical circles. C.f. *Ritratti di Umanisti* (Florence, 1967), pp 41-67. Also see Giorgio de Santillana, 'Paolo Toscanelli and his friends', *Reflections on Men and Ideas* (Cambridge, Mass., 1968).
26. Alberti, *Della Famiglia,* Bk. II, p. 149.
27. These three things - all essential to Alberti's estimation of the relation between man and nature - metaphorically reproduce the three images of the one God that the philosopher Cusanus repeatedly describes. This is important because Cusa himself greatly stressed an analogy between the human capacity to know, and the divine quality, the power to create, the act of creation together with the reality of creation. When men make what is potential real and actual, this can be seen to occur in steps or stages, but in God actualization is unified in a threefold image. First, if we take creation as our focus, *God can do;* second, but simultaneously in the nature of God, *it can be done;* and three is the *knot* that unifies and binds Father and Son, and this knot is the Holy Spirit. Here the power is unified with the act and the reality. If the human mind and spirit is to be seen

in finite and sequential parallel, then within these limits *man can do*. If the harmony of nature is seen in a similar parallel, then *it can be done*. What this means is that man has been given the capacity to know, and nature is so made that it is knowable, but actualization must be brought about and this is Alberti's recognition process. In the full biological and spiritual way that Alberti saw it, recognition is the *knot* that binds and unifies reality with knowledge. Thus within spatial and temporal limits human knowledge is infinitely perfectible and real. In pointing out this metaphor, I am not suggesting a secret theological passion in the occupations of Alberti. The stress for Alberti is in the adoption of the analogy between divine creativity and human knowledge and works. This is essential to the Renaissance artists' idea of themselves, of perfectibility and progress and of genius.

28. J. Gadol, *Alberti*, p. 106.
29. Leon Battista Alberti, *On Painting*, trans. J.R. Spencer (New Haven, Conn. 1956, revised 1966), Bk. III, p. 93; my italics.
30. Alberti, *Architecture*, Bk. IX (239).
31. *Ibid.* Bk. IX (239).
32. *Ibid.* Bk. I (33).
33. E. Panofsky, *Renaissance and Renaissances in Western Art* (Uppsala, 1960), p. 26.
34. Alberti, *Aedificatoria*, Bk. VI, ch. ii (115).
35. J. Gadol, *Alberti*. For a superbly clear evaluation see chapters 4 and 5.
36. His method was one of comparing beautiful bodies and gathering the ideal proportions for a man from the best features of these bodies. The passage about this in the *Statua* is reminiscent of a much earlier passage written in the treatise on painting where Alberti recounts that Zeuxis, an ancient painter, chose the features of beauty from five beautiful girls. Presumably, his source for this story was Cicero. Cf. Alberti, *On Painting*, Bk. III, p. 93, and see Spencer's note, p. 134. Alberti tells a similar story in the treatise on statues. But this time it is about an ancient sculptor who had been employed to make a statue of their goddess for the *Crotoniati*.
37. E. Panofsky, *Idea,* pp. 15, 57.
38. Alberti, *Of Statues,* trans. John Evelyn, first printed 1707, pp. 70-73, found in *A Parallel of Ancient and Modern Architecture*, by Roland Fréart *Sieur de Chambray*. Cf. also Alberti, *Of Statues,* trans. Leoni and Burtoli (London, 1739), pp. 33, 34.
39. *Ibid.* p. 74. Cf. also A. Blunt, *Artistic Theory in Italy, 1450-1600* (Oxford, 1962), first pub. 1940, p. 14, n. 3. Alberti invented a device consisting of a series of circles and plumb lines. With it the sculptor could measure, in terms of height

and projection, the contours of any figure or three-dimensional object.

40. E. Panofsky, *Meaning in the Visual Arts* (New York, 1957), first pub. 1955, 'The History of the Theory of Human Proportion as a Reflection of the History of Styles', p. 95.

41. R. Wittkower, *Architectural Principles in the Age of Humanism* (London, 1952), pp. 90-99, especially p.96. In the arithmetic progression the second term is greater than the first by the same amount that the third is greater than the second: (b - a = c - b), e.g. 4, 6, 8. In the geometric progression the ratio of the first term to the second is the same as the ratio of the second to the third: (a:b = b:c), e.g. 4, 6, 9. The harmonic mean is defined by the formula $\frac{x - y}{y} = \frac{z - x}{z}$ and it is represented geometrically by Fig. 1.

$$\frac{BC}{AB} = \frac{CD}{AD}$$

AC = x
AB = y
AD = z

42. Alberti, *Architecture*, Bk. IX (250).

43. Cf. A. Blunt, *Artistic Theory in Italy, 1450-1600*, pp. 1, 21, 22, and especially p. 18.

44. S.K. Heninger, Jr., *Touches of Sweet Harmony: Pythagorean Cosmology and Renaissance Poetics*, Calif. 1974, pp. 193, 194; cf. by the same author, *The Cosmographical Glass: Renaissance Diagrams of the Universe*, Calif. 1977, chs. iv, v.

45. Cf. A. Blunt, *Artistic Theory in Italy*, p. 17.

46. Alberti's method of comparative selection resulted in detailed observations of the body including the numbers of bones, the muscles and the junctions of the nerves. Cf. *De Statua*, p. 74.

47. A. Blunt, *Artistic Theory in Italy*, p. 17.

48. Alberti, *On Painting*, Bk. III, p. 93.

49. *Ibid.* Bk. II, p. 65.

50. *Ibid.* Bk. II, p. 77.

51. Washington, D.C., 1960. *Passim.*

52. Paolo Rossi, *Philosophy, Technology, and the Arts in the Early Modern Era*, tr. S. Attanasio, New York, 1970, pp. 137-38.

53. Wittkower, *Architectural Principles*, p. 95.

54. K. Clark, *The Nude* (Edinburgh, 1957), first pub. 1956, p. 13.

55. Wittkower, *Architectural Principles*, p. 4.

56. E. Panofsky, *Renaissance and Renaissances*, p. 28.

57. On the question of size, Alberti believed that were the appropriate instruments available, it would not be impossible to make a statue as big as Mount Caucasus in perfect proportion. And

because the proportions would be devised by strict observation and prescription, one half of this statue could be made in Egypt, and the other half in the mountains of Carrara, and then they could be fitted together. Alberti, *Of Statues*, trans. J. Leoni (London, 1755), p. 271.

58. Alberti, *On Painting*, tr. J.R. Spencer (London, 1956), *passim;* cf. especially n. 8 on p. 133.

59. Alberti says that the foot was Vitruvius' measure.

60. R. Allers, 'Microcosmos from Anaxamandros to Paracelsus', *Traditio*, vol. 2 (New York, 1944), pp. 321-22.

61. Cf. chapter two, pp. 57-8, for an analogy of correspondence between the earth and man.

62. Alberti, *On Painting*, p. 73.

63. E. Panofsky, *Renaissance and Renaissances*, p. 123.

64. J. Gadol, *Alberti*, p. 42.

65. J. Gadol, *Alberti*, p. 75.

66. *Ibid.*

67. E. Panofsky, *Renaissance and Renaissances*, p. 126. In pictorial space continuity is implied in two ways. One, because any point in a perspective image is determined by three co-ordinates. The other, because the diminution between the magnitudes in a perspective image is constant and can be expressed by a recursive formula. Alberti's actual procedure for construction is described very clearly in J. Gadol, *Alberti*, pp. 44-52.

68. Cf. chapter two, pp. 76-8, and chapter three, pp. 109-11.

69. J. Gadol, *Alberti*, pp. 27, 68, 69.

70. Cf. chapter two, pp. 68-74.

71. A. Lovejoy, *The Great Chain of Being*, pp. 55-56.

72. A. Lovejoy, *The Great Chain of Being*, p. 58.

73. *Ibid.* p. 59.

74. The term hierarchical applies to the social order here, not to the positing of a metaphysical hierarchy at different levels of the cosmos. Alberti's social hierarchy is largely conceived of in aesthetic terms with some metaphysical overtones, in that social harmony is seen as an aspect of natural harmony. In society also, harmony will be achieved by a proper balance between the parts.

75. Alberti, *Della Famiglia*, Bk. I, p. 39.

76. Baussola LeMano Maria, *L'Ideale estetico del Trattato 'Della Famiglia' di L.B. Alberti* (Rapallo, 1956), pp. 39-68.

77. Our interest is in the aesthetic ideals of the *Della Famiglia* because they illustrate Alberti's consistent application of natural harmony to different aspects of reality.

78. P.H. Michel, *La Pensée* de Leon Battista Alberti (Paris, 1930), pp. 267-68.

79. Alberti, *On Painting*, p. 75.
80. Cf. chapter two, p. 84.
81. Alberti, *On Painting*, p. 75.
82. Alberti, *I Libri della Famiglia*, tr. R. Watkins (Columbia S.C. 1969), Introduction, p. 18.
83. A. Lovejoy, *The Great Chain of Being*, p. 115.
84. A. Lovejoy, *Chain of Being*, pp. 108-109; and W.P.D. Wightman, *Science and the Renaissance* (Edinburgh, 1962), vol. 1, p. 125.
85. Girolamo Cardano, *De Vita Propria Liber*, tr. J. Stoner; Estotilant was in Northern Labrador (New York, 1930), pp. 189, 314.
86. This is a general reflection that is not taken from one individual example. The tensions in individuals could show in any number of ways. So that Galileo, for instance, was concerned to persuade the church and others about the truth of heliocentricity and of the motion of the earth. But at the same time we must realize that his own faith in the harmony of nature had not been shattered when he became convinced of the Copernican view. In fact, it is more probable that Galileo was anxious to persuade the church that a real belief in divine order in the universe was not even vulnerable to threats posed from alterations in men's understanding of their physical circumstances.
87. Here rational is meant in the way we commonly understand it, but not as a value judgement. The practices calling down powers from the heavens, and those using close experience, magnifying it, and generalizing from it, were not really all that separate and distinct from each other in early modern thought.
88. Cf. chapter two, p. 86.
89. P. Lavedan, *Histoire de l'Urbanisme (Renaissance et Temps Modernes)* (Paris, 1941), pp. 9-12. Also H. Rosenau, *The Ideal City* (London, 1959), p. 36.
90. R.M. Douglas, 'Humanisme et Réformation, b) Genus Vitae and Vocatio', *XIIe Congrès International des Sciences Historiques*, Rapports III, Commissions (Vienna, 1965), pp. 75-86.
91. Michel, *Pensées*, pp. 296-97.
92. Roland Fréart de Chambray, *A Parallel of the Ancient Architecture with the Modern* (London, 1723), p. 27.
93. Edition of London, 1723, p. 15. This edition contains also de Chambray's essay, and Evelyn's translation of Alberti's *De Statua*.
94. W.P.D. Wightman, *Science and the Renaissance*, pp. 26-27.
95. A. Stokes, *Art and Science (A Study of Alberti, Piero della Francesca and Giorgione)* (London, 1956), p. 29.
96. Alberti, *Aedificatoria*, Bk. VI, ch. 2 (115).

2
LEONARDO DA VINCI AND UNIVERSAL HARMONY

Nothing is the force that renovates the world.
Emily Dickinson

The temporal move from Alberti to Leonardo da Vinci (1452-1519) does not break the climate of thoughts and assumptions seen in the last chapter. Certainly society changes, and changes significantly. However, the harmony of nature, the meaning of art in terms of that harmony, the creative role of the artist, the value of art as an imitation of nature, these and many other related themes continue in the thinking of Leonardo.

These themes have come to light here because Alberti's view of the meaning of the artist's role was invested with them. Still, the themes are themselves suggestive of an even more diverse set of suppositions that seem to have played a general part in creative thinking in the early modern period. The analogy between the whole and the parts of nature, the analogy between nature and art, parallels betwixt and between specific art forms, the analogy between macrocosm and microcosm, and even the idea of God as the creator of the universe and of man as the subject who perfects or recreates its model in the mind - all of these notions both reinforce creativity and are, in some ways, basically related to each other. They are similar either in their form and/or in the sorts of effects that they are presumed to have upon human sensibilities.

Certainly, these are very general assumptions and they can only be appreciated through bringing forward many examples of their use. However, insofar as it can be so, my focus is on the assumptions. Thus, in citing from Alberti, Leonardo and others, I am not trying to write a mini-history about them, or about the culture of the Renaissance. Assumptions can only be made visible in terms of the thoughts of those who held them. But once they are more visible, it might be possible to appreciate a whole new area of both stability and change in cultural history.

The rhythmic quality of nature's cycles

In the first chapter I described Alberti's belief in an ideal order, the parts of which were mutually analogous. Leonardo, also, believed in this principle. He devoted his life to attaining knowledge of its manifestations in nature and to describing them in a rigorous record of observations. He believed that what we generally call art and science (pictures, descriptions, written observations, mathematical proofs, and experiments) combined with each other to make up different aspects of such a record of nature. However, any comparison of Alberti with Leonardo will show definite differences between the modes of expression of their points of view. These differences are not the result of a clash between their basic conceptions of natural harmony, but are implicit in their different applications of the idea. Alberti desired knowledge of the principles of nature to apply them in the creation of works of both beauty and usefulness. Leonardo had this same desire, but he also sought knowledge with no other clear purpose than that of his wanting to know. Alberti had been occupied with questions of structure, architectural, pictorial, and even social. Consequently, his frequent use of analogy can be seen to be based upon common formal and structural features. Questions about growth and movement are less apparent.

Leonardo was also concerned with structure, both in painting and more generally, and so there is an essentially formal element in the way he formulates his analogies. But Leonardo was as much intrigued by growth and by movement as he was by structure and form.

Leonardo frequently draws an analogy between the microcosm, man, and the macrocosm: in this instance the earth (more commonly it was the whole cosmos). The preoccupations of his imagination are revealed here as he compares them with respect to the processes of growth and decay. This is not simply a structural analogy based on abstract proportions. Some of the parallels made are based on organic, therefore developmental, properties. At other times, when he is engaged with a problem of seeing how something works, he draws mechanical analogies. A number of examples of this sort of analogy gives his overall view of natural harmony a mechanical cast. The universe appears in the role of a super-ideal mechanism. The mechanism also had a maker, and so God or, at times, a personified Nature, is envisaged by Leonardo as the ideal inventor and artist, analogous (with qualitative distinctions, of course) to man: here again a microcosm but now in his creative and reasoning capacity. So the range of Leonardo's application of the analogy is much wider than Alberti's, and this increased range is not really theoretical but is a reflection of Leonardo's interests and unique capacities. Leonardo's view still involves the assumption of a pattern of formal relations, formal relations that he somehow mysteriously animates by viewing forms progressively.

Leonardo's most typical general expression of the analogy between microcosm and macrocosm is organic and has Aristotelian inspirations. For example, 'Nothing originates', where there is no 'sentient', 'vegetable', or 'rational life'. He compares the frequent renewal of feathers on birds to that of hairs on animals, to the grasses in the fields and to the leaves on the trees. He continues:

> . . . So that we might say that the earth has a spirit of growth; that its flesh is the soil, its bones the arrangement and connection of the rocks of which the mountains are composed, its cartilage the tufa, and its blood the springs of water. The pool of blood which lies round the heart is the ocean, and its breathing, and the increase and decrease of blood in the pulses, is represented in the earth by the flow and ebb of the sea; and the heat of the spirit of the world is the fire which pervades the earth, and the seat of the vegetative soul is in the fires, which in many parts of the earth find vent in baths and mines of sulphur, and in volcanoes. . . .[1]

In these correspondences drawn between physical properties of the earth and physical properties of animals, Leonardo describes a natural condition which involves parallels between entirely structural features as well as between patterns of motion and change. The structural features of soil, and rocks, for example, are analogous to flesh and bones. There are also analogies made between patterns of action and interaction. These comprise the operations of physical things. Thus, breathing and the beating of the pulse are similar to the ebb and flow of the tides. The overall characteristics of growth and decay operate in the parts and in the whole of the being, as they do in the parts and in the whole of the earth. These characteristics appear frequently in Leonardo's notes.

Many of Leonardo's analogies based on natural structure and function show that both constancy and repetition exist in nature. Thus, the renewal of the grasses and of human hair and nails, the motions of the tides, growth and, of course, death - all these things can be observed as characteristic of the natural condition at all times. But, at the same time, we can also observe that they operate in cycles or repetitions with regard to specific parts of the earth, or to the individuals concerned. So that there are always tides, but the tides of different seas do not coincide with each other in terms of time, and the heart always beats, but not every heart in unison. These are various ways of saying that, while at any one time some are born, others wither and die, but birth and death are constant characteristics of nature. The recurrence of natural operations gives nature a rhythmical quality. The basis of rhythm is reliability (the predictable occurrence of the instant and duration of the next beat). So it is not strange that one of the earliest expressions of the idea of the predictable and reliable occurrence of natural phenomena was formulated in an analogy between music and nature. This Pythagorean analogy came to be expressed in a great variety of ways. Leonardo's writings show how this early analogy between music and nature was compounded by the addition of animal and mechanical analogies. The seventeenth- and eighteenth-century analogy of nature with the machine or the time-piece has a basic similarity to the old Pythagorean analogy. Seventeenth-century natural philosophers including Newton still thought in terms of both the musical and the mechanical analogy. Long before them, Da Vinci certainly did. The repetition and recurrence of patterns both of structure and of operations, in inanimate and animate nature, assured Leonardo that man could observe in his own life's experience the principles and the workings of true natural laws.

Since Plato used it in the *Timaeus,* the image of the world as a living thing has been just as potent as the complementary idea of nature as constructed on a basis of mathematical harmony. The Creator as architect or geometer did not essentially differ from the Creator as the author of life; rather, life itself could be a kind of divine geometry. Now it is important to realize that whatever may have happened to these two models in later history, the vision of the universe as an animal and the vision of the universe as a harmonious construction had been philosophical relations to each other. This reminder has to be voiced insofar as the mathematical analogy has been marked by some historians as having given rise to mechanical analogies, and these have been seen to be very important in the development of early modern science.[2] But the animal analogy has had a more doubtful reception because elements of mystery are contained within it. The soul of the world was more difficult to get at by scientific methods than the geometry of parts and their operations. However, looking back in this way gives an over-rationalized view of it all. For while no one will deny the fruitfulness and popularity of the mechanical parallels used in early modern science, yet no one should fail to see that both brother images were equal sources of inspiration in some creative Renaissance minds. The functioning of parts in the animal universe and in man was often viewed within mathematical and/

or mechanical terms. The integration of those parts and the
real unity of the whole remained in a spiritual area. A mechanical analogy was often supported by the unvoiced assumption
of the wider spiritual one. In the course of time, however, men
increasingly left this spiritual region to faith. But, in terms of
Leonardo, any separation of one image from the other would
abuse the character of his imagination. As some historians have
indicated, he may not be the archetypal early scientist, but
whatever the fruits of his creativity were, they were all
developed from the full range of his imagination. Thus, Leonardo's more general biological parallels are one type of expression of the wider macrocosm/microcosm analogy, and this vision of the earth and of man and of other living creatures forms
a persistent image in the notations of Leonardo. Such an image
may have directed his imagination towards his highly original
evolutionary types of observation in geology. It is not possible
to say whether it actually did. But, it is possible to study
Leonardo's biological analogies in specific contexts. Perhaps
some instances of their application will give a clearer picture of
the significance of this sort of image for him.

The tree of veins

This analogy is drawn between the human circulatory system
and the structure of a tree. Leonardo used it to demonstrate
that the veins originate from the heart and not from the liver,
as was generally accepted by Galenic authorities. The analogy
was suggested in the following observation by Mondino (1270-
1326) in *Anathomia*:

> Note that the verna chilis (vena cava) hath her origin from the
> heart since she is united to the substance of the heart and doth not
> go through it, but is greatest next her base and root, like to the
> stock of a tree.[3]

Leonardo took up this analogy:

> The heart is the root which produces the tree of the veins, which
> veins have their roots in the dung, that is the meseraic veins, which
> proceed to deposit the blood they have acquired in the liver from
> which the upper veins of the liver are nourished.[4]

We can see the importance of this application of the analogy when
we consider its details. The plant, he writes, cannot grow from its
root, because it existed before the root. And in the same way the
veins proceed from the heart, not the heart from the veins,

because the heart existed before the veins. This can be observed. The greatest thickness in the veins and the arteries is at the junction they make with the heart; the farther away they grow from the heart the thinner they become, and they are divided into smaller and smaller branches. This analogy is also represented figuratively in the drawing of a heart whose superior and inferior vena cavas are compared with a nut and its plumule and radicle (embryonic stem and root); another drawing of man's vascular system is simply labelled the 'tree of veins'.[6]

The analogy here is made between organic things, but its details show a basically formal concept with additional dynamic elements. The pattern of forms in the growing plant can tell us something about the pattern of forms in man's vascular system. Also knowing the correct structure of the system can suggest something about its manner of functioning. Leonardo implies such a possibility, but does not explore it. When we reflect on it, this specific version of analogy (between the circulatory system and the tree) appears less strange and remote than Leonardo's more general analogy. For now we are prepared to accept structural similarities in natural things without proposing cosmic models. The basis for Leonardo's feeling that the tree and the circulatory system were analogous in the features essential to this case is supplied by his assumption that this pattern of the growing plant is typical in nature and that it is therefore reasonable to imagine its repetition in a completely different context, the body. Hence, this example of analogy is similar to the first example mentioned in the general introduction, between the motion of sound waves and ripples on water, because Leonardo accepted an even more general analogy between all motion in air and in water.

What may this sort of analogy-making have meant in terms of the development of empiricism? Here Leonardo was led, by the use of this particular analogy, to a scientifically more accurate observation, viz.,that the veins and arteries originate from the heart and not from the liver. Therefore, is it possible to suggest that his general assumption of an analogy between parts of nature was instrumental in enabling him and perhaps other contemporary natural philosophers to make scientific discoveries? This framework did have qualities that made some productive effects likely; but, if it were not possible to see the framework as a direct instrument of progress, this does not mean that it was without historical consequence. It was the great stimulus for many unique creative imaginations. On the whole it is better not to try to evaluate the analogy of nature in simple progressive terms. And, if I now did so, this particular example could show it acting in both ways. It served as a suitable image for Leonardo in his location of the central point of the vascular system. But, historians

have also suggested that he might easily have progressed further
here and formulated a full theory of circulation. If this might
have happened then Leonardo would have had to reject
completely the parallels that served him in the above example.
His image of 'ebb and flow' in nature in general, and of the
movement up and down of the sap in a tree in particular,
provided analogies that make circular images difficult. So, the
models he used would have had to have been rejected or, at least,
been made subordinate to other models. Leonardo's following
words suggest the rising-falling image was deeply impressed in
his consciousness:

> The waters return with constant motion from the lowest depths
> of the sea to the utmost height of the mountains, not obeying
> the nature of heavier bodies; and in this they resemble the blood
> of animated beings which always moves from the sea of the heart
> and flows towards the top of the head; and here it may burst
> a vein, as may be seen when a vein bursts in the nose; all the
> blood rises from below to the level of the burst vein. When the
> water rushes out from the burst vein in the earth, it obeys the
> law of other bodies that are heavier than the air, since it always
> seeks low places.[7]

Keele, however, does give instances where, partly by the aid
of the analogy between parts of nature, Leonardo did make
scientific progress, namely by discovering the form of the upper
as well as the lower ventricles of the heart.[8]

The grandchild of nature

The analogies that Leonardo makes between parts of nature
are closely related to those that we have seen Alberti make between nature and art and between the various arts. All of these
analogies depend upon the idea that nature and the arts that
imitate it embody consistent principles that typify absolute values. These principles are compounded together in the whole
order of nature and have analogies in all the groups and their
parts. At all levels the integration of parts in various lesser
wholes contains some analogy with the integration of all parts
in the greater whole of nature. Thus the harmony of one small
song can evoke the truth of the harmony of the spheres. Similarly, a beautiful landscape seen while ascending a mountain
can evoke the beauties of some of Virgil's lines in the mind of a
beholder. Apparently these poetic lines could be seen as
divinely inspired because they conveyed specific beauties that
were in some way analogous to natural beauty. These are ways

in which examples like these were regarded in the Renaissance, and this sort of point of view extended and reinforced the medieval practice of drawing analogies between parts of nature. Hence, the motion of a single projectile could embody a principle of motion in space altogether. And, as we have just seen, the forms and operations of growing plants may have analogies in the forms and operations of the systems of living creatures. Analogies go back and forth between the arts and sciences and nature. One art form can evoke another art form or embody some principle of nature, and it is possible for one natural process to explain another apparently more mysterious natural process. Leonardo's belief that motion in air will be like motion in water belongs here. This view can apply to the sciences; for example, Leonardo saw the principles of geometry as the first principles of painting. Real surfaces and the relations between them, and represented surfaces and the relations between them, all obeyed the guiding laws of geometry. Leonardo knew that the science of geometry was abstract in the mind but he also saw it as continually being perfected within physical examples, especially in the practice of painting. At the core of all of these examples of Renaissance analogy-making there is the assumption that qualities like harmony, truth, goodness and beauty are expressed directly in nature and also that the ultimate source of these qualities transcends nature. The expressions divine beauty and divine harmony are not merely superlatives, they refer quite literally to qualities that have a divine origin. In some Renaissance minds, these qualities also existed as eternal archetypes; but for others the transcendental character of these qualities was sufficiently conveyed in the thought that nature was designed, made, created. Leonardo was this sort of man. He wanted to understand nature and not to journey into supernatural realms. He was sceptical of doctrine, and thought that men's supra-physical ascents were more outrageous than the flight of Icarus. Indeed such a flight was conceivable as its principles were available from physical nature. But metaphysical flights represented withdrawals into unguided fantastic territory. Still, he does not state that this sort of territory does not exist. Instead Leonardo has a belief about the capacities of the human mind. Nature is knowable and accessible to the mind. Thus while some Florentine Neo-Platonists were busy making new maps for the elaboration and security of their excursions into supra-physical territories, Leonardo, apparently within the influence of the epistemology of Nicholas of Cusa, preferred to perfect his view of the territory he believed he was given to understand. But nature was not godless territory. Both the mind and nature were designed by God, and the principles brought to light by the study of nature were absolute.[9] So the implications of Leonardo's sort of faith extend far beyond what we would now consider a simple statement of faith and then getting on with it. With Leonardo we are not dealing with the conception of a distant providence. Rather we have the divine principles directly immanent in the operations and forms of nature, and at the same time these principles are transcendent in God. The orderly principles of nature have been implanted there from an absolutely eternal source. Thus, all motion tends towards rest, but in Leonardo's terms we have got to understand that rest also pre-exists motion as a divine principle, and infinity pre-exists time. The experience of nature is an interlude within eternity, and yet eternity does not merely surround that interlude; the interlude is in it in an intimate way. Each minute anticipates the next minute, and so on, in unlimited number. The hand of the designer is the only hand that holds the stop-watch in this series, and even if the design may be finite as against the eternal, the designer, God, is by definition eternal. Certainly Leonardo does not attempt to journey into these metaphysical territories; instead, he relies on them and walks in them because these truths are partially expressed in the parts where he walks. Thus absolute principles comprise Leonardo's assumed spiritual place, and if his concept of nature is not located in this wider metaphysical space, then we will see that it makes no sense in the terms that Leonardo chooses to describe nature. Hence, I am suggesting that Leonardo's Dantesque statement describing painting as the grandchild of nature and truly related to God is a genealogical statement. The fact that he saw the painter as a creator after the divine creator is not a romantic notion but an epistemological idea. For, it involves his assumptions about reality and his views about how men can discover and know more about reality and also make real creative contributions to it.

In the following sections I deal with examples of Leonardo's analogies that involve rather abstract concepts, concepts of continuity, time, infinity, and nothing. These appear difficult in themselves but they are highly accessible because Leonardo's imagery is dominated by the most general arithmetical and geometrical concepts. If we move from a point to its extensions we will move with Leonardo's thoughts and if we are prepared to view that point as the invisible impression of the finger of God we will also move with Leonardo's imagination. It is rather as Cusanus puts it in the third book of *The Idiot*, 'Concerning The Mind': human minds are images after the divine mind, but creatures and things of the world are not images. An image possesses the quality of mind/soul and the capacity for intelligence. The rest of the things that exist are temporal explications of the divine in the world, and they are also both contained and combined within the divine creator. Therefore everything that exists contains some analogy with a divine attribute, possesses something of God, but nothing resembles God. The whole of nature itself is an active and integrated sum of divine attributes, principles, or ideas. These attributes can reveal the work of God to men; his work in material, in space, and in time. But men must also see that works, materials, space, and time are all combined and contained in one who is at rest, immaterial, ever-present everywhere, and eternal. God cannot be surmised from his analogies in nature. The analogy between the mind of man and God is the most intimate likeness to God expressed in nature, but this is only insofar as the perfecting of human understanding and works can be compared with the divine work of creation. No sum of concepts in the human mind can describe God. However, men can understand and describe ideal qualities as they exist and are expressed in nature. Hence the perception and experience of nature will inevitably stimulate men to perfect their knowledge of reality. God's creation is accessible to men, and as they develop their understanding of that work, men also gradually understand more and more of God through the medium of nature. Nicholas of Cusa put men in the intellectual position of having to walk through nature, and to understand its principles in precise detail in order to get beyond. There isn't any other road on this side of the gates. Thus other possible forms of understanding are left to eternity, and they are not discussed. We can see how in Cusa's terms they would not be explorable. There is only one direction to go in and it is the direction that Leonardo da Vinci took. I think that Cusa's attitude towards knowledge goes a good way in describing Leonardo's personal attitude toward the study of nature. Only, in Leonardo most of this goes without saying.

Cusanus describes the human mind as having conceptual powers, and the relation of mind to the things of nature to some extent parallels the relation of the divine mind to everyone and everything. This means that men can generalize from experience. They can classify, organize, separate experiences within different categories, and characterize all types of experience through reason and understanding. Even though things and objects exist purely and simply in themselves in the world, men can organize their concepts drawn from these things, remember them, and continually perfect the understanding of them in the mind. If God's ideas are eternal in God, men's ideas span time through memory and teaching.

Men's immaterial and abstract ideas are formed and contained
in the mind and are also applied and developed in and from
the world. An example of this is found in the work of a geometer's drawings. For him, the drawings depict his conceptions of
the implications of extending a purely abstract point. He and
his predecessors experienced surfaces in nature, and from real
surfaces, outlines, and points men developed the science of
geometry. Thus, minds generalize from nature and they reapply their generalizations both conceptually, in the development of abstract sciences, and practically as well as conceptually
in activities like the arts and crafts, invention, engineering and
in all human skills. This is a progressive idea of knowledge.

In the following chapter I will illustrate how Cusanus saw the
mind in possession of special faculties for the understanding of
the signs of God in nature. Whatever the mystical overtones
are, his view depicts the mind as possessing an objective gift
that uses the experience of nature as its primary stimulus and
source. The cultivation of human understanding must be
empirical. These valuable thoughts that were bound to attract
attention in Florentine technical and artistic circles, and did,
were all conceived of by Cusanus in a manner that is very alien
to us now. Just as Leonardo's naturalistic religious paintings
convey an air of super-reality in their atmosphere, all of
Cusanus' modern theory of knowledge was even more explici-
tly conceived of in a super-real atmosphere. He rests all of
these points about the mind and nature upon a curious contrast between God and all the rest. But we must not place these
apparent opponents on the opposite ends of a scale; for we
must also start out by assuming his assumption, that all the rest
that is creation is also in God. Cusa does an unusual overlapping of abstract concepts with the experience and vision of
nature. For instance, if in your imagination the complete form
of one building could be contracted back to the initial single
dot on the drawing board where it was conceived and planned,
and if that dot could be seen to imply the existence of an
abstract point in the mind, then we could conclude that within
the conception of the point lies the whole potential of the building. Now transplant this imaginary experiment from our temporal experience, that occurs successively, to an immaterial region of timelessness. There, in that super-physical region, the
point might be seen to contain the whole building, no longer
just potentially, but truly and completely. Thus we see that
things as they appear in the world look opposite and different
from the things as they actually are in God. For, the abstract
point in the timeless region is just a metaphor for God.

From Cusanus' assumption that everything in nature is going

to look opposite from the reality in God, certain connections between contrasting qualities can be made. He draws these connected-contrasts for us in his dialogue on the mind. He sees that number in nature explicates unity in God, and similarly, motion explicates rest. Time explicates eternity, and time, once more, explicates the present. Here, the present is conceived of as an abstract point; for when the instant that is actually the real present arrives, it has, in fact, already passed. Thus the present only exists in the form of our anticipation of the next instant. Here it is expressed by Cusanus, and later in this chapter I will illustrate how Leonardo handles time in exactly this way. Composition explicates simplicity, greatness explicates a point, inequality explicates equality and diversity, taken out of the material world and space, and time, explicates identity.[10] Cusanus also writes that motion is the explication of a moment. This crossing of spatial and temporal concepts is typical for him. He did it before in a grand way, in his treatise on learned ignorance where he proclaimed the indefiniteness of the universe. But this is complex and involved and I will have to explain it later. His handling of time works by analogy with geometrical and spatial concepts, and this is true for Leonardo too.

If these concepts seem to be totally alien, frame them in artists' terms. In the Renaissance some saw the diversity of forms in nature as the expression of beauty, and natural beauty was the explication of divine excellence, or concord in mundane music was seen as the expression of divine harmony which was the explication of unity in God. Remember, Alberti said that true beauties were rare, yet beauty was seen to exist. If beauty is a principle of nature it must originate in the excellence of God. Thus leaving aside Cusanus' great preoccupation with the coincidence of all of these apparent opposites in God, we can turn to his vision of the source of human understanding, nature. Here we find divine and absolute principles embodied in the pluralities in nature, and in the sequences of nature's activities. As given from God, the human mind develops its ideas from the stimulus and content of nature and from reasoning about all of this. Then here is the territory of Leonardo's search, not just nature in the way we understand it to be, but nature as it was seen to be, the finite expression of divine creation. Certainly Cusanus' distinction between mind and all the rest in the created world resembles some notions that we can discover in the way that Leonardo actively proceeds with intellectual problems. This context makes some of his apparently mysterious remarks and allusions seem more sensible. It will take me some time to draw this out, as the influence of Cusanus was more acted out in Leonardo's grappling with the arts and sciences than it was spoken of, or directly referred to in writing.

Continuity as a basis of analogy

Leonardo was interested in the living movement of forms as well as in their static conditions. The practice of cinemato-graphic drawing has suggested to historians a manner by which, beginning with static form, he developed a precise catalogue of motions in the transitions between one formal state and another. Some copies of Leonardo's drawings in the *Codex Huygens* seem to illustrate the method by which he studied the dimensions of an upright human body as they altered in con-tinuous movement. 'In these drawings,' says Professor Panof-sky, 'Leonardo fused the theory of human proportions with one of human movement.'[11] However, Leonardo's awareness of continuity and of motion as a continuous process is not always easily discerned. In some instances, his awareness of the con-tinuity of the surface of a thing does not involve its movement. A purely mental and progressive kind of visualization was applied to things which were static. Indeed this kind of visuali-zation was developed in the practice of painting in perspective. This is also the form of mental visualization evoked by the metaphysical geometry of Nicholas of Cusa. Thus, there may be a point of appeal here, insofar as artists who were inventing and learning the techniques of representation in perspective in the fifteenth century might have easily been attracted to the work of a philosopher who spoke about more universal matters in their language. In any case we can understand that every form of continuity does not imply actual movement but only a progressive relationship. In the following analogy that Leonardo draws between painting and geometry both discip-lines share the same basic structural forms that are built up from points to lines to surfaces. The depiction of these forms is static, the painting does not move; however, the mental vision by which the forms originate and are constructed is progressive and continuous. Here is Leonardo's formulation of this analogy:

> The science of painting begins with the point, then comes the line, the plane comes third, and the fourth the body in its ves-ture of planes. This is as far as the representation of objects goes.[12]

And:

> Take, for example, the continuous quantity in the science of geometry: if we begin with the surface of a body we find that it is derived from lines, the boundaries of this surface. But we do not let the matter rest there, for we know that the line (in its turn) is terminated by points, and that the point is that (ultimate unit) than which there can be nothing smaller.[13]

Therefore, 'the point,' he continues, 'is the first beginning of geometry, and neither in nature nor in the human mind can there be anything which can originate the point.'[14] ,

Neither *nature* nor the *human mind* can originate the point; and yet that original point must exist for material surfaces to exist. So God is the originator of the point, or indeed the point of origin.

Here Leonardo's manner of expressing himself stands close to the imagery and to the geometrical metaphors of Nicholas of Cusa. The imaginative recreation of physical surfaces in the geometrical terms of point, line and plane, the infinite number of possible forms that might be developed from these terms, and/or the imaginative reduction of forms back to an abstract point of origin gives us a complex image that is at once both continuous and discrete. The continuity of form begins with a real dot or point; however the origin of the point is not physical. In and above this, the point is not just a mental abstraction. The mind can conceive of it in a manner; but we are told that the mind cannot originate it. What is conceived therefore, is an abstraction known only from a reduction of the ramifications of that abstraction: from the bodies' surfaces, the planes, lines, and points of the science of geometry. However, the real attributes of the originating point are not in the mind. And the real point is not an entirely geometrical concept although it is derived from an analogy with a geometrical point. Instead it is an image that is applied to validate the whole science of geometry, as well as the reality of the actual surfaces of nature, and even the imitations of those surfaces in painting. Not of nature, not entirely of mind, that real point has to correspond to the quality unity, a divine quality.

The implication of a discrete and qualitative leap to unity is not the only metaphysical concept that can be drawn from Leonardo's wording. He also implies two different sorts of infinity, partial and absolute. Partial infinity can inevitably be drawn from the continuous and unending number of possibilities presented in the geometry of surfaces that Leonardo outlines. But the second implication of infinity is entirely qualitative. The origin of the point, or unity must be seen to be both transcendent and immanent in physical reality for physical existence to be, in fact, real. Leonardo accepts it as real, and his overlapping of continuous and discrete concepts places an immaterial point that originates from super-reality into the human mind, hence into actual physical reality as well. By similar implication, he also places all the bodies of nature, and all the surfaces that might possibly be conceived of back into that supra-physical point; because ultimately those bodies and surfaces cannot be entirely reduced to purely geometrical terms, or to any other terms that can wholly originate in the mind. The point, unity, must therefore also be absolutely infinite. It pre-exists the mind and nature, and all that exists in nature, and all that can and might be conceived of in the mind. All this is contained in that one point. *Hence the way that Leonardo characterizes his origin of the point in the analogy between geometry in nature and geometry in painting, suggests far wider metaphysical parallels between the origins of geometry, and the creation itself.* As the abstract point that originates from unity is the original quality from which all subsequent points, lines, and surfaces are developed, so the simultaneous unity and infinity in God is the original quality that gives rise to all the diversity of physical beings and things. In his geometrical conception of the painting, the artist, in a finite and limited way, creates just as God creates.

These metaphors are entirely like those of Cusanus who symbolizes creation, the mind, and the creator in metaphysical terms that are almost all developed from geometry. And the metaphors also contain a supra-physical and highly intellectual conception of the validation and spiritual vivification of all physical existence. I intend to continue to explore the appeal of these images in the following chapter.

As I mentioned, it is not necessary to apply the concept of continuity to motion and to moving things in order to understand that applications of this concept require us to visualize progressively. In continuity itself there is implied a mental movement and this is present even when this notion is applied to things which are objectively motionless. Envisioning in continuous terms involves men in making up their minds either to build up a whole or break it down for purposes of analysis. Anything to which the concept can be applied is necessarily understood as consisting of an accumulation of continuous sections, parts, phases, or stages, etc. It is especially clear that analysis in terms of continuity usually involves mental progression (or the reverse) and that applying continuity requires mental movement when we contrast it with more static concepts.

For instance, proportion makes us aware simply of a relationship. If we visualize the compared objects as a whole afterwards, then we have added continuity to the original conception of proportion. When continuity is applied, whether it is to still things, like the surface of the body, or to moving things, like the motion of the body, the whole object of its application is seen in terms of accumulation. This can be a purely geometrical accumulation of points, lines and surfaces, and this geometrical accumulation can be complemented by a physical, or physiological, one as well. Thus, the still surface of the body can be viewed as a whole specific complex of unbroken points, lines, and surfaces; and, in a similar manner, the walking motion of the body can be viewed as both an unbroken accumulation of points on the hypothetical path of the movement, and, at the same time, as an unbroken order of changing positions of the parts of the body that are moving. The cycle of this progression completes the whole movement.[15]

The contribution of bones, muscles, nerves, and of the mind to a movement can also be visualized within terms of connectedness. Many of Leonardo's physiological quests were devoted to the refinement and perfection of his own understanding of specific operations in the body, operations imagined in continuous terms. Thus, the continuity of forms and of operations was an inspiring type of visualization that gave direction to Leonardo's eyes and mind as he attempted to trace some specific patterns within the operations of nature. His particular vision of continuity was derived from a Cusan and mathematical strain of Neo-Platonism.[16] I believe that this strain had had great appeal for the artist of the fifteenth century; however it was not the only strain, as we can see from Michelangelo. In Leonardo's works he shows us how a mathematical source of inspiration can also be filled out and applied, at least metaphorically, beyond the region of number, or of outlines of forms, or of paths of motion. He frequently applies such an image to a problem without any mathematical content. This image of continuity directed his mind to the interconnectedness which he assumed to be at the basis of the order and operations of all natural things. Thus, he saw his task was to expose the steps or specific details of a continuous action or object, and then to arrive at a scientific description in terms of the physical material of the thing under study. The muscles of a bird in a continuous action in the body perform a sequence that makes the continuity of the flight possible. Physiology is interwoven with aerodynamics in a flowing image that presents nature as Leonardo saw it. As he peeled off layers from the surfaces of things, the stuff of reality, the materials of a body would

demonstrate their own statement of the law of continuity. This
is a viable and universal vision of analogy between the parts
and the whole of nature. The materials look different from
each other but they behave in a similar manner. Rock and bone
are different, and yet Leonardo made them play the same role
in structure and support; or, to frame the analogy in a more
conventional way, the harmony of tones in music can be seen to
parallel the harmony in the sequences of the seasons, or in the
four ages of man.

Originally, the continuity of forms or of things in the world
had been expressed in an Aristotelian idea and the assumption
of this connectedness between all aspects of being had also
been absorbed by Neo-Platonists. The notion was undoubtedly
attractive to them as it could be seen to complement
Pythagoras' and Plato's idea of mathematical harmony. Neo-
Platonists continued mingling these ideas, and they eventually
came to be expressed in a great variety of contexts and in an
even wider variety of ways. By the Renaissance, notions of continuity and harmony can be found in astrology, alchemy,
magic, in many aspects of philosophy, as well as in mathematics
where they had always had Platonic inspirations. The
philosopher Cusanus expressed the continuity of nature in
largely geometrical terms but in addition to questions of weight
and balance he also applied his terms to metaphysical questions
from which he drew some amazing physical conclusions, and
also to questions about the mind. In Leonardo, the most obvious application of continuity is in the geometry of surfaces and
of pictorial perspective. But Leonardo was also inclined to
assume wider applications of this concept and to draw universal
implications from it. Among the many inspirations of Leonardo's whole view of reality I see the ideas of Cusanus as having a
primary place in Leonardo's imagination. Perhaps the
mathematical philosopher had had his greatest appeal in the
studios of Verroccio and others, while later, Michelangelo's
apprenticeship in the atmosphere of the Medici gardens had
been coloured by somewhat different philosophical inspirations. Workshop and court were never the same, and Ficino's
translations of the Hermetica and of Plato had their effects in
the later part of the fifteenth century. By then, Leonardo had
already ripened in a different way and it is not surprising that
he was not attracted by the dominant strain of Florentine
Neo-Platonism.

Certainly, during the fifteenth century many other
philosophical inspirations were being expressed alongside of
Cusa's very abstract and individual Neo-Platonism. Visions of
continuity seen between occult forces operating in nature also

inspired Renaissance men to attempt to understand and to manipulate nature. The confirmation of human manipulative power was of essential importance in the psychology of early modern science. Such confirmation did not come from any single source. So out of all of the possible ways of construing the continuity of forms and of operations in nature and the harmony of nature, Leonardo chose a mathematical and geometrical way. And yet he did not concern himself very much with pure mathematics. The applied mathematics of design and perspective and engineering was a different matter. Whatever his activity, however, his imagination was coloured by mathematical concepts. Thus, Leonardo re-read the implications of these concepts back into a whole wide range of characteristics in physical reality. This means not just into abstractions of motion and of form and shape, but into the phenomena of light and of colour, into flesh, muscle, bone, and earth, into all the stuff of nature. Much of the actual intellectual problems that occupied Leonardo were developed in Aristotelian sources, yet the imagination that processed this content was geometrical at its core. With this imaginative pattern Leonardo believed that the materials and the operations of nature could be understood and be expressed in the sciences. Nature could be given creative additions by men that paralleled the real examples of nature herself. This is an honest belief in the progressive and manipulative powers of the human arts and sciences.

Historians have rightly remarked that Leonardo was a bad publicist for progress. He seems to have read the implications of his work back into his own ego. He had a withdrawn personality and appears to have been more concerned with solving for himself the dilemmas of how and what the mind could know than he was with the problem of informing and educating his fellow men. Some historians mark his mentality as expressing a stage of pre-scientific consciousness; but I do not know how they separate this from the straightforward conclusion that Leonardo did not relate to other men easily. Later, in an age of much more public science, Isaac Newton only expressed himself very carefully and had to be urged to publish by a few devoted followers. Was he, too, exhibiting a stage of pre-scientific consciousness? The fact is that Leonardo believed in the powers of *the* mind, not just in his mind, although he was enthralled with that. So here is the power to manipulate nature expressed without enlisting the services of any occult forces. The immanence of God was, in fact, so great in Leonardo's idea, that any visions of intervening spirits would have created a definite and superfluous overcrowding both of nature and of super-nature.

However, I am not saying that Cusa's or Leonardo's mathematical images were either more scientific, or more of an inspiration in the philosophy of science than those of other styles of Neo-Platonism. Although Galileo's imagination seems to have worked along similar lines, this would be too facile a generalization to apply to the intricate and varied atmosphere that was the nurturing ground for early scientific attitudes. Occult philosophies were appealing and they kept many great minds trying again and again to grasp and to manipulate reality. Cusanus' visions also had their own unique creative appeal, and in and above this they had a scientific purity and simplicity. But history plays tricks; and in the sixteenth century Giordano Bruno was happily combining what Ficino and Leonardo could not have combined.

No path to the early progress of science is entirely clear or simple, and many combinations of ideas were inspiring - for example, Leonardo combined the miraculous transformations of Ovid's *Metamorphoses* with an empirical study of nature that had the effect of slowing down the seemingly instant metamorphoses into something that approached his anticipation of evolution in nature. Later, Kepler's interests were clearly occult, but Galileo's mostly not so. Cartesians kept the soul above and outside of their mechanical explanations; still, the soul made those explanations meaningful. Also, followers of Baconian traditions kept divine providence in their minds as they practised the method. And still, in the eighteenth century, occult traditions and humanistic ones were playing important roles in the psychology of science. For example, literary and historical traditions were providing a great deal of the conceptual material for early psychology. So while it is possible for historians of science to single out certain practices and arrangements as suitable for and encouraging to some progressive features in natural philosophy, it is not easily possible to do this quite so definitively with more general assumptions and wider traditions in ideas. The practice of experimentation that was developed in the general fields of physical studies and chemistry in the second half of the seventeenth century, was of undoubted value for the development of knowledge and for the progress of a whole tradition of practice in science. Whereas, by contrast, the fruits of a tradition like humanism are more varied. The effects of humanists' studies could be different as these were absorbed by varying conditions and by different minds. Thus, Erasmus and Francis Bacon were influenced differently; and yet it is not possible to write off these less tangible inspirations because of their devilish ubiquity. Inspirations derived from mathematics, and medicine, from astrology, alchemy, magic and from humanism often changed sides, now encouraging and even providing the supporting framework for scientific pursuits, now preventing even the remote possibility of something scientific happening.

Geometry and time

In another analogy, one between geometry and time, Leonardo's analysis is similar to that of the previous analogy between painting and geometry. But, there is one extremely important qualification that makes this analogy different. Geometry, we are told, is a science applied to continuous quantities (*quantita continua*), to things that have substance (*materia*);[17] painting deals with the same. But time has a different nature. Time is not a truly continuous quantity.[18]

Before proceeding it is important to realize that Leonardo took over Aristotelian distinctions between continuous and discontinuous quantities. Geometry dealt with the first and arithmetic with the second.[19] Thus, when he tells us that geometry is not wholly applicable to time he also implies that, for him, time is in some basic way unlike space. Geometry is applied to both space and objects, but only the geometrical first principles apply to time, and even this application is only by analogy with the application to space and to objects.

> The point may be compared to an instant of time, and the line may be likened to the length of a certain quantity of time, and just as a line begins and terminates in a point, so such a *space of time* begins and terminates in an instant. And whereas a line is infinitely divisible, the divisibility of a *space of time* is of the same nature: and as the divisions of the line may bear a certain proportion to each other, so may the divisions of time.[20]

Painting and geometry involve the representation of features that are actually demonstrated in material things and in the spatial relationships between them. The applicability of these sciences to material things seems to have had great significance for Leonardo with regard to the contrast of geometry with time. Although the points, lines, angles, planes, and solids represented in geometry are abstractions in themselves, both painters and geometers apply them to things of substance and it is these things that have corporeal extension and demonstrate continuity. Thus: 'The smallest natural point is larger than all

mathematical points, and this is proved because the natural
point has continuity, and anything that is continuous is infinitely divisible; but the mathematical point is indivisible
because it has no size.'[21]

Time does not have continuity in the full sense of this word.
For Leonardo, time is both indivisible and immaterial, meaning
that the instant, *now*, is an abstraction and a limit of time, just
as the mathematical point is a limit of a line.[22] Point and line
are abstractions when applied to things that have corporeal
extension, and point and line are abstractions analogous to the
movement of time. But what actually is time? Time is described
by *no qualities* outside of motion. By means of the motions of
the physical spheres or of the hands on the clock men can perceive and measure time. But what is time? Leonardo leaves
time in the same shadow as St Augustine did. Leonardo's
strange notation, 'describe the nature of time as distinguished
from the geometrical definitions', leaves even more mystery.[23]
There is a hint of eternity here.[24] It is rather like Leonardo's
special point that has no origin in nature or in the mind. When
Leonardo goes on to make descriptive remarks about time,
what he really comments upon is time's passage. He records the
continuing extension of its limits or duration, instant by instant.
And therefore, the abstractions of point and line are applied to
an existence which reveals itself through motion and change
but which has no other describable qualities of its own.

A thought may occur to us; that we could add that space, as
far as geometry goes, might also possibly be counted as having
no qualities either. Why did Leonardo qualify time as not being
a continuous quantity in the full sense of the word, and not do
the same for space, whose elemental substance or material, as
far as the geometer is concerned, counts for nothing outside of
its proximity to a material surface? Certainly, proximity is the
answer. For the surface of a material object gives the space
around it physical limits. Space, insofar as the painter or the
practical geometer approach it, is defined by the material
objects in it. Thus a relation between space and objects is not
only described in abstract terms of point and line but in terms
of plane, angle and solid. In other words, although geometry is
not concerned with the material or substance of space
(Leonardo was aware that this was air), it is concerned with its
limits, and these limits give space dimensions. As we have seen
in the perspective drawing, space considered with objects
receives the same dimensional treatment as actual material
bodies. Thus, in terms of the representation of surfaces, space
lends itself to being treated just like a material body. This is
why Leonardo has geometry deal with continuous quantities

('take, for example, the continuous quantity in the science of geometry') which, he says, are substantial ('geometry which represents its divisions by means of figures and bodies of infinite variety such as are seen to be continuous in their visible and material properties') and makes no exception for space whose substance is for the most part invisible.

Like space, time has limits, too, but only one-dimensionally along a single line. In a partial analogy with space, time may be said to be given definition by physical movements or events, just as space is by physical objects, but the *before*, the *now*, and the *after* are its only dimensions and these occur along a single line.[25] When Leonardo says it is because geometry deals with things of *material* that it demonstrates full continuity, he is in some ways a little misleading. It is not primarily the material in itself but the fact that an object or an area has three-dimensional surfaces and limits that interests the geometer.[26] It is by analogy with *corporeal extension* that geometry can describe both motion and the relation between space and objects. Continuity is fully explorable because material objects have limits, space has limits in terms of these objects and geometry deals in all three dimensions. Both motion and time, which is measured by motion, derive continuity, insofar as they have it, from this analogy with corporeal extension. 'Before' and 'after' in time rest primarily on the analogous distinctions of the 'here' and 'there' positions in space which are successively occupied by a moving body. The continuity of time is derived from the continuity of motion, which, in turn, depends on the actual continuity of corporeal extension.

There are additional aspects of Leonardo's ideas about space which, in some respects, put space closer to material bodies than to time. But despite these it is important to remember that Leonardo, like Alberti, dealt with space quantitatively, and that the conventional Aristotelian idea of proper place had in effect entirely given way to geometrical conceptions of space. Therefore I am not suggesting any regression on the part of Leonardo to these conventional ideas. On the other hand, I wish to tentatively suggest that the vestiges of these physical ideas are apparent in Leonardo's notes and that these might just have had some small degree of influence on Leonardo's treatment of space as a continuous quantity.

Although it is true that space has no visible surface, except in terms of the limits it shares with material bodies, it does have some degree of material substance because it is filled with the element air. This element may be thought of as demonstrating continuity in the same way that a visible and less diffuse material body can. As a painter Leonardo was aware that air was not

always entirely invisible. He explains that the artist should not
make small figures which are at a great distance from the eye
in the same finished way that he would make a nearer figure:
'...The object is small by reason of the great distance between
it and the eye, this great distance is filled with air, that mass of
air forms a dense body (*grosso corpo*)which intervenes and pre-
vents the eye from seeing the minute details of objects.'[27] Air is
actually seen in a close analogy to water, as an elemental
medium through which visual images project themselves.

> Just as a stone flung into the water becomes the centre and cause
> of many circles, and as sound diffuses itself in circles in the air;
> so any object placed in the luminous atmosphere, diffuses itself
> in circles, and fills the surrounding air with images of itself. And
> is repeated, the whole everywhere, and the whole in every smal-
> lest part. . . .[28]

The idea that the air is filled with images was part of an elaborate theory of vision of the time. But here I wish only to suggest that the atmosphere is a characteristic of space that can be
seen as having a material or substantial quality. Thus space,
when thought of in an elemental rather than a purely geometrical capacity - this space had physical qualities like other bodies
and unlike time. I do not imagine that this view actually introduced confusion into Leonardo's application of geometry to
space, but it may have influenced the distinction he seems to
have made between space and time.

Many remarks of Leonardo seem mysterious. What is one to
make of an allusion to time as something outside of geometry?
Is this mental doodling? What is he talking about when he
writes that the point does not originate either in nature or in
the mind? His peculiar remarks about the point and about time
are not at all senseless if we compare them with his unusual
comments about *nothing*. At first these also seem to be somewhat nonsensical, that is, until one applies some of the imagery
of Nicholas Cusanus. Then they are made sensible. And even
the remarks about the mysterious origin of the point and about
time apart from motion are sensible, but only within this wider
philosophical context.

Formerly, such mysteries had been attributed to the fragmented and uncommunicative character of Leonardo's
notebooks, and also to his habit of leaving things in the air. But
whatever he left in the air, it was not without an internal meaning and logic of its own. Now I am not speaking about scientific
correctness, but about a mind that expresses itself meaningfully
in terms of its own hypotheses. There is no good reason to
believe that Leonardo was silly, and there is much good reason

to believe he was not entirely haphazard in what he said to himself. His remarks about nothing seem to be beside the point. Why should a thinker and painter who was attracted to natural philosophy, but avoided speculative philosophy, speculate about the character of nothing? I am suggesting therefore, that his nothing plays some real part within his natural philosophy.

'Nothing' exists in terms of its proper place

> Nothing, in short, is given only in relation to what is, and even the idea of nothing requires a thinker to sustain it.[29]

This talk about nothing arises from Leonardo's remarks about nothingness and his specific placement of nothing in time.

> What is called nothingness is to be found only in time and in speech. In time it stands between the past and the future and has no existence in the present; and thus in speech it is one of the things of which we say: 'They are not, or they are impossible.'
>
> With regard to time, nothingness lies between the past and the future, and has nothing to do with the present, and with regard to nature it is to be classed among things impossible: hence, from what has been said, it has no existence because where there is nothing there would necessarily be a vacuum.[30]

It seems to be clear that nothing has no physical location because Leonardo did not believe that there was a vacuum in nature.[31] However, nothingness is given theoretical place and is not permitted to exist as a free-floating concept in speech. It is not simply described as the conceptual opposite of something.

The theoretical place of nothing is found in time. I believe I can show that Leonardo posited a similar concept of nothing in the relation between space and objects. Both in time and in space, the concept of nothing is described by an analogy with the zero or the nought in arithmetic. Because nothing has no physical existence, the concept of nothing could have little meaning without this analogy.

> Amid the vastness of the things among which we live, the existence of nothingness holds the first place; its function extends over all things that have no existence, and its essence, as regards time, lies precisely between the past and the future, and has nothing in the present. This nothingness has the part equal to

the whole, and the whole to the part, the divisible to the indivisible; and the product of the sum is the same whether we divide or multiply, and in addition as in subtraction; as is *proved* by arithmeticians by their tenth figure which represents zero; and its power has no extension among the things of nature.[32]

In other words, what the arithmeticians ascribe to zero informs us about the 'essence' of nothingness and, therefore, of nothingness with regard to time. This placement of the zero between the past and future, but with no existence in the present, seems to be somewhat comprehensible in terms of Aristotle's dynamic interpretation of nature. Because all nature moves between the potential and the completed, that potential at once is and is not. However, the light that this sheds is not very bright for it is not at all clear why amid the plurality of things in the world nothing should be given *first place*. All things do not happen in nature because men anticipate them; so why should nothing, that can only be a concept, be given a first place? Nature may move between the potential and the completed but men must derive their anticipations from nature. The potential in nature is not a nought, or a zero, or nothing. Nature is what it is while it is so. Potential and actual are categories that emerge from reflection about nature; they belong to the mind. Thus, only men's concepts of as yet unplayed actions can be signified by zeros. And Leonardo also tells us that nothing has a function over all things that have no existence. Now he is either telling us nothing about nothing, or he is telling us about *no material thing* and about no concept that can be expressed in quantitative terms or be entirely derived and developed from any existing physical entity.

It is not at all puzzling for a natural philosopher to deal in abstract sciences, for the principles of these sciences are demonstrated in nature. But when he talks about an idea that is immaterial, a concept, and that idea does not originate from nature, because nothing doesn't exist in nature, the effect is dizzying. The point at which he places his 'essence' of nothing, between the past and the future but without place in the present, sandwiches everything between nothing. This is true; for I will shortly show how he puts his essence, a 'medium' of nothing, at the limits between space and objects as well. Then if Leonardo's nothing does not exist, nevertheless it is certainly all-pervading. If he is not to be thought nonsensical here, then we must suppose that he is referring to a power of the mind, and not just to the mind as a physical entity, but to the human intellect that must also be seen to have spiritual qualities.

Where can we seek spiritual qualities of mind that enable men to interweave and embody what is material in what is not material? This is all done in the curious terms of connected contrasts, where real surfaces are seen absorbed in an abstract point, and where the sequences of time are also absorbed in the *now* which is a concept like the point. The point, or the essence and actuality of potentials, in these examples, is discrete from natural extensions and it looks opposite to them. Numbers are divisible. Nothing is indivisible; or, we might say, all the divisibility of number is absorbed in and descends from its indivisibility. For example, I shall soon quote fully a passage from Leonardo wherein he says you must think of a whole composed of a thousand points, and then divide some parts of this quantity by a thousand. The thousandth part, Leonardo maintains, would also be equal to the whole of the point. The instant now is no time, yet men's assimilation of time proceeds from the concept now. Leonardo has said that this now has no existence in nature just as he has also said that nothing in the mind or in nature can originate the point. Therefore I think that the *now* seen in the mind ultimately originates in eternity, and time proceeds from eternity, and is encompassed in eternity. The point seen in the mind originates in unity, and points, lines, and surfaces and material solids proceed from unity. And they are also encompassed in unity. Proportion and harmony also proceed from unity; and number itself proceeds from unity as motion does from rest. These are Cusa's images. In their terms Leonardo's nothing appears to be a metaphor for all that is not material. God is not a thing but is actuality, quality and essence. As the image of God, the mind is not a thing, yet the mind can incorporate quantities because of its own powers or qualities. The mind sees a 'medium' of nothing around everything. Divine immanence forms the sandwich bread around and between and in everything; and divine transcendence is the origin and the end of everything.

It is not at all unthinkable that Leonardo possessed some general framework of these images and they do make sense of his remarks pertaining to what is continuous, or what can be entirely derived from a continuous quantity, and what cannot. The following is Cusanus on the mind pertaining to time: [my brackets]

> By the (mind's) assimilative power of the complication of now, or the present, it (the mind) hath the power to assimilate itself to all time. . . .[33]

By to assimilate he means to absorb and to incorporate. It must also be added that this power of the human mind is but an image of the ultimate assimilative power of the divine mind. Men may incorporate the past and the future in the abstract now, God creates and incorporates all time in eternity. Man's concept reflects and projects in sequence, both backward and forward, so that the memory of the past can be seen to culminate in the now, and the anticipation of the future can proceed from the now. God creates and incorporates all time, everything, all at once. Thus, perhaps for Leonardo the present, that is, now, is not the zero, but rather the zero analogically indicates a limit of the potential instant that is to come. This limit may be like a spiritual breath, but it also has conceptual meaning in that men know that it is about to pass despite the fact of its non-existence.

This statement and its background can be made still clearer by recalling and elaborating Leonardo's analogy between the instant in time and the point, and the path, or motion of time and the line. Despite his statement that nothing could be found only in time and in speech he actually does also place nothing (in a similar notional way) in spatial relations.

> And the point does not partake of the substance of the surface. And supposing you imagined a whole composed of a thousand points and divided some parts of this quantity by a thousand, it could very well be said that this thousandth part would be equal to its whole. And the point may be compared to zero or nought, the tenth cipher in arithmetic, which is denoted by an O. . . . The nought itself is worth no more than nothing; and all the noughts of the universe are equal to one single nought, both as regards their substance and their value.[34]

Thus the instant and the point have no physical substance and no numerical value; they are both invisible and immaterial. They are not really subject to quantitative values or terms. In them the divisible is equal to the indivisible, the part to the whole, and the whole to the part. *Opposites coincide in them.* In arithmetic the zero is the symbol for these conceptual characteristics or non-characteristics. Somehow Leonardo seems to have believed that the zero in arithmetic ought to have at least a theoretical parallel, a position in *material* reality. Perhaps it is because the zero is a metaphor for unity and eternity in super-reality that he placed it at the limits of a given space or in time. Certainly, in the case of space, these limits are identified by Leonardo as something spiritual *(ma si può nominare più presto cosa spirituale).*[35]

> The boundaries of bodies are the least of all things. The proposition is proved to be true, because the boundary of a thing is a surface, which is not part of the body contained within that surface; nor is it part of the air surrounding that body, *but is the medium interposed between the air and the body, as is proved in its place.*[36]

The boundary of a body has a theoretical limit which is the equivalent of nothing. This theoretical 'medium' is not actually necessary to bodies in space. For geometry, it is quite sufficient to be aware that conceptual points and lines are not physical but are abstract symbols derived from the extension of material bodies. The nought or the nothing is not a symbol of that extension at all, but only of the intellectual recognition that corporeal extension has limits. Thus the placement of nothing at the limit of time and of bodies in space is superfluous to the actual situation. We know that geometrical points and lines are abstract and immaterial, but it is not therefore necessary to posit a 'medium' or nothing 'in its place', around everything in actual space.[37]

The vision of the progress of time as parallel to the motion of an object in space heightens men's awareness of the state of becoming rather than of being. The spot where the object will next be, the *there*, the instant which is yet to come, the *after*, represent the discrete break-off or limit of something that is more generally being seen in analogy with a continuous quantity. So material things and even time are seen to have quantitative attributes, but the essence of these things, essence experienced in the mind, is not quantifiable. This point or this essence is symbolized by a zero; and this analogy between the zero and the point is based upon the discontinuous nought expressed in arithmetic. The point, or place, or instant is actually nothing, and the wider implications of this analogy with the zero are spiritual and not physical. Thus, amazingly, nothing is given definite location or place with regard to something. Then it is fairly certain that Leonardo looked at the actual world within terms drawn from analogies with the concepts of geometry and of arithmetic. He is not unique in thinking of these analogies and associating these sciences with the very order of nature. Pythagoreans, Plato and other Neo-Platonists did before him, and Alberti too; however, Leonardo is outstanding in his zeal to give precision to these visions. I think that his placement of the zero at the limit of time is particularly interesting, for it shows him making a purely theoretical point about an entity which in itself is unknown, except by means of its passage, by means of a partial analogy drawn from corporeal extension. Yet he has already told us, time is not a continuous quantity. The placement of the zero there can satisfy nothing except Leonardo's own conceptual framework. Then this might represent his vision of the non-physical character of the mind. And if so, it does ultimately imply the relation of nature to God. The zero concept in the human mind partially reflects or just signifies the ideas combined in unity in the

divine mind. Therefore placement of these zeros brings us
closer to a sensation akin to religious and aesthetic satisfaction,
rather than to something that has most to do with the practical
applications of geometry or arithmetic.

The artist is like the creator:
his works are like nature

The concepts of good proportion, infinity and continuity
appear frequently in Leonardo's writings, and these concepts
are frequently viewed as the analogous elements in different
things, and especially in analogies between the different disciplines. The continuity of corporeal extension was the basis of
Leonardo's analogy between geometry and painting. Now the
concept of harmonic proportion forms the basis of another
analogy, one between music and painting. 'If you say that
music is composed of proportion, then I have used similar
means in painting. . . .'[38] Thus both painting and music involve
proportion, and both painters and musicians employ proportion. Behind this there is the assumption of the existence of
truly good proportions. Despite the fact that receding objects
appear to touch each other, he says: 'I will nevertheless found
my rule on spaces of twenty braccia each, just as the musician
who, though his voices are united and strung together, has
created intervals according to the distance from voice to voice,
calling them unison, second, third, fourth and fifth, and so on
until names have been given to the various degrees of pitch
proper to the human voice.'[39] Leonardo is referring to his
theory of diminution (see Richter (99-106)). In it, objects of
equal size that are placed so as to recede from the eye at regu-
lar intervals of, say, twenty braccia each diminish to $\frac{1}{2}$, $\frac{1}{3}$, and $\frac{1}{4}$
of their size, in harmonic regression.[40] Both in the 'Paragone'
(34), and in general remarks on perspective (102), Leonardo
stresses the artist's practice. So he centres his expression of the
analogy as much on the act of perceiving and creating both the
degrees of diminution and the harmonious musical intervals as
upon the actual proportions that are involved. The ideas come
to light through recognition. Leonardo's introduction of the, I
the creator, point of view into his analogy between music and
painting illustrates two levels of analogy-making that I have
been talking about. One is that good music and good painting,
like nature itself, must result from a proportioning. The other
is that the composer or painter, like the creator himself, em-
ploys proportions in his creations. Leonardo's general inclination

to stress the artist to God aspect of this analogy has implications in terms of Leonardo's own personality. These will become clearer in a later chapter. The twofold structure of this analogy indicates Leonardo's full conception of man, the microcosm, within the analogy of nature.

Naturalism and the imagination

An awareness of continuity can be observed in Leonardo's works even when he does not actually use continuity as the basis of an analogy between different parts. For instance, the concept of continuity can be detected as being applied in two different ways in Leonardo's idea of painting. A naturalistic painting, drawn in true perspective, demonstrates one application of continuity, that is, that between objects and spaces. To this application Leonardo adds another, that the physical actions portrayed within the painting should be conceived of as one phase of a whole physical action.[41] The continuity of this whole action is demonstrated in reality or experience. In the following section I will explore Leonardo's conception that represented actions should be thought of as portraying a phase of real actions.

This application of continuity demands an imaginative extension of the actions portrayed, both by the artist, and, possibly, by the viewers. So, this continuity of motion or action has little to do with the painting as a physical object. Similarly, the painting's content, meaning now simply the arrangement of forms on its surface, does not in itself demonstrate Leonardo's application of continuity to the actions. This is because these arranged forms exist simply as a pattern when they are not elaborated by our extending their actions in our imaginations. If the design is represented in perspective then it will demonstrate the continuity between objects and spaces on the picture plane. But once again this is not the application of continuity to the actions that Leonardo talks about.

Leonardo distinctly posits our making an imaginary extension of the physical consequences of the actions which are represented at only one stage. This extension is to be made first and foremost by the artist who abstracts and contrives it, and then possibly by the viewers for whom it has been designed. By this means the physical actions in the picture are seen as being continuous; but, of course, they are not. They are frozen. The continuity which is being imagined in these actions exists and is demonstrated in experience alone, not in the picture. Only real motion can actually be seen to be continuous. However, when men relate their experience of motion to the representation of actions in the painting, the actions can be imagined as demonstrating the same continuity as in physical reality. So, if an artist started off by accepting Leonardo's suggested goal, that of implying a real physical continuity of action in the painting, the artist would have to substantiate this end or purpose with specific types of study. His subject matter would be both the static and moving forms of things. Changes of form and of place, and other physical indications of change would all become interesting. He would not only have in some degree to know these things but also to acquire the necessary artistic techniques to produce naturalistic portrayals of these things. By means of these studies he would be able to implant symbolically his suggestion of the continuous nature of actions portrayed within the picture. Then once again Leonardo's whole conception of the painting indicates that the analogy he made between art and nature was more than just formal or structural. He saw all nature in stages of transformation. It was a developing and moving entity and he wanted to imply this vital characteristic of nature within the painting which is really a static and formal arrangement. Through the science of painting he froze at one instant a multitude of movements and actions that he saw to be continuous. For him his choice of the instant represented one of an infinite number of choices for he saw the divisions of any continuous quantity as infinite. Thus around and in everything there is this mysterious implication of infinity and God is never forgotten.

In this case Leonardo was engaged in the observation and intellectual comprehension of movement in nature for the sake of the painted representation, and for his theory of painting. At other times Leonardo was engaged in the same intellectual activities, but his intentions were not connected with representation. He was observing some aspect of nature out of a desire for a clearer apprehension of the thing itself, observing nature for its own sake. Although Leonardo's goals differ in these two activities, his intellectual approach to the problem shows a similar blend of observation with conceptualization, and the formulation of his understanding the problem, primarily in pictures and also in words. Some reference to Leonardo's approach to natural observations for their own sake may clarify his attitude towards the specific application of natural observation to the painting.

In his study of Leonardo's work on 'The form of movement in water and air', Sir E.H. Gombrich has noted that Leonardo's depictions of moving water were not intended to be simple reproductions, but rather, that they served as tools of formulation, both for his own understanding, and for the expression of what he understood.[42] Professor Gombrich describes one of Leonardo's drawings of water falling upon water as a picture of his ideas about this subject, not a naturalistic reproduction of the phenomenon.[43] This example is consistent with the general character of Leonardo's study of movement in water and air. He even listed an immense number of words that could be used to describe water.[44] This was not just a simple verbal exercise any more than the drawings in this study were just representational exercises. Both were parts of a grand attempt to comprehend and describe the most complete range of circumstances applicable to moving water. In the light of Gombrich's observations let us turn back to the problem of what Leonardo was doing when he advised the artist to study nature in order to learn to make an imaginary extension of the continuity of physical actions. Leonardo always saw problems of depiction in the wider context of the problem of knowledge. Depiction was really like creation.

All of the features of the picture represent a formulation that reveals the painter's knowledge, his understanding; it is not just a simple copy of something that has been seen. Hence:

> Painting can be shown to be philosophy because it deals with the motion of bodies in the promptitude of their actions, and philosophy too deals with motion.[45]

So each activity portrayed must be part of a whole and complete physical action, not because every phase of this action is to be represented; but because, in each instance, the action must be as completely understood as possible. Without this scientific understanding the image would fall short of Leonardo's artistic standards.

It shoud be clear, therefore, that the true analogy with the continuity of physical movement in nature exists in the artist's mind. The painted scene presents the viewer with a phase of the painter's understanding, and that understanding holds the model of nature. The execution of the picture is a process of knowledge, a perfection and expression of understanding.

An example can clarify the importance of the role of the viewer's imagination in Leonardo's assessment of the meaning of the painting. It would be easy to decide that one part of the naturalness of a painting comes from the descriptive capacities of the medium. Oils enable the artist to portray real things more realistically than pencil, or pen and ink. But this is not completely true, and the reason is that an educated viewer makes an unconscious adjustment to the medium and judges in terms

of the characteristics of that medium. Leonardo knew this and
he depended on it, and on another similar adjustment on the
part of the viewer. The viewer could accept the artist's suggestions that the portrayed actions were indeed absolutely natural, and that, therefore, they could continue. Certainly, viewers
needed to be educated both visually and also by theory. However, they were thought to be capable of appreciating the
implied wholeness of the naturalistic image. This kind of
imaginative extension of the action had not always been the
intention of artists. Just think of the illustrations in medieval
illuminated manuscripts. Even when the content represented
was a phase of an action, it was the thematic, not the naturalistic qualities of the action that the artist intended to present. He
wanted to show the proper activities of the hours and the seasons, not the science of movement.

   Thus, from the point of view of the analogy, it is even more
forcefully clear that, during the fifteenth century, the ideal of
the imitation of nature centred on naturalistic representation,
as well as on metaphorical and iconographic forms of imitation.
This event, the real but temporary stylistic importance of direct
representation, brought about important advances in natural
philosophy. Implied in these was an epistemological point that
far outlasted the style. For, long after artists gave up
naturalism, the notion of building the model of experience in
the mind continued in the learned world. So even after stylistic
trends changed, the general effects of Renaissance naturalism
on philosophy continued. Man's inner eye had been directed
outward in specific and scientific ways, and the event that had
begun as a stylistic innovation had lasting effects on the whole
approach to nature.

   Leonardo did not predict these lasting effects, but he was
certainly aware that the painter was calling man's attention to
nature in a new way.

The painter competes with nature

No matter how suggestively any painting portrays a given
phase of real action, it does not demonstrate the continuity of
that action. It only suggests it. Perhaps Leonardo would have
enjoyed the possibilities of artistic photography, especially
motion picture photography. But without the benefit of this
technology he remarked about the one aspect of painting
which least conformed to nature. In fact, he set an extremely
high value on the artist's ability to give permanence to a physi-

cal state which represented only a passing moment in reality.[46] On this count, Leonardo placed painting above both poetry and music because it could present a simultaneous and whole vision of an event which the other art forms could only represent either in sequential or in partial and allusive form.[47]

Music can supply the simultaneous experience of harmony, but only fleetingly. Because of its fleetingness Leonardo relegates music to an inferior position to painting.[48] Yet Leonardo was well aware that this fleetingness was actually in the characteristics of the model itself. Both in physical movements and in more gradual evolutionary tendencies, nature presents precisely this harmonious but ever changing panorama of experience.

It is interesting that Leonardo should especially praise the one aspect of painting which, no matter what else its virtues, was in fact a limitation of its powers of imitating both how men experienced nature and how nature, in fact, operates.

> Oh wonderful science, which can preserve the transient beauty of mortals and endow it with a permanence greater than the works of nature; for these are subject to the continual changes of time which lead them to inevitable old age! And such a science [painting] is the same in relation to divine nature as its works are to the works of nature, and for this it is to be adored.[49]

This rather strange placement of the painting above nature suggests that Leonardo, like Cusanus, placed mind above nature; or, given the fact that the human mind is a divine image, it is still a part of nature, though separate from and above all other parts.

Leonardo said that the works of nature 'are subject to the continual changes of time', and this statement is reminiscent of Cusanus' idea that nature could only express itself in a continuous series, but that mind could both reflect back to the past and anticipate the future.[50] In other words, with the groundwork of its knowledge firmly based upon the study of nature, the mind has the capacity to range, to draw conclusions, to make generalizations or laws, hence to have a truer knowledge of the principles operating in nature. The rest of nature can only manifest itself instant by instant in terms of playing out its laws. In this ability to comprehend the idea of nature, the mind bears a likeness to the divine mind.

Painting can preserve the harmony of forms and the integrity of a single moment, but it can only suggest either evolutionary development (e.g. in Leonardo's drawings his contrasting youth and old age) or physical movements. For all his praise of the powers of painting for giving permanence to things that would otherwise wither or change, and for his slightly contradictory point of praise, praising the power of painting to imitate nature naturalistically, Leonardo reserves his highest praise for nature itself.[51] Even then, he also writes: 'The painter strives and competes with nature.'[52] One aspect of Leonardo's own competitive attitude, placing mind above matter, is illustrated by his praise of the superior ability of painting to confer permanence on things at a particular moment.

Mechanical analogies

Another important mode of expression of the analogy between the whole and the parts of nature is mechanical. Leonardo included mechanical models together with the structural and organic ones that he saw operating in nature. Kenneth Clark describes Leonardo's mind as a mind that moved from mechanism to organism.[53]

Earlier we have seen that Leonardo's analogies were not always scientifically successful (e.g the tree of veins was only partially successful). But analogies like this one can still show us habits of mind, habits that are important to the historian trying to comprehend Leonardo's mentality. The following example of one of his mechanical analogies falls into this category, because it turned out to be incorrect. However, scientific or not, it is still a pertinent example that illustrates Leonardo's manner of thinking out problems in natural philosophy.

Leonardo drew an interesting analogy between the workings of organ pipes and the sound producing action (he thought, of the trachea) in animals. The example is typical of the way that he applied mechanical models to organic contexts. He took the principle of length and width of the pipes, and the effects of these on the pitch of the tones produced, and he applied them to the human trachea, which he, falsely, thought produced sounds.[54] He was incorrect in several respects. Principally because he did not know about vocal cords in humans, and consequently he misapplied the results of experiments that he made on swans and geese. The things that he looked for in his dissections of throat and chest were also erroneously predetermined by his misconception. He remarked:

> Note well the use of the trachea and how it disposed itself to make high, middle and low voice. And what muscles produce these. Consider if the muscles between the oesophagus and the

spinal column of the neck can, by their contraction, press the oesophagus against the flexible part of the trachea, where there is a deficiency of the rings. And also note if the movement that produces the size of the trachea in its contraction may not be made by the lateral muscles of the neck.[55]

Clearly, this is all wrong; yet if we look beyond the history of scientific successes to the history of the scientific outlook we see that this approach, by analogy, was sometimes fruitful. The mechanical principle, the tests and dissections, the mind's reasoning on the basis of the known evidence were all there. An important bit of missing information accounts for this particular failure. However, brief reference to the range of subject matter that Leonardo is known to have used in this single analogy will give a clear view of his bringing together ideas and information from different disciplines.[56] First, there was his understanding of the technology and art of musical instruments and of music. He constructed and played a magnificent lyre. Vasari movingly describes how Leonardo built it, mostly of silver, in the shape of a horse's skull. On a sheet at Windsor (no. 19115), Richter observes Leonardo referring to a book where he treated the mechanics of instruments in detail; this reference is located near calculations of the sizes of organ pipes. The book is lost, but Richter cites several examples of Leonardo's experiments in this field from the manuscripts.[57]

His experiments with the structure and mechanics of instruments were not only directed to investigating instruments alone, but also to the general phenomena of sound. Leonardo's interest in this has been mentioned in the introductory parallel between sound waves in air and wavelets on water. The following examples show his mingling of questions about instruments with wider questions about sound:

> Just as one and the same drum makes a deep or acute sound, according as the parchments are more or less tightened, so these parchments variously tightened on one and the same drum will make various sounds.

And:

> The stroke of a bell will be responded to and will move somewhat another bell similar to it. And the string of a lute will be responded to and will move another similar string of like voice in another lute. And this you will see by placing a straw on the string similar to the one that is played.[58]

Returning to the analogy between organ pipes and the presumed action of the trachea, this not only illustrates Leonardo's interests in instruments and in the physics of sound but also his work in anatomy and physiology. He experimented with the production of the human voice and concluded that differences in vocal pitch could not be accounted for by activities of the tongue. He further concluded that the tongue had twenty-four muscles, and that these corresponded to the six muscles that compose the portion of the tongue that moved in the mouth; also, that when a, o and u were pronounced successively without pauses between them, the lips should be gradually closed, being open widest when sounding a, closing somewhat for o, and still further for u. Indeed it could be demonstrated that all vowels were pronounced with the farthest portion of the false palate which is above the epiglottis.[59] And there is more than this involved in Leonardo's investigations in the physiology of voice production. In the manuscripts at Windsor there are explanations of how the alternate expansion and contraction of the thorax works like a bellows and drives the air through the lungs and trachea. There are studies of the muscles of lips and tongue, in addition to those mentioned before on vowel production.[60] Leonardo also was the first to successfully demonstrate that air did not pass into the heart through the trachea. He disproved the Galenic hypothesis, that air entered the left side of the heart from the lungs.[61]

Thus, it appears that Leonardo's analogy between organ pipes and the presumed voice-producing action of the trachea presents at least three of his major interests, the mechanics of music, the physics of sound, and animal and human physiology. It is open to historians of science to reach, perhaps rather diverse, estimates of the value of this analogy. As far as Leonardo's immediate inference drawn from it, the analogy was imprecise and therefore misleading. However, in my judgement there is at least one other important frame of reference in which this example shows something that was significant in the development of modern thought. It illustrates (and perhaps helped to promote) the cross-fertilization of ideas and methods from different sorts of studies, upon which the scientific revolution so much depended. Like Alberti before him, Leonardo pooled ideas, methods and information under the influence of his general assumption of analogy. The principles of the whole would be expressed in the parts, and the principles of human arts and works were valid insofar as they reproduced natural principles. Why else might organ pipes tell men about the voice?

The two roles of man

Because Leonardo's modes of thinking are related to his more general assumptions about nature, it is important for cultural historians to understand the nature of that wider view. . . .To do this it is necessary to focus also upon his view of man within nature, and aspects of that view have already been illustrated. A further chapter about Leonardo will go into the more personal features of this view.

In Leonardo's cosmic vision man takes both active and passive parts. Both parts are seen in the terms of the related group of analogical assumptions that confirmed the harmony of nature. As a being, man holds in himself correspondences with the parts and the whole of nature. Simultaneously, he is the only natural (as opposed to supernatural) being known to have reason and consciousness of himself and of the order of surrounding nature. In the spirit of this view Leonardo writes:

> . . . For the works of man are to the works of nature as man is to God.[62]

Here man's active role is indicated; he is the creator of works. This can be contrasted with the view that places him in his passive posture, as a creature of the world. Leonardo writes:

> Thus, in fifteen figures (based on dissections), you will have set before you the microcosm on the same plan as, before me, was adopted by Ptolemy in his cosmography; and so I will afterwards divide them into limbs as he divided the whole world into provinces; then I will speak of the function of each part in every direction, putting before your eyes a description of the whole form and substance of man, as regards his movements from place to place, by means of his different parts. And thus, if it please our Great Author, I may demonstrate the nature of men and their customs in the way I describe his figure.[63]

Passive man is seen as a mechanism.[64] And, at the same time he is a divine creation, a superior invention, a superb work of art.

By contrast, instead of the invented, active man is the inventor, the artist, the builder, thus an imitation and likeness of either the creative principle of nature and/or God.[65]

Leonardo's active and passive men occupy twin places, and still find their ultimate unity within the framework of the analogy of nature. Traditionally, there was a sharp division between the mind or rational faculty of man and any other possible object of study (and this also includes man). This fundamental division between mind and matter is definitely weakened within Leonardo's vision of natural harmony. Just as Alberti once assumed that a recognition process, a secret argument imprinted in the mind, accounted for man's ability to distinguish causes within the multitude of received sense impressions, so Leonardo went further and acclaimed the intelligent use of the senses as the best way of perfecting the understanding.[66] The issue of a qualitative gap between the images of the senses, images from the material world, and the intelligence of the mind, the purely mental image, does not arise with Leonardo. The relation between eye and mind is direct. The eye both informs and confirms the mind. Leonardo even interpreted the anatomy and physiology of the nervous system in this manner.[67] Thus, the remarks of Ernst Cassirer are particularly apt when he calls attention to the closeness between human perception and human understanding in Leonardo's thinking.[68]

Both the active and the passive view of man had the science of representation as their point of departure in the fifteenth century. In the theory of that science the assumptions were woven, that nature was harmonious, that principles of natural harmony could be seen and understood, that human understanding, represented by the mind of the artist, was somehow analogous to divine creativity. In the spirit of all this, Leonardo proposes the metaphor of a deity for the science of painting:

> ...The deity of the science of painting extends over works human as well as divine insofar as they are bounded by surfaces. . . .With these she prescribes to the sculptor the perfection of his statues. By drawing, which is her beginning, she teaches the architect to make his edifices agreeable to the eye, she guides the potters in the making of various vases, the goldsmith, the weavers, and embroiderers. She has invented the characters in which the different languages are written, she has given the symbols to the mathematician, and has described the figures of geometry, she teaches opticians, astronomers, mechanics, and engineers.[69]

The grand analogy

Since the analogy between the whole and the parts of nature was an on-going assumption in western thought, there is a tendency for historians to take it for granted and to imagine that it was only a slight factor in any significant change. Doubt has already been cast on such a position. Clearly, revivals took place, and notions of harmony tended to be reinterpreted in terms of specific cultural urgencies. Thus the reinterpretations show the shifting meanings and the historical role of this wider framework of analogy.

When stripped to its outlines the harmony of nature indicates that men ordinarily assume that they live in a world informed by an order that is regular enough to anticipate, or to look forward to anticipating most basic natural events. In any version of the analogy between the whole and the parts of nature the same assumptions of harmony, repetitiousness and predictability appear. Mostly, these assumptions were elaborately formulated, meaning that in and above their affirmation of regularity various descriptive elements were added to expose the order. Historians of science have appraised some of these descriptive elements as having been more troublesome than productive. For example, hierarchical distinctions in the cosmos, sacred numbers and controlling spirits eventually had to be disregarded because they no longer described nature in a satisfactory way. While not attempting to label such beliefs, either as barriers or contributors to progress, I am concerned to call attention to the fact that valuable assumptions about natural orderliness were associated with them. Thus, it is possible to imagine elements of the analogy falling into disuse while, at the same time, others were preserved precisely because they confirmed the preoccupations of those who evoked them. The family of assumptions, here represented primarily by the analogy between the whole and the parts of nature, were associated with disciplines like astrology, alchemy, and magic. These have been labelled pre-sciences and, by less generous historians, pseudo-sciences. However, it would not do to suppose that every aspect pertaining to these subjects was irrational, or that the men who upheld them were unreasonable. So, the association of the analogy with them does not, in itself, place the analogy in the position of having had an indifferent or negative effect on developing ideas.

By itself, the notion of natural harmony can tell us little more than that we can assume that the sun will rise tomorrow, that the seasons will pass in the same order, etc. It is not possible to use the naked concept, so to speak, in order to try to appreciate its role in the history of thought. But, that role can be revealed and appreciated from the various contexts in which the analogy, or some version of it, was evoked. The idea of looking at it through specific examples already suggests that the analogy is likely to have been more than just a bare assumption of order. Although this is not so for all phases of culture from that of the ancients to the present, it is certainly likely to be so at times when the notion was popular, when it was being reformed and re-expressed. Historians must be prepared to take these revivals seriously and to attempt to see why harmony suddenly mattered and the exact ways in which it did matter. If Alberti's and Leonardo's versions were significant for their modes of thinking, and they were, then possibly Descartes or Newton's versions might have been similarly meaningful.

This chapter has shown Leonardo's vision of nature and art to have been one of harmony. However, if the point of view is changed from his assumptions about nature to his personal attitudes towards nature, as it will be in the chapter that follows next, a different and less harmonious picture will emerge. Leonardo's harmonious view of nature was not complemented by a harmonious personality. Yet, the tensions of that personality were not wholly subjective but represent some of the more general tensions of his age.

Notes to Chapter Two

1. Leonardo da Vinci, *Literary Works,* ed. J.P. Richter (Oxford University Press, 1939) (1000).
2. Paolo Rossi, *Philosophy, Technology, and the Arts in the Early Modern Era,* (New York, 1970), Appendix 1.
3. As quoted by K.D. Keele, in *Leonardo da Vinci: On Movement of the Heart and Blood* (London, 1952), p. 99.
4. *Ibid,* p. 100.
5. *Ibid.* p. 100.
6. *Ibid.* figs. 37, 38.
7. Leonardo da Vinci, *Literary Works,* ed. Richter (849).
8. K.D. Keele, *Leonardo: On Heart and Blood,* pp. 126, 127.
9. B. Rackusin: 'The Architectural Theory of Luca Pacioli, 'De Divina proportione chapter 54', *Bibliothèque d'Humanisme et Renaissance,* XXXIX, Librairie Droz S.A. (Geneva, 1977), pp. 479-502.
10. Nicholas Cusanus, *The Idiot,* 'Concerning the Mind', Bk. III, ch. iv, Sutro Branch California State Library, Occasional Papers, Reprints 19, p. 34.
11. E. Panofsky, *The Codex Huygens and Leonardo da Vinci's Art Theory* (London, 1940), pp. 122-125.
12. Leonardo da Vinci, *Literary Works,* ed. Richter, 'Paragone' (2)
13. *Ibid.* (1). I am interpreting the process of analogy-making broadly as comprising the drawing of any similarities, likenesses or samenesses between different things. The differences which distinguish the things can be so small as to make them simply different individual examples of the same genus. On the other hand they may be so great as to encompass all the overt differences between geometry and painting. Despite their differences both practices share the same science of the presentation of surfaces. So with respect to that science they are analogous to each other.

14. *Ibid.* 'Paragone' (1). A mathematical point is notionally indivisible and not quantitative, but the mind's idea of it is derived from nature and the analysis of real solids. Here Leonardo indicates that this derivation is not adequate to originate the point. The point is not a concept but it is the actuality prior to extension and motion and time. This discussion is advanced in Chapter 3.

15. E. Panofsky, *Codex Huygens*, pp. 126,127.

16. Cf. Paul Lawrence Rose, 'Humanist Culture and Renaissance Mathematics of the Quattrocento', *Studies in the Renaissance*, vol. XX, 1973. Even Ficino respected mathematics. p. 53.

17. Leonardo da Vinci, *Literary Works*, ed. Richter, 'Paragone' (1).

18. *Ibid.* (916).

19. *Ibid.* vol. I, p. 31, n. 2.

20. *Ibid.* (916); my italics.

21. *Ibid.* (44).

22. *Dictionary of Philosophy and Psychology*, ed. J.M. Baldwin (New York, 1902), 'Time,' cf. p. 699 '. . . time is never actual in any of its parts, for the momentary "now" taken strictly, is no part of time, but a limit, the beginning or end of a period.' Compare this with Leonardo da Vinci in Richter (46): 'The point being indivisible, occupies no space. That which occupies no space does not exist. The limiting surface of one thing is the beginning of another . . . .'

23. Leonardo da Vinci, *Literary Works* (917).

24. P.J. Zwart, *About Time* (New York, 1976), pp. 34-37; here he explains that 'before', 'now' and 'after' notions of time can be regarded as 'highly elementary and primitive', meaning they are fundamental to humankind and are derived from experience. However, Leonardo's *Now*, like his special point, is not seen by him to be derived from experience.

25. That line is never totally perceivable, either, for the before depends on memory and the afterwards depends on hypotheses made from the experience of the past.

26. Of course, materiality affects the surfaces and limits of a thing. But it is these surfaces and their limits that are described in geometry, and not the material itself. Hence space has surfaces and limits with relation to the objects in it, but the material of space, the air, is of no interest to the geometer. But, it is of interest to the painter with respect to other problems of representation.

27. Leonardo da Vinci, *Literary Works* (568).

28. *Ibid.* (69).

29. *Encyclopaedia of Philosophy*, ed. p. Edwards, 'Nothing', p. 524; cf. Rosalie Colie, *Paradoxia Epidemica: The Renaissance Tradition of Paradox*, (Princetown, N.J. 1966), pp. 24-7, 29-30, 151, 222, 225, 228.

30. Leonardo da Vinci, *Literary Works* (1216)
31. *Ibid.* (1214).
32. *Ibid.*(1216).
33. Nicholas Cusanus, *The Idiot*, Bk. III, chap. iv, Sutro Branch California State Library, Occasional Papers, Reprints 19, p. 34.
34. Leonardo da Vinci, *Literary Works*, 'Paragone' (1). This is the expression of a notional device for the construction of perspective drawings.
35. *Ibid.*(47).
36. *Ibid.* (49); my italics.
37. Cf. chapter three, pp. 126-132.
38. *Ibid.* 'Paragone' (34).
39. *Ibid.* 'Paragone' (34). Cf. (102).
40. *Ibid.* vol. I, p. 78, n. 34.
41. E. Panofsky, *The Codex Huygens*, p. 125.
42. D. O. O'Malley, ed., *Leonardo's Legacy, An International Symposium* (Berkeley and Los Angeles, 1959), p. 174.
43. *Ibid.* p. 176.
44. *Ibid.* p. 178.
45. Leonardo da Vinci, *Literary Works*, ed. Richter, 'Paragone' (9).
46. *Ibid.* 'Paragone' (33).
47. *Ibid.* 'Paragone' (19), (25).
48. *Ibid.* 'Paragone' (32).
49. *Ibid.* 'Paragone' (32).
50. E. Cassirer, *The Individual and the Cosmos in Renaissance Philosophy*, first publ. 1927. (New York, 1963), pp. 39-41.
51. Leonardo da Vinci, *Literary Works* (837).
52. *Ibid.* (662).
53. Kenneth Clark, Leonardo da Vinci, revised ed. Penguin Books (1958), p. 13, and see also p.17; and J.H. Randall Jr., 'Leonardo da Vinci and the Emergence of Modern Science', *The School of Padua and the Emergence of Modern Science* (Padua, 1951), p. 137.
54. Leonardo da Vinci, *Literary Works*, ed. Richter (832).
55. J.P. McMurrich, *Leonardo da Vinci the Anatomist* (Baltimore, 1930), p. 193.
56. J.H. Randall, *Padua and the Emergence of Modern Science*, pp. 117, 129, 138.
57. Leonardo da Vinci, *Literary Works*, ed. Richter, vol. 1, pp. 70-71. Richter thinks that one of the drum drawings might show a precursor of Savart's wheel for analysis of pitch and frequency of vibration.
58. *Ibid.*(1129), (1129a).
59. *Ibid.* (832).
60. *Ibid.* vol. I., pp. 71-2.

61. This shows a link between the trachea dissections and his dissections to find how air entered the heart. He followed the bronchi to their smallest branches imbedded in the lung. He also inflated the lungs of geese and, besides linking the sound produced by the escaping air to a possible pipe-like function of the human trachea, he also found that no air passed directly from the lungs into the pulmonary veins and into the heart. Cf. K.D. Keele, *Leonardo, On Heart and Blood,* pp. 49, 50.

62. Leonardo da Vinci, *Literary Works,* 'Paragone' (22).

63. *Ibid.,* (798)., cf. also J.P. McMurrich, *Leonardo, the Anatomist,* pp. 85-90, and E. Panofsky, 'Artist, Scientist, Genius: Notes on the Renaissance Dämmerung', *The Renaissance* (New York, 1953), pp. 155-158 and K.D. Keele, *Leonardo, On Heart and Blood,* pp. 34-6.

64. Leonardo da Vinci, *Literary Works,* Richter, (797).

65. E. Cassirer, *The Individual and the Cosmos,* p. 165.

66. Leonardo da Vinci, *Literary Works,* Richter, 'Paragone' (6). Certainly, he knows that reason can have knowledge without confirmation by the senses, as in mathematics. But when men adopt correct and intelligent procedures of study, the senses inform the mind. They do not inevitably mislead it. The frame of reference is not completely forgotten: 'The senses are of the earth; reason stands apart from them in contemplation.' (1145).

67. Martin Kemp, 'Il concetto dell'anima in Leonardo's early skull studies', *J. Warburg and Courtauld Institutes,* vol. XXXIV, 1971, p. 115-135.

68. Ernst Cassirer, *The Individual and the Cosmos in Renaissance Philosophy,* first pub. 1927 (New York, 1936), p. 161.

69. Richter translates *la caratte* as ciphers, but symbols seem more appropriate: Leonardo da Vinci, *Literary Works,* Richter, 'Paragone' (27).

3

THE INFECTIOUS IMAGINATION OF NICHOLAS OF CUSA

> ...While reason must seek in nature, not fictitiously ascribe to it, whatever as not being knowable through reason's own resources has to be learnt, if learnt at all, only from nature, it must adopt as its guide, in so seeking, that which it has itself put into nature.
> Immanuel Kant

By way of things certain we arrive at the unknown

Speaking about imagination is always difficult. We accept it as a real mental faculty. And we even accept that there are styles or trends in the images of the imagination just as there are styles in drawing and writing. Yet unless a thinker is so self-revealing as to tell precisely what it is that he imagines, visualizes, or even day-dreams, we are left to ponder and gather from his thoughts, habits, and environment in order to make hopefully intelligent conjectures about the images of his imagination. Some guesses are almost certain. So when I write that both Alberti and Leonardo saw nature and human works in terms of a prior assumption of harmony of the whole and the parts of nature, few will object. But this does not get me very far either. In holding this view they were not different from a host of other Renaissance men, men of entirely different interests and intellectual capacities. Even so, despite the popularity of the assumption, we have also seen a real intimacy between this general and common feature of many imaginations and the entirely specific thoughts and works that each of these men accomplished.

Frequently historians treat such a popular assumption as a theme that describes the cultural background of persons and/or events. By contrast to this sort of reference, historians tend to view original thoughts, innovative actions, and new situations as forming the dynamic and essential parts of history. When pertaining to thought, the core of the history of ideas for a period is usually seen as standing out and is necessarily placed somewhat apart from the general background. However, if both descriptive terms, intimacy and background are simultaneously applied to this most general of all assumptions then the reader should feel uncomfortable. Yet this is just what I have been doing. For when Leonardo uses movement in water to study and hypothesize

about movement in air, he uses the analogy between the whole
and the parts of nature in an intimate way, a way that enables him
to reason by analogy about a specific problem and to express his
views with precision. Yet his, or anyone else's private use of this
grand analogy ought not to detract from the fact that the general
assumption was truly at the back of a massive body of thought
within the early modern period. The error is to imagine that
general concepts and assumptions, concepts that often form the
setting or back-drop for historical events, cannot at the same time
move forward and participate in the formation of events. This
great plasticity of the grand analogy makes it seem like a nose of
wax. Indeed it was a nose of wax. But the way that we find the
assumption moulded within the context of certain ideas actually
influences the ideas, giving them definition and character. Thus
the analogy between the whole and the parts of nature could be of
great importance and this is not only as a source of inspiration
and reassurance. It could even be vital within the conception of
important and original ideas.

This sort of problem of interpretation dramatizes the curious
paradox of imagination. If we free ourselves from the old
assumption of a mere image-making faculty, we must admit that
the problem of evaluating imaginative images can play wicked
tricks on historians. The images can be superficial to creative
expression, conventional schemes applied conventionally. Yet,
the images that stir the imagination, whether these be privately
formulated or general and popular images, all cannot be relied
upon to remain superficial to originality. If it is abstracted from
content an imaginative assumption can seem so general as to
appear to mean only a loose and universal thing. After all, what is
the harmony of nature if not a most general notion? But we know
that it was not always employed in a way that restricted it to its
most general terms. Fertile minds could use the analogy to draw
new conclusions about specific artistic and scientific problems.
Thus, when Alberti viewed his theory and practice of perspective
as a scientific description of vision and of the presentation of
reality he was not thinking in mere generalities. His use of the
analogy made it possible for him, first, to appreciate the
importance of perspective, and then, to view all works, including
works of art, as potential parts within the grand design. This is
how works could be on a par with nature. Here a universal
assumption was participating in important and original expression.

Now in the shadow of some of this original expression I have
placed the subtle influence of another fifteenth-century thinker.
I have alluded to Nicholas of Cusa and suggested that his ideas
about reality and human knowledge attracted both Alberti and

Leonardo. The same attraction is also possible, indeed probable in the case of Brunelleschi and others in contact with Cusa's mathematician friend Toscanelli.[1] For Alberti and Leonardo, I have shown how this might be so by comparing Alberti's view of the creative process with Cusa's conception of mind. I also compared Leonardo's notions of space, time and infinity with Cusa's idea of being and reality.

I want now to continue in this vein, to explore the imaginative content of Cusan images and the possible historical role of that content. But this is not because I think Cusa was the primary influence within all of the intellectual problems that confronted Alberti and Leonardo. This might have been so in the case of Luca Pacioli and other mathematicians. However, for Alberti and Leonardo the influence was rather one of orientation than of the posing of specific questions. For example, Alberti absorbed the Cusan notion of a power of knowing in the mind but he did not directly address himself to questions of epistemology. Cusa was different from these Florentines. He was neither painter, nor engineer, nor anatomist. More churchman than city-dweller, he can be seen to belong to entirely different dimensions of activity in this era. His stunning corollaries of movement, the philosophical conclusions that played havoc with the accepted physics and cosmology of his time have been amply celebrated by eminent historians such as Ernst Cassirer and Pierre Duhem. Certainly, I am not seeking to exclude either the differences between the Cusan himself and the highly secular strain in Florentine thought and activity at that time, or even the wider implications of Cusa's attack on Aristotelian logic and cosmology and the fact that Florentines did not celebrate him by name for initiating that attack. These things are there, and yet Cusa's infectious images and metaphors made him capable of influence in a world that was not entirely his own world. This influence was not exclusively derived from the number of earth-shaking corollaries attached to the end of Book II of *De docta ignorantia* in 1440. Still, we should remain aware that the view of space in the corollaries is largely dimensional or geometrical rather than qualitative and that this generally corresponds to the treatment of space by perspective painters. However, Cusa's effect was more general, affecting the vision of the grand relationship between man and nature and God.

As I have said before, imagination has its styles, and so I see Cusanus as the generator of a most original style of visualization. This had quick influence during his lifetime and shortly afterwards. The historical implications of this influence work in two general ways. The first way is usually acknowledged. His corollaries of motion seem to have foreshadowed Copernicus's theory in 1543, the impact of Tycho's new star in 1577, points that Galileo made using his telescope in 1610, and some of Kepler's work before 1609.[2] The sun and the earth were saved or regained for men by Cusa long before John Donne's ever-quoted First Anniversery of 1611, '. . .The sun is lost. . .'. This is because Nicholas of Cusa's philosophy had a unique quality that made his line of thinking able to prevent disorientation in a vast and indefinite universe, in a state of being without a knowable beginning, essence, or end, and ultimately, in a mysterious immanent and transcendent God. Although later, Cusan concepts were combined with magic in Giordano Bruno's philosophy, and achieved their wider popularity therein, his conceptions by themselves provided the vital elements for maintaining the integrity and importance of the human mind within the universe and in super-reality. Ultimately, that reality was not spacial or temporal, it was non-directional and could not entirely be known. For most people, this maintenance of the integrity of the mind was one of implication rather than one brought about by a direct grappling with Cusan notions. However, in the instance of some of the Florentines, and especially of Leonardo da Vinci, I think that the Cusan practice of learned ignorance actually confirmed the ambitious character of their universality. The spiritual ingredients in Leonardo's works are truly Cusan. Cusan theology was acceptable to the Church in his time but it was also abstract, unique, and little understood. Leonardo's religious posture has this very same strangeness. It will take some time to expand and explain my thoughts about these matters.

The contemplative posture that Cusa called learned ignorance required men to apprehend the greater truth of the divine mystery, or, as he expressed it from inspirations from negative theology, to apprehend the greater truth of nothing. Nothing stands as a symbol without attributes. It signifies the essentially unknown and unknowable character of the origin, substance and end of being. For the moment, let it suffice to say that the practice of learned ignorance had qualities that could maintain and preserve the value of finite minds within an indefinite universe and eternal reality. Cusan epistemology created a unique option for the investigator of natural phenomena because The Divine Word was present in all parts and in the whole of the natural universe. The way to achieve the state of mind called learned ignorance involved a thinker in a process of knowing parts of the universe by reasoning, comparing and contrasting things, and then, as a consequence of this first limited sort of knowing, of achieving an apprehension of the limits of knowing. This awareness is seen as a kind of negative knowledge, knowing what you cannot know; and it has to be ripened by constant practice. More of this below. For the moment we see that men could know the real world progressively if not completely and the very process of doing so initiated a contemplative process wherein men became wise by knowing their own ignorance. Now even if the planet earth were to dance a gavotte men could not lose this sense of the importance of their own mental processes, of the true power of their minds and souls within the Divine Maximum.

It is a pity that the counter-reformation Roman Catholic Church did not understand things from a Cusan point of view, as did Cusa's friend Pope Pius II (Aeneo Sylvio Piccolomini 1405-1464). Then they would have understood the attack on their unity in more wholly political and doctrinal terms, and perhaps they would have seen that they did not need to be vulnerable to shifting scientific views. Galileo had got this right.

This moves me nearer to Cusa's second monumental contribution, now, not of a view of motion that contradicted the accepted Aristotelian ideas, but one of substantial food for the modern imagination. Thus, I make the claim and will take some time over explaining and illustrating it. I am convinced that the Cusan view of knowledge confirmed practitioners, men like Toscanelli, Brunelleschi, Alberti, and Leonardo. Therefore, the effects of Cusan originality live on, to some extent, in the context of the works of these people. Their orientation, their view of human knowledge in relation to reality, their vision of creativity and of the divine creation itself were gleaned from the dramatic and vivid images of Nicholas of Cusa. Cusa was a unique mystic. He was so confirmed in his view of the expression of the divine mystery as limited within the individual parts and the whole of nature, and also in his view that the mind was gifted with an intellectual sensibility that could take it beyond the examples of nature, that he himself could confront the problem of knowledge of nature with something akin to a scientific attitude. At the same time, and most important, within the same act, he simultaneously worshipped the creator. Before him, bold statements of empirical method were rare* but here we have his formulation and it is quick, concise, and evocative:

> When we use an image and try to reach analogically what is as yet unknown, there must be no doubt at all about the image; for it is only by way of postulates and things certain that we can arrive at the unknown. But in all things sensible material possi-

*This does not refer to practices but to the general consideration of questions of knowledge and method.

bility abounds which explains their being in a continual state of flux. Our knowledge of things is not acquired by completely disregarding their material conditions, without which no image of them could be formed; nor is it wholly subject to their possible variations; but the more we abstract from sensible conditions the more certain and solid our knowledge is . . .[3]

This attitude to method is similar to Leonardo's. Conclusions had to come either from mathematical demonstrations or clear and certain evidence that began with the senses. In some ways Cusa's point of view is even somewhat Baconian; although, Bacon tended to express himself in a baroque and decorated style and he was not mathematically inclined.[4]

One infinite exemplar

Now that Cusanus has been trumpeted and announced I have to bring him to the fore-stage and say what I mean to continue to do with his thinking. First, glancing back at the earlier chapters, what I have said about Alberti's and Leonardo's use of analogy developed from studies of their works. Their use of analogy is revealed in these studies and does not entirely depend upon the possible inspiration of Cusan ideas. Even so, it is clear that I believe in the likelihood and potency of such inspiration. This is especially true in the region of assumptions about the mind, the creative process, and about the wider meaning of knowledge. Now I am not really writing about Cusa's analogy between the whole and the parts of nature for its own sake, rather, I am attempting to clarify some of the historical importance of Cusa's thought and in this way possibly to develop the characteristics of a Christian Platonism in Florence that was different from the later Neo-Platonism of Ficino's Academy. Therefore, I will be exclusive in what I say about Cusa, about a mind that was too diverse to be wholly described in this context.

If the effects of Cusa's imaginative style are to be made plausible, it is necessary to tell some general things about his life and writings. I see these effects as consequent upon the attitudes of some mathematicians, artists, and thinkers not as sources for the development of a new school of philosophy. Only an exploration of the curious style of Cusanus can reveal how it was possible for him to maintain a viable form of Neo-Platonism without a belief in eternal archetypes, in the 'Ideas'.

Without such archetypes men had to rely on non-introspective modes of recognition. However, if Cusa had rejected the Platonic scheme altogether, he would have lacked the fuel for his whole rejection of Aristotelian physics. As it was he originated a unique style of thinking that combined rationalism and empiricism with mystical contemplation. He developed this from a reliance on specific gifts or qualities of the mind. The examples were in nature only and the power in the mind. Evidently, a modern outlook was developing in the speculative writings of a religious mystic and Platonist. Cusa is very clear about his rejection of the archetypes:

> A plurality of distinct exemplars is then absurd, for each would be to the objects modelled on it the infinitely true exemplar, but infinite truth can only be one. One infinite exemplar is all that is needed and one alone suffices.[5]

Nicholas of Cusa was born Nicholas Krebs* in Kues across the Moselle from Bernkastel in 1401. Probably through the influence of Count Theodoric von Manderscheid, he was sent to Holland to Deventer to study with the Brothers of the Common Life. This was about twenty years after Thomas à Kempis.

This is not an attempt at an intellectual biography of Cusa. I just want to identify some of his experiences and inspirations, and some sources of his ideas. This is generally less known than the background of Alberti or Leonardo.

Cusa attended universities in both Germany and Italy. In about 1416 he became interested in the Christian Neo-Platonism of Meister Eckhart (1260-1328). This early contact with Eckhart's ideas is fascinating; for, it was Eckhart who both thought and spoke specifically about concepts of time. And radical notions of motion, space, and time are concepts that link Cusa with the mathematicians and artists of Florence.

Eckhart spoke of the *Now* moment as something that contained all time within the present.[6] I have already indicated a similar thought in the example of Leonardo da Vinci's use of the zero, his idea of nothing as a symbol for the present that really has no duration in time. I also associated this symbol, nothing, with Cusa's general extension and assimilation of time from the *Now* moment. That moment was a conceptual point, and a special sort of point. Not one that was abstracted from the line representing the unfolding of time, instead it was *actuality*, the point from which time unfolded. It was an origin, a

*Other versions: Khrypffs, Krypffs, Cryfts.

point prior to the line. So finding a fifteen year old Nicholas at grips with Eckhart can illustrate how very early in life Cusa began to respond to the specific ideas that were to fire his own mature imagination. It also suggests that we note something of importance in the atmosphere of religious Neo-Platonism before the fifteenth century. In pondering the contrasts between material extension and spirit, and between time and eternity, religious thinkers were casting the relativity of all human experience under the aegis of concepts of space and time. For example, in 1277, in the council of the doctors of the Sorbonne, Averroes' notion of space or place was declared to be heretical. This was because the doctors felt that the recognition of an absolutely immobile body, immobile even for God, was not possible because it was incompatible with the fundamental ideas of theology.[7] If rest is a quality of God, the universe can only hold bodies that are more or less in motion, relative to each other, but there will not be a body that is absolutely at rest. Grounds like these are apparent in Cusa's corollaries of motion. But Cusa did not leave these things simply within the context of theological disputes. He shifted them to questions of knowledge and to statements about the universe.

The terms proximity and distance only temporarily apply to man and do not apply to God. Cusanus established this but *his elaboration of this point was one of an already existing cultural emphasis.* Notice this emphasis in the way that Eckhart conceived of time and of the creation:

> Time comes of the revolution of the heavens and day began with the first revolution. . .To say that God created the world yesterday or tomorrow would be foolishness, for God created the world and everything in it in the one present *Now.* Indeed time that has been past for a thousand years is as present and near to God as the time that is now . . .[8]

Here Eckhart makes two points about time. Time comes from the revolution of the heavens. Thus, the time that men experience depends upon a regular motion. Edkhart expresses this idea just slightly differently from St. Augustine. Augustine also noticed the comparative character of men's awareness of time. Men measured time by movement. Augustine also remarked that any motion might be used as a measure of time. Time could be seen to pass for a potter at the wheel, and this would happen even if the revolutions of the heavens stopped.

Eckhart's second point about time is that flow, a continuing line, or the journey of the world passing through a medium of time, and other images like these cannot apply to time when men consider time in the light of what God cannot be less than. God cannot be less than eternal, and this is not by his *becoming eternal* but by his *being so.* So time can be understood to not pass when men think of God and of the divine creation. Thus, absolute time is all-embracing and ever-present. It does not descend from motion, but motion itself descends from time. Men have nothing to signify this, only nought, no duration or the figure zero. Their apprehension of this condition is an awareness of essence without form. Their actual knowledge of absolute time does not exist, and yet it is possible for them to be certain that absolute time is real.

Originally, men were intended to ponder the religious import of these contrasts between knowledge and awareness and this was largely in the form of a devotion. It was a spiritual exercise developed to teach men how to ripen their own appreciation of the divine mystery. The *devotio moderna* and its historical counterparts all subscribed to this aim of personalizing religious contemplation, of perfecting the most intimate awareness of the contrast between the universe and the divine mystery. These aims and methods are supreme in Cusa's practice of learned ignorance.

At the same time, and in addition to these things, Cusanus began to think about the practical implications of the identification of the world's time with the motion of material bodies. He gave philosophical treatment to this aspect of the problem and, as we know, he introduced some astounding conclusions.

Historians are already aware that Cusa's attack on Aristotelian concepts of space coincided with fifteenth-century artists developing a new theory and practice of perspective. Perspective itself has also been associated with practices of land surveying and map making, all processes involving the geometrical conceptualization of space. Space was described in terms of pure dimensions in perspective pictures and it was constructed in relation to the eye of an observer. Nicholas of Cusa was not ignorant of these artistic developments. He studied map making when in Padua and his close associates Piccolomini and Toscanelli were, among other things, cartographers. As in perspective pictures, in Cusan cosmology, space possesses no qualitative or hierarchical features in terms of its proximity to bodies. In the picture it is given dimensions but not virtues by the environing objects. In the Cusan cosmos space is homogeneous despite its proximity to the stars, to the sun, to the moon, or to the earth. Historians have been aware of these things, yet they can never be overemphasized. Following upon this, they are far less aware of Cusa's preoccupation with time. First, he had the devotional preoccupation that we have

observed in the Eckhart examples. In and above this he also
had practical concern with the world's time. In 1436, before *De
docta ignorantia,* he proposed a reform of the calendar along
lines resembling those adopted later under Gregory XIII. So
the question how to calculate and measure time by the motion
of the heavens or indeed, as in Augustine, by any motion, was
not remote for Cusanus. He and others associated the measurement of space with the placement of the eye of an observer.
But, as far as I know, Cusa alone also associated the experience
of time with the observer's position or place in the physical universe.

Time and space are not exactly the same in any two places

This surprising association appears in the context of a discussion about natural philosophy. It is a remark about the possibility of achieving absolute precision in the science of astronomy.
Unlike the association between space and the eye, the Cusan
association of time with place did not become a scientific theory
until Newtonian concepts were modified by Einstein. In Cusa,
the relativity of motion and of the measurement of space and
time comes in the form of a curious statement of philosophical
awareness. This was not formed into a real new theory of the
universe but it was a philosophical reflection that Cusa expressed with as much certainty as Eckhart had, when he distinguished between time in the physical world and absolute time.
Despite the fact that these reflections were supported on
theological grounds, the historical effect was one of loosening
the hold of conventional conceptions of space and time and of
reinforcing the geometrical approach to cosmology and
physics. We must not expect to find Cusa in 1440 thinking like
Copernicus in 1543.

Cusanus is speaking about the position of the science of
astronomy and what he thinks here is no less important than
what he thinks in a related passage where he maintains that the
earth must move. He says:

> It is impossible to have precise knowledge of the plan of the
> heavens with regard to any sort of place or with regard to the
> rise and setting of the stars or of the elevation of the pole and all
> that lies around it. Since the factors of time and space cannot be

precisely the same in any two places, it is evident that precision in detail is by no means to be in the judgement of astronomers.[9]

The expression of this thought is couched within the terms of geocentric astronomy. Here, the earth was at rest and in the centre, and fixed stars were in the heavens. In the sense of this model Cusa then speaks about an elevation of the pole. However, this must really only be a mode of communication for him. Actually, he contradicts the existence of any fixed points in space: '. . .the poles do not exist'.[10]

You will remember that time is described by movement, and Cusanus points out that movement itself can only be detected by reference to a fixed point. But the only fixed point that can exist is in God. Evidently, this cannot be a location in space. It is a spiritual quality. As Cusa puts it:

> It is only by reference to a fixed point - poles or centres - that we are able to detect movement, and we take such fixed points for granted in our measurements of movement. By reason of these assumptions which we make, we find ourselves involved in error on all points, and because we do not question the notions the ancients had about centres, poles and measurements, we are puzzled when we discover that the stars are not in the position indicated by their system.[11]

Passages like this one give progressively minded historians a great deal of trouble. Often, Cusa's immediate effects are looked for directly in cosmology and astronomy, while actually, they appear to have been in mathematics and in the epistemological assumptions of fifteenth century Florentine artists. Many historians of science balk at Cusa's assertion of the impossibility of being accurate in astronomy. But this has to be understood for what it is. It is an expression of learned ignorance. In so far as God is seen to be the centre and circumference of the universe, it is not possible to measure motions accurately because there are no fixed points in the universe. However, the universe is not chaotic either and Cusa is not maintaining that astronomy is futile. Like geometry and music, astronomy has to be understood in the following way. Precision exists only in God. It is the truth of God. He is the equality that precedes, and that contracts itself in the harmony of the universe. He is the unity that precedes, and that contracts itself in quantity in the universe. He is the rest, the absolute fixed point, that precedes and that contracts itself in motion in the universe. Thus, the accuracy that Cusa talks about is absolute and therefore impossible for men. However, Cusa does not imply that men should leave off their geometry because physical forms cannot attain perfection, or music because music making cannot be truly harmonious, and the harmony of composition cannot express equality, or even astronomy, because the universe is not precisely describable. *In the imprecise examples that men study they find both the resemblance and the contrast to absolute reality. These are the terms of all human knowledge.* If men did not study the examples they would have no sources of knowledge whatsoever. The mind perfects from experience. Thus Cusa's point is that astronomers ought to practise learned ignorance and *not be bound by accepted theories* when they ought to know better. They can perfect their knowledge while they must still realize the approximative character of all the sciences. This is learned ignorance. But to despair of study and science would only be pure blind ignorance. It would also mean sin: the despair would amount to doubting God's *word,* his knowability and love. As far as I know, Cusa never recommended that.

In this discussion Cusanus concludes that all physical bodies must move; thus, the earth moves. Bodies are also made up of differing proportions of the same material, thus, they can be lighter or heavier, drier or wetter, hotter or colder than each other, but not qualitatively different from each other. Space has no virtues or qualities but only dimensions from the point of view of an observer looking at objects or bodies in space. The universe is homogeneous, and the measurement of space, time, and motion depends upon the observer's point of view. There is no absolute time or space except in God. Now natural philosophers did not immediately rush forth to draw from this; however, the very fact that the statement could be made shows a loosening of the whole conventional framework in ideas about physical reality. Cusa was not the prophet of classical science but perhaps he was something of a seer in terms of present physics and cosmology.

I do not want to press this biographical point of Cusa's having come to some kind of intellectual terms with Eckhart in 1416 and having written these things in 1440; note only, speculation about notions affecting these problems and preoccupations was alive in his early world. It does seem plausible that an intellectual environment that habitually contrasted man's extended, fluctuating, and temporal reality with a unified deity and an ever present eternity could invite the kind of speculation that Cusa entertained, especially when that environment had already placed human consideration of the differences between physical reality and God within terms of the experience of space and time. Cusanus was original because he shifted the problem from a theological appreciation of the mystery of God to an *intellectual* appreciation of the implications of that mystery within nature. This is an order of originality far greater than that of later thinkers who produced more coherent cosmological systems. To some extent he was helped by new preoccupations within the environment. For example, Cusa's Paduan association with the mathematician Toscanelli allowed for mutual preoccupations with map projections and with the science of perspective. The placement of the eye of the observer came to be seen as crucial for determining a picture's construction in linear perspective. Perhaps then, if the placement of the eye was crucial for a scientific awareness of terrestrial space, Cusa drew an analogy with cosmic space. In a homogeneous universe reality would present itself to the perceiver in terms of the position of that perceiver.

A Renaissance career

During the years after 1416 Cusa continued his studies in Padua. There he met and became the lifelong friend of Toscanelli. He also made a journey to Rome and was at Cologne in 1425. During these years Cusanus did many different sorts of things, the sheer variety of which supports my view of him as one who had a Renaissance career, despite some theological preoccupation with concepts that had been developed earlier. He was one of the first to question the Donations of Constantine and to describe them as an eighth century forgery. He became a doctor of law and mastered Latin, Greek, Hebrew and Arabic. He studied mathematics and also maintained certain literary and philosophical passions. Among these were his reading of Proclus' commentary on Plato's *Parmenides* and also an interest in the writings of Ramon Lull. Cusanus gained an early reputation as a serious theologian and thinker and he also began what was to be an outstanding executive and diplomatic career in the church. He was ordained in 1430 and represented Ulrich von Manderscheid at the council of Basle. There he took the conciliar position, as did his geographer friend the future Pope Pius II. Later, in Cusa's case by 1438, they both changed their minds about this. During their lifetimes they were mutually involved with church problems and intellectual problems, and this complementarity continued until death, which strangely came for both in 1464.

The importance of Cusa's early years is that they provide us with a whole fund of associations so that his conceptual leaps do not appear in isolation from the rest of his world. For, when commentators are not celebrating Cusanus' radical corollaries of motion and their implications for the cosmology of the late sixteenth and seventeenth centuries, they are frequently characterizing his thought as essentially medieval. Certainly this is not completely wrong. Some of the theological questions were old but are we then to regard things like Pico Della Mirandola's writings about being and God, *De ente et uno,* as also medieval because an old point of speculation is continued? The attempt to classify Nicholas of Cusa both as a medieval mind and as the prophet of the new cosmology is clumsy, not because there is no truth in both of these images but because they are ill knit and do not really tell us much about Cusa's mentality, not to speak of his audience. Certainly his great desire to make distinctions between human knowledge and experience and a mysterious and divine reality was part of both an ancient and a medieval commitment of minds to this problem. Still, much of what Cusanus thought and wrote also had direct and immediate appeal in his lifetime. A swift assembly of points can bring this timeliness into the light. Cusa confirmed the value of human life and of the body for the soul, and he stressed the role of the senses in the whole process of apprehension. The stress on provocation of the mind from an initial apprehension of nature was conventional enough; not so was Cusa's practice of learned ignorance. Here a style of contemplation began with the senses. Knowledge of the world was seen existing within wisdom, instead of being seen as an illusory charm obscuring wisdom. Thus, men were intended to know the images of experience with all possible certainty in order to begin to apprehend the limits of their knowledge outside of experience. The intuitive leap to an apprehension of God as the one in whom all opposites coincide is only possible in the light of an anterior struggle to understand diversity and plurality in nature. These convictions facilitated the appeal that Cusan metaphysics had to persons like Paolo Toscanelli. Cusa admired works and workmen. His books on wisdom and the mind are set within the market place. The historian Eugenio Garin characterized Toscanelli as having the mind of a spice merchant.[12] I imagine the philosopher whose father had been in commerce and who selected a spoonmaker as his personal representative in his books on the mind did not fail to see real importance in a spice merchant's mentality. Without going into detail about it, I will allude to Cusa's career in the church, for it is the diplomatic career of a Renaissance man.

First for the council, then for the Pope, Cusanus rose to a
highly important position in the church. As cardinal of San
Pietro in Vincoli and, ten years later, in 1458, as vicar-general
of Rome, Cusanus and his friend Pius II typified some of the
most enlightened leadership the church ever had in times of
trouble. Both internal troubles and the pressure from the
westward-moving Turks made this a time of great crisis. A
despairing letter from Piccolomini (the later Pius II) to Cusa, in
May 1453, when Constantinople was on the point of falling,
echoed the Cusan's own long-term concern with the unity of
Christendom. He had written his *De concordantia catholica*
twenty years earlier.

Cusa spent much of his active and travelling diplomatic
career trying to bring about substantial reforms within the
church, trying to bring about the fulfilment of the pastoral
needs of the times, as well as confronting the menace of Islam.
How then can we think of him as an essentially medieval man?
If anything, sometimes he truly anticipates the future, for
example, when he considers all beings, even possibly beings living on other stars, as either examples or images of God. The
distinction between an example and an image is one of mentality. Only intellectual beings possessing mind are images of God.
In the light of this Cusa also saw all religions as containers of
some portion of divine truth. No religion could be outside God.
The Catholic church, however, expresses the truest and fullest
image of divine reality on earth. This is the tone of Cusa's book
on the Koran, his *De cribratio alchorani*, written in 1461, just
when the Roman church was suffering at the hands of the
exponents of that scripture. Most Catholics were inclined to
view the Koran as so much devil's work. But for Cusa all religions were the rays of one sun, and Christianity was an all
embracing truth that included all the other truths within it.
This is how Islam was to be regarded. Neither essentially evil
nor enemy, it was a rising star to be included within the greater
light of an even higher sun. Pius II actually attempted negotia-
tions with the Sultan in terms of Cusa's vision of the meaning
of the Koran. Evidently, these two leaders were willing to place
their own theological and philosophical conclusions upon the
negotiating table. The immediacy and intimacy of their commitment to their intellectual values is clear.

The artist's philosopher

In his *Études sur Leonardo Da Vinci*, Pierre Duhem compared
specific material from the notes of Leonardo with Cusan con-

cepts.[13] Cusa's mathematical and scientific writings provide many studies that could have been further developed by Leonardo.[14] It is not my intention to follow these through. Instead of showing a translation of specific studies from Cusa to Leonardo or to other Florentines, I am trying to show that some of the early fifteenth-century artists of Florence may have adopted a kind of philosophical posture from Cusanus. His is the wider view of mind, nature and reality that seemed to have made the most sense to persons committed to developing geometrical space and naturalistic representation. Thus, the two universal men of the fifteenth century, Alberti and Leonardo, appear to have taken their assumptions about the powers and processes of the human mind from Cusa. They were also confirmed in their wide-based belief in the importance of human creativity. And above all, their personal sense of the meaning of nature within greater spiritual reality seems to have been expressed in tones and colours that could only be Cusan. Historians credit Cusa with substantial contributions to mathematics; his attack on Aristotle's physics and cosmology generally appears to anticipate the new cosmology of the mid-sixteenth and seventeenth centuries. But in and above Cusa's impact in these areas, I believe his most immediate intellectual role was that of the artist's philosopher.

All human arts are certain images of the infinite and divine art.[15] This is his view of the value of every example of knowledge in this world, and regarding the arts and crafts he repeats it over and over again. The arts and crafts have been processed by the mind and therefore they represent a perfected knowledge, in and above the examples in nature. Some passages of *De docta ignorantia* are highly evocative of the mood, style and content of passages of Leonardo. We are all familiar with the following convictions from Alberti and Leonardo; here however, they are expressed by Cusanus:

> Who could help admiring this craftsman (*opificem*) who is spheres and stars and in the vast stellar spaces employs such skill that, with no discontinuity, achieves in the widest diversity the highest unity. . . .[16]

It was Alberti's point that men were intended to admire divine works, the divine art in the design of the universe. Cusa frequently speaks in this way, and when he does he is in direct dialogue with the contemporary artist.

> It is His will that the vast admirable contrivance of the universe (mundi machina) should lead us to admiration of Him.[17]

The creator is compared with the human artist. Leonardo da Vinci wrote that he gave degrees for the diminution of objects in a perspective picture much as a musician gave notes as specific tones in a continuum of sound. The human arts are images of the infinite divine art. They are analogues to each other; and the purest and most essential basis of all of their analogies lies in the use of number. This is so because God used number in the creation of the universe. Art is close to nature then, and the whole of nature is a divine work of art.

If we look at the Renaissance from a future perspective, looking backward so to speak, all this seems to be a very old song; however, if we remember that we are in the 1430s and 40s looking ahead, then the forceful pronouncement of the high status of the human arts by Cusanus justifies the vision of him as the artist's philosopher. The Aristotelian hierarchical cosmology has gone, and so has the low status of the human arts and crafts. Common use of the abstract sciences of number, the grasp of harmony, the need for proportion in the making and design of anything at all, these things are the essence of the analogy between human creativity and the divine creation itself.

> Behold how the infinite unity of the sampler (God), cannot appear (in the physical world) but in an apt proportion, and that is in number. For the eternal mind doth act, as a musician which would make his conception sensible; for he takes many voices, and brings them into a proportion agreeing to that harmony, that in that proportion the harmony may sweetly and perfectly appear, when it is here in its place, and the resplendence of the harmony is varied according to the variety of the proportion that is fit for it; and the harmony ceaseth, when the aptitude of that proportion ceaseth. From the mind therefore is number and all things.[18]

Certainly it would be foolish to ignore the role of Renaissance humanism in also confirming the higher status of arts and of artists. The reading of Roman rhetoricians, especially of Cicero, was highly instrumental in supporting this raised status of the arts. Cusa even participated in this activity and, in addition, he and both Alberti and Leonardo were persuaded that the use of number and proportion must be the essential point around which to base arguments praising the arts. The first principle of the science of painting is geometry; the numbers that please our ears also please our eyes and delight our minds. These are familiar thoughts from Alberti and Leonardo. In all of this

mathematical imagery there is an association between proportion, perception, and the mind. Nicholas of Cusa did not simply esteem the arts on the basis of past tradition, and on the
basis of a common-sense appreciation of the culture of his
time; in addition, he provided a real framework upon which
men could explore and examine the analogy between art and
nature. A full view of this can only be gathered from a wide
view of Cusa's ideas. However, the intimacy that existed between images supporting practices in the arts, and images of the
powers of the human mind might be communicable from the
following example.

Recall a device recommended by Alberti for making a drawing in true perspective. The artist places a glass, like a window,
between his eyes and the objects to be drawn. He traces them
on the glass, and their proportions are represented in perspective from his point of view. In all this the eye acts as a vital
agent that informs the artist's mind how the objects appear on
the glass. The mind unifies this information and conceives of
the whole picture, and then brings about its execution. Now
this is not unlike a related explanatory device that was used by
Cusanus for describing what it is that actually is in the mind.

In the mind, Cusanus sees, not innate ideas, but a capacity or
gift of understanding. He compares what is in the mind with a
glass or a mirror. This reflects all the perceived sensible forms
brought before it. It reflects the imagination that has been stirred by these perceptions, and it reflects the reasoning or
judgement about all of these things. But this ultimate power of
the mind is not dead, instead it is a living mirror; God did not
make it passive, but active. It is not a purely reflective power, as
with the images on a real mirror or traced on a window; it is
also a power of understanding. This power compresses all that
happens between the eye and the mind when the viewer is perceiving the shapes in the window. In this mirror of the mind
the many shapes, and the proportions they display in terms of
themselves and of each other in space, are placed against an
understanding that recognizes harmony within the diversity of
things. This power is capable of distinguishing the objective
qualities of things from the proportions that they present to the
eye that is fixed and viewing the things from just one specific
place. This ability to recognize, understand, and harmonize
within the mind is from God. All multiplicity is unified in the
divine understanding. As he sees it, Alberti uses his window or
perspective plane not to alter the objective reality of the scene
before his eye but to explain and represent that scene as it presents itself to the stationary eye. In a similar way Cusa uses a
mirror to illustrate how it is that many viewpoints, many eye-

views, can actually be composed within one unified picture in the mind. That picture is not passive, like shapes on a glass; it is active, like forms seen by the artist's eye are understood both objectively, and also from the point of view of his eye. Only then are they recreated on the picture plane.

> He that considers in himself the power of a looking glass, how it (the whole power of the glass) is before all *quantitio*, if he conceive it alive by an intellectual life, in which the sampler of all things (God) shineth, may make a tolerable conjecture of the mind.[19]

Without experience the mind is empty of images and therefore of notions. It is like the eye in the dark, the eye that can see but is not yet seeing. *This intellectual potency is, in fact, a more economical and elegant possession than a range of innate ideas.*[20] Thus, men have a capacity to conceive from the truth of God when the mind is first stimulated by perceptions, stirred up to imagination, and drawn into reason. The mind is made so that its seeing is indeed an image of God's knowing. This is how painting is truly God's grandchild. And this is how the admiration of God's work in nature is consequent to the pleasures received from being able to recognize well-contrived forms.

Nicholas of Cusa re-evoked the maker of the *Timaeus* and following Pythagoras, Boethius and Vitruvius he saw his God as an artist and an inventor.[21]

> When we measure the size and analyse the elements and study the behaviour of things, we make use of the sciences of arithmetic and geometry and even of music and astronomy. Now these same sciences God employed when he made the world. With arithmetic he adjusted it into unity, with geometry he gave it a balanced design upon which depends its stability and its power of controlled movement; with music he allotted its parts that there should be no more earth in the earth than water in the water, than air in the air or than fire in the fire, so that no element could be wholly transmuted into another; whence it comes that the physical system cannot sink into chaos.[22]

and:

> God has set up the elements in an admirable order, for he created all things in number, weight and measure. Number appertains to arithmetic, weight to music and measure to geometry. Heaviness is kept in place by the action of lightness . . . . In setting up these things eternal wisdom employed an indescribably accurate proportioning.[23]

Then, on the purely practical level, men who had some task involving proportioning should refer to these divine and guiding sciences. This is what Leon Battista Alberti recommended in a chapter on proportions in *De re aedificatoria:*

> . . .There are very useful considerations in practice to be drawn from the musicians, geometers, and even the arithmeticians. . . .[24]

On the human level proportioning occurs in a series of human acts. An individual can achieve advances in balance and harmony in his lifetime; for example, harmony in personal life, in civic life, in various works, in the perfection of his understanding. But within the divine creation the harmony of the universe arises out of a limitation of the mysterious unity of God. No perfection of human proportioning can match His indescribably accurate proportioning and His complete intermingling of the four elements. Cusanus suggests that men might underestimate God if they did not realize that the elements necessarily had to exist mixed and intermingled with each other. This contradicts the Aristotelian view of the hierarchy of the elements. There cannot be a truly pure element, only a relatively lighter mixture of the elements. The accepted scheme of the elements which tends to separate them and move them towards their proper and increasingly higher places in the cosmos is wrong. We do not have a low earth with a ring of water encircling it; air is not above and pure fire uppermost; for: 'Fire. . .is immersed in things and without them cannot exist.' Nor can earthly things exist without it. 'But God alone exists absolutely.'[25] Here we have it again, the vision of the comparative nature of all physical reality in the wake of a conviction of the pristine perfection of God. Cusa illustrates his mingling of the elements with an old and highly evocative analogy. It is the same as the one used by Leonardo in his comparison between the earth and man.

> And he (God) related one element with another in such intimacy that one must necessarily dwell in another. The earth, as Plato says, is like some vast animal whose bones are stones, whose veins are rivers, and whose hairs are the trees; and the animals that feed among those hairs of the earth are as the vermin to be found in the hair of beasts.[26]

Here we see that the animal image can be as effective for expressing a new scientific idea, the intermingling of the elements, as are its kindred mathematical and mechanical images.

Learned ignorance, a style of contemplation

The originality of Leonardo da Vinci is in no way diminished

by the suggestion of a connection between Cusan realities and
Leonardo's assumptions about nature and mind. Rather it will
serve to illuminate things that Leonardo did not elect to explain fully. Leonardo made masterful philosophical remarks in
his notes; but he was also rather mysterious, neglecting to connect his insights on speculative matters. Clearly he did not feel
this to be his task and this might be because a connected statement had already been made by another. Leonardo seems to
have been acting out his wisdom rather than publicizing it.
There is a philosophical direction in his writings, and, with
some differences of emphasis and interest this looks very like
the wisdom of Cusa's learned ignorance.

Many of the pre-occupations of Cusanus, it is true, should be
distinguished from those of Alberti and Leonardo. Even in scientific matters, Cusa's first concern was to distinguish and contrast an attainable area of knowledge in physical reality with the
ineffable God who was not knowable. Although both Alberti
and Leonardo would have confirmed the inscrutability of God,
their intellectual commitments were not primarily expressed in
a contrasting of God with all the rest that is from God. They
wanted to know how nature worked and to use their knowledge for the perfecting of human understanding and human
works. This part of the desire was certainly not alien to
Cusanus; but his commitment to this was only one part of an
even grander desire. Cusanus wanted to describe and clarify
the extent and the means by which men could know the
world. Beyond this, he wanted to distinguish this sort of
knowing from the way that men could apprehend God. Within
Cusa's philosophical task, knowledge itself was inevitably
associated with knowability. Hence, characteristics of the knowable world and of the rational means or methods of knowing
form a great portion of the content of Cusa's thinking. At the
same time, the mysterious and true reality of God provides
the philosophical buttress of all Cusanus' meanings.

The following is one of Cusa's procedures for explanation.
He explains a generally accepted point and then contrasts his
explanation with a quality that cannot be known in all of its
attributes; for example, the quality of perfection. This must be
seen as a divine quality. Now ask how knowledge can be ignorance?

> In every enquiry men judge of the uncertain by comparing it
> with an object pre-supposed certain, and their judgement is
> always approximative, every enquiry is therefore comparative
> and uses the method of analogy.[27]

This is clear as far as it goes. But then Cusa brings this acceptable point up against a metaphysical truism. Men do not understand but they do apprehend that God is infinity. No known thing can be compared with infinity. In fact, infinity is beyond all comparisons. At this very point we are meant to recognize that what he says of infinity, of its unknowableness, must be true. For we have just accepted the point that judgement takes place by making comparisons. When we realize the difference between how we do judge or know and how we do not know, in so far as our means of knowing cannot pass a qualitative barrier to our understanding, then we have practised learned ignorance. This is a true practice not a fixed realization. It must continue throughout life.

Rest, unity, infinity, and other pristine qualities are beyond reason, for reason teaches men that contradictory things connot be true at the same time. If reason is applied to God it can only confirm some attributes and deny others, good and evil for example. But God is good, and evil is good in God just as the curve is a line in infinity. There are no contradictions in God, and God can be described as the coincidence of opposites.

All of this must seem far from either Alberti or Leonardo; but the impression is misleading. Both Alberti and Leonardo believed that qualities like goodness, or harmony, or truth were universal in nature and were from the divine creator. Shortly below I will discuss Leonardo's conception of an infinity that is totally above any quantifiable comparison or expression. His image is very like that of Cusanus. As for the absolute qualities, Erwin Panofsky has rightly pointed out that Leon Battista Alberti did not think of them as innate archetypes or Platonic ideas. What Alberti did conceive of seems to be much more like Cusa's *knowing power* in the mind. If there are universal qualities the problem is how to recognize them? The mind must be equipped to do so and Alberti said that it was so equipped, somewhat mysteriously, and beyond the area of personal judgement. The sampler for all things is God and from God's absolute nature qualities descend that are serially expressed in the parts of nature. These qualities are united only as they are simple and one in God. Thus, neither Alberti nor Cusanus make any mention of an intermediate world soul. Alberti took us straight from the eye to the mind and I think he also looked straight from nature to God. Cusanus denied the existence of a world of archetypes outside God. Remember also that Alberti saw a sense of honour and of goodness and of truth existing in the mind and acting like a kind of conscience. If this inward sensitivity is compared with anything else, it is more like Cusa's knowing power than it is like the innate ideas or like purely empirical judgements. The value of such purely worldly

judgements would lie only in the judge and in his peers, so that
a better idea could not be said to be approaching the best, but
only to be better in terms of values posed by the culture that
gave rise to the idea. But Alberti says he is not doing this.
Beyond taste, he refers to a certain faculty of knowing.

In the light of this it seems plausible to assume that Alberti
was attached to the Cusan variety of Christian Neo-Platonism.
This version eliminated the archetypes intermediate between
God and nature. It also replaced innate ideas with a given
capacity to see, and it placed the world soul in God as a simple
whole, and also in nature, only within the individual forms of
the separate parts. Then it is clear, Cusa's Neo-Platonism is
very different from that of the later Florentine Academy.

> The Platonists, then, were wrong in regarding Universal Neces-
> sity as a Mind inferior to the Creator; it is the Word, the Son
> equal to the Father in the Deity, to whom is given the name of
> Logos or Reason because He is the reason why all things exist.
> So the Platonists' theory about the images of forms has to be
> completely discounted, for there is but one infinite form of
> forms and of it all forms are images.[28]

The word soul is real but it is not viewed in the way that
Platonists habitually see it. Here is the way that Pico della
Mirandola described it:

> Antiquity imagined three worlds. Highest of all is that
> ultramundane one which the theologians call angelic and
> philosophers the intelligible.... Next to this comes the celestial
> world, and last of all this sublunary one which we inhabit.
> ...The third (world) is moved by the second, the second is gov-
> earned by the first. . . .[29]

Here the intelligible forms are actual and above the world and
they determine the motions of the cosmos, and these, in turn,
the motions and activities on earth.

Cusa sees differently. He rejects any agency between God
and the Universe. In the angelic mind the divine limitation is
not the same as in the human mind; in the sun the divine limitation is not the same as it is in the earth. Yet these beings and
bodies are all in Him as He is, and He is in them as they are.
None of these forms is the actualization of the other forms.
The analogy between the whole and the parts of nature
descends only from the Word of God. Cusa writes:

> The soul of the World has, in fact, to be regarded as a universal
> form which contains within itself all the forms; yet it has only a

contracted (more or less limited) actual existence in things and in each thing it is the contracted form of the thing as we said previously of the universe (whole in God and at the essence of the form of each part of nature). Therefore the efficient and formal and final cause of all is God, who in one Word creates all things however different they be; and every creature owes its existence to this creative act of God and for that reason is finite Thus between the absolute and the finite there is no mean, as was imagined by those who regarded the Soul of the World as the Mind whose existence was posterior to God's but prior to the existence of the finite world.[30]

This appears to be the model Alberti has in mind when he assumes that absolute principles are expressed directly in nature and are recognized by an intellectual faculty in the mind. His indifference to Florentine Neo-Platonism, most probably on the basis of its hierarchical concepts, should be clear.

Evidently, when Nicholas of Cusa writes about The Word he does not mean simply the birth of Jesus Christ in historical time. Beyond this birth, Cusanus is speaking about the eternal existence of Christ in God. The three persons that co-exist as one in God can only be seen to exist conjointly in the universe. This is why men view the creation as the beginning of the universe, and the historical birth of Christ, as both God and man, as the beginning of the possibility of personal salvation. However, there is bound to be temporal confusion between finite and infinite reality. The ultimate reality of The Creation is not that of an action in time; for, The Creation is in God as the Word, and the Word does not commence in time. Creation is a divine act. God possesses unity and contractability. Contractability is a divine capacity to limit unity or His absolute simplicity in the creation of the physical universe, and also in all parts of the universe as the form or the essence of each part. God is beyond time, and the universe, as it is in God, is in eternity. Naturally, this is confusing; however, God must be seen to be both immanent in nature and transcendent or above nature. From the point of view of one in nature, we might say He is immanent and transcendent at the same time. Realizing, however, that He is absolutely beyond nature, we can only say all things are eternally in Him and He is ever present. Cusanus had a rather high-powered way of putting all of this. He thought that everything in the universe was in the divine *complicatio*. Every varied thing was eternally unified in God. Also, the universe and everything in it was from the divine *explicatio*. Everything descended from a divine limiting principle and thus the Word, or Christ, makes the reality of creation an event in time.

An uncluttered image of nature is couched within these metaphysical concepts. God is the eternal present, and the whole of nature is in God. From the Word or the Son descends the limiting principle. And He contracts Himself in all the parts of nature, not his whole essence in each part, that would be impossible; rather Himself in the part as the origin and end of the form of the part. Thus, absolute equality is in God, and through the grace of His contractability, harmony is in the whole and in the parts of nature.

Nicholas of Cusa saw God as accessible to men through nature and the scriptures and the Catholic church. While the church is the best interpreter of scripture, and the best representative of the kingdom of heaven here on earth, the mind is the interpreter of nature. Reason makes comparisons and contrasts and draws analogies from experience; gathers and holds the idea of a genus or of a species. Beyond this, everything is unified in God. Analogies in nature can only be apprehended with the human eye and mind. For example, there is no archetype man, save with Christ, but the mind certainly makes the species man. In man, the analogy between the parts is not one of likeness from part to part, it is rather one of belonging to a whole, to man; and the whole essence exists in God. Therefore the foot is not like the eye; yet, as both parts are immediately in man, they are analogous. The same is true of the analogy between parts of the universe.

Reason works by comparison and contrast. Therefore no sum of knowledge can add up to a knowledge of the unity of God. The knowledge of reason is also limited when it comes to understanding the beginning, essence and end of each thing. What men are left to know is the divine contraction as it is expressed in the parts of the universe. This is a real and valid knowledge. However, it also only takes place in serial form. But for Cusa, the serial and summary is not the only road to wisdom, even though it is a road that *must* be walked by all who wish to attain wisdom. Beyond the partial knowledge of reason, men can understand being and reality by the practice of learned ignorance.

For example, if men first really see that in the world things are known only by number, weight, and measure, and then they ask by what number, ounce, or inch, can they describe unity, then they place themselves up against a limit in the continuity of their knowing. They have shifted from knowing by quantitative means to a question about a non-quantifiable quality.

It is the same if they bring all extension up against the limit of an originating point. That point is not derived from extension, but originates extension, is not a quantity but a quality.

This way of questioning causes a mixed psychological and intellectual confrontation between what men see they can know and rationally explore in the mind, and what they can conceive of, but cannot explore or really know. The continuous practice of such confrontations induces the state of mind that Cusa called learned ignorance.

Cusanus saw it as the grace of God that human minds could conceive of things that they could not really know. They could, for instance, form metaphorical conceptions of the coincidence of opposites. In order to see that the circle must be the same as the straight line in God, one must increase the size of a circle in the mind. As the circle grows larger the curvature of the circumference decreases. The largest conceivable circle has a circumference of the smallest curvature. Now comes the leap from quantitative notions to a qualitative state. Beyond the largest possible circle, conceive of an infinite circle. Since the circumference of the largest possible circle already had the smallest curvature, the infinite circle must have no curvature. Thus, the infinite circle is the same as the straight line; or we see that the circle and the line must be the same in God. Cusanus devised many such illustrative metaphors and all of them play upon the fact that quantitative notions do not work in absolute infinity. This is why Cusa said that reason provided foods that sharpened the appetite the more that it was filled. The more that men tried to know, the more they wanted to know even more still, and the more they also practised their learned ignorance. The most ardent investigator of nature might be cultivating his learned ignorance; for the more men know, the more they crave the first principle from which all else descends. *Therefore learned ignorance is a practice and style of mystical contemplation that depends upon a prior commitment to rational knowledge and to the investigation of nature and experience.*

> ...We must attribute the perfections of the infinite figures to the simple Infinite, which cannot possibly be expressed by any figure. Then, whilst we are groping in the dark, our ignorance will enlighten us in an incomprehensible fashion and enable us to form a more correct and truer notion of the Absolute.[31]

This reminds me of the practice that Leon Battista Alberti used in order to recognize the beauties of the human form. Beauty was in the mind of the artists as they perfected it from the example bodies. They had no innate idea of it, but they were also not giving their personal opinion of beauty. They were attempting to *see* beauty. The secret discourse in their minds was a power

of knowing. So in Alberti the analogy between the whole and
the parts of nature is visualized as Cusanus visualized it.[32] A
column or a porch is not analogous to the whole building *qua*
column or porch; but as these parts are intimate with each
other within the architect's concept of the whole building, they
are analogous. Beauty is in them as it descends from the artist's
mind, wherein it was perfected from nature. The actuality of
beauty is in God.

Perhaps then some of the early fifteenth-century artistic circles cultivated a *Platonism that was more Cusan than Platonic*. It is
possible that this point of view was primarily brought out
within discussions in these circles, and that its enthusiastic
advocate and teacher was Cusa's close friend Paolo Toscanelli.
Thus, at first, the influence of Cusanus was not directly explored by philosophers; but rather, it was appreciated in
philosophical discussions within the artistic community.

The direct and wider historical impact of Cusa on philosophy
comes much later when he was taken up by Giordano Bruno. It
is also conceivable that Cusan thought experiments and
mathematical concepts may have reached Galileo, perhaps
through the medium of Luca Pacioli's *De Divina proportione*, a
work Vincenzo Galilei may have known. But, except for Bruno,
this is all guesswork.

Negative theology and nothing

Because historians have largely come to identify Renaissance
Platonism with the preoccupations of Ficino's Academy, it
seems easier to place Cusa in the context of medieval thought
than in the Renaissance. This, I think, misleading placement
can also come about through noticing his unconventional
humanism. For, although he did some important work along
the same lines as some humanists he was not primarily
occupied with the revival of classical literature as such, except
for mathematics. Furthermore, although he shares common
sources with later Renaissance Neo-Platonists he makes a rather
different blend from them. Foremost among these sources are
Plato's *Timaeus* and writings of Aristotle, Cicero, Vitruvius,
Ptolemy, Plotinus, Dionysius the Areopagite, Proclus, Boethius
and St. Augustine. In addition to these common sources Cusa
was influenced by the personal mysticism of The Brothers of
the Common Life and by the sermons of Meister Eckhart. It
was from these sources, not common with the later Florentine
Platonists, that Cusa was attracted to the presumed relation
between contemplation and understanding, and to the prob-

lems of negative theology, knowing what God was not. These certainly are medieval themes but to imagine that they were also being developed in a medieval mind is misleading. We might just as well say that Dürer was a purely Gothic artist.

Compared with Cusa, almost all other styles of mystical contemplation move quickly inward to a psychic and spiritual territory. One draws in or withdraws in order to ascend and see. But Cusanus used his unusual immanent and transcendent deity to make the concept of knowledge non-directional. Men might descend to God at the essence of things or rise up to him; they could reach out to God and move in to him. For, God is both the essence and end of all things; in the cosmos He is centre and circumference, all in all and all all at once. In this case the knowing process is not just a simple ascent from particulars to conclusions, nor is it an ascent moving away from the particulars of experience to an inner psychic territory of spiritual insight. Instead it runs a curious zig-zag course between the senses and the various capacities of the mind, from particulars to conclusions, from conclusions to desire, from desire to perfected notions, from the multiplicity of these notions to a further desire for simplicity. Knowing men would know more and, seeing the limit men desire the source and origin.

It is not surprising that he was accused, though wrongly, of being a pantheist. Still his was a unique process blending understanding with spiritual apprehension. A process that was both empirical and rational and with a further shift to the spiritual before the conclusion of any major question. It could do the work of validating the chores of artists, engineers and natural philosophers. So whatever medieval legacy Cusanus assimilated, his view of knowledge was an original view that answered many of the pressing cultural urgencies of the Renaissance.

> Up, therefore, says our learned ignorance and find Thyself in Him. Then, since all things in Him are Himself, nothing can be wanting to thee. To approach the inaccessible light is not in our power.[33]

Dionysius the Areopagite (a supposed follower of St. Paul, dates range roughly between A.D. 300 and 500) believed that men could only know certainly what God was not. In this vein, He was not essenceless, lifeless, reason or unreason, not body or figure or form. None of these qualities could exist without God and yet God *is not them*. All bodies and figures and forms are from Him, He is in them, not in them as they are, but in them as He is. For, as Eckhart wrote:

> God acts at large above being, animating himself. He acts in
> uncreated essence. *Before there was being, God was; and he is where
> there is no being.*[34]

No being, still all being is from him. Shortly below I will compare this idea of *no being* with the concept of *nothing* as we
have encountered it in Leonardo's notes. Clearly this no being
is in firm association with actual being, and yet it is beyond
being:

> God is something that must transcend being. Anything which
> has being, date, or location does not belong to God, for he is
> above them all and although he is in all creatures, yet he is more
> than all of them.[35]

The one who is no being is in all individual things and still is
more than any of them, more than all of them. Could these
attributes, or indeed non-attributes, indicate the lines along
which Leonardo was thinking when he wrote that amid the vast-
ness of all existing things, the existence of nothingness had
first place?[36] Could Leonardo's nothing, that somehow curi-
ously exists, be a symbol or hint of the non-region of no being,
of the unknown and the unknowable? Eckhart thinks further
about the unknown:

> As one saint says: 'If anyone imagines that he knows God and
> his knowledge takes form, then he may know *something* but it is
> not God.' Thus when I say that God is not being and that he is
> above being, I have not denied him being but, rather, I have
> dignified and exalted being in him. If I find copper (or being) in
> Gold (or non-being), it (the copper) is in a *medium* more precious
> than itself.[37]

This medium of gold, here the symbol for precious non-being,
reminds me of the strange medium of nothing that Leonardo
placed at the limit of time and also between all objects and their
surrounding spaces. Rather than gold a better metaphor for
non-being would be the zero or nought of arithmetic. True, the
zero is not precious, but it does have the curious quality of representing no known number while still being at the beginning
and at the end of number. It is the conceptual source and
origin or number, and thus, it is intrinsic to all that follows. It
can be seen as a medium in terms of its place. Leonardo da
Vinci sees the notion nothing as the glint of an instant; it is
the same as St. Augustine's and Meister Eckhart's present without duration. Leonardo also placed it, or recognized it, in its
non-attributes, right at the edge of surfaces. Not of surfaces,
but rather, the surfaces and the spaces between them within

nothing. Nothing is either in nor of space, neither in nor of extension but Leonardo visualized all of these things in a medium of nothing.

This view is really wholly Cusan:

> God's being, which is unity, is not abstracted by the mind from things, nor is it united to or immersed in things; it is, therefore, beyond anyone to understand how the plurality of things is a development of the unity which is God. If we consider things without Him, they are as number without unity: nothing; if we consider Him without things, He exists and the things do not; if we consider Him as He is in things, we are regarding things as something else in which He exists - an error. . . we saw that the being of a thing is from the Being, God, and cannot, therefore, be 'other' in the sense of being totally different; if we consider a thing such as it is in God, then it is God and Unity.
>
> *All that remains for us to assert is that the plurality of things is due to the fact that God is in nothing.* Take away God from the creature and you are left with nothing; take away the substance from a composite being, the accidents also disappear and nothing remains.[38]

Leonardo's treatment of actual physical space and time is quantitative. As quoted, he even thinks about *a space of time.*[39] His space of time is analogous to the line and is infinitely divisible. However, then Leonardo contrasted this quantitative measurement of time with the mysterious reality of time. This is the instant that has no duration and that is indivisible, just as the point is. This instant looks very like the now-moment in Meister Eckhart's theology. And Cusanus was the thinker who drew the parallel between the now of Eckhart and the point. Perhaps then a largely theological notion became absorbed in a metaphysical view of nature for some of those early theoreticians of perspective that were also exposed to Cusan thinking. Toscanelli should not be underestimated as the advocate and publicist of this. Cusan philosophy made appealing sense of the notional terms of the perspective painter's work. The analogy between art and nature may have its substance in the fact that both were seen to begin and to develop from one formless point. Just as the essence of all surfaces was the point that was nothing, so the essence of the stone or of the vegetable was in an eternal quality that was also just nothing. The artist uses empirical methods, yet he creates after God. He does not approach God as God is no-form but he approaches the reality of nature, God's works. This view may represent the non-doctrinal kind of reverence that can be seen in both Alberti and Leonardo.

It is not surprising that Leonardo raised temporal questions in the terms of spacial concepts. He was inclined to compare space, time, and motion and to see how far the analogy with material extension could be pushed. Time is one dimensional, space and bodies three. He did not add time to them to make a fourth. But he saw that the instant equalled nothing and that it could be called zero. The point that originated extension was the same. If non-being or beyond being were substituted for nothing here, we would be saying that Leonardo saw every existing thing in a reality that was not ultimately material but spiritual, *'ma si puo nominare presto cosa spirituale.'*[40] Space and time exist in a spiritual medium that is not quantifiable. It makes real sense if we are willing to view Leonardo's nothing as a notional descendant of Eckhart's not-knowable one, and of Cusanus' one from whom all else descends, the absolute maximum and minimum.[41] Negative theology has married itself to the mathematician's point so that knowing what God is not can illuminate what human knowledge is and also what its limits are.

Leonardo's placement of nothing at the limits of both space and time only makes complete sense within the terms of learned ignorance. The mind cannot originate the point. The point is actual. Conceptually this point representing nothing is not to be confused with the absence of anything or with a vacant space, it is non-space, it is what is not known. Leonardo writes:

> Nothing exists apart from occupation of space; it follows that nothingness and a vacuum are not the same, for the one is divisible to infinity, and nothingness cannot be divided.[42]

St. Augustine began the confusion about time by emphasizing that the past does not really exist. It can only have existed when it was the present. But the present has no duration, it is nothing; and clearly, the present that has past must also have been nothing. Also, the future cannot be said to exist yet.[43] Men can anticipate the future; however, their anticipation can only come about in the present, and, once more, the actual present has no duration.

We seem to be getting tied up in some kind of knot; for if according to these lights, past, present, and future do not really exist, then everything that takes place in time is taking place in nothing.

At the same time, being is real. All the Platonists accepted this as so. Existence is not an illusion, but because it apparently takes place in time, in a context that has no attributes except in the mental experience of its passage, true being must really exist in eternity.

The nothing that is a metaphor of the limit of time indicates the everything that makes existence possible. This is God who is non-being and who is in and beyond being as a mystery. Like the finger of Leonardo's ecstatic St. John who points upward in space to no definable thing, the limit that Leonardo saw at the edge of time indicates the existence of the unknowable divine reality. It is the origin of the point, and the non-being that Eckhart saw, and even more precisely, it indicates the coincidence of opposites presented in the vision of Nicholas of Cusa. As Cusa says:

> All time is comprised in the present or *Now*. The past was present, the future shall be present, so that time is only a methodical arrangement of the present . . . The present in which all times are included is one, it is unity itself. So too is diversity contained in identity.[44]

The application of theological concepts to nature comes to Cusa in the form of explanatory metaphors that are frequently mathematical. Motion is in rest in the way that a line can be said to be in the point. Like the present *Now* Cusa saw movement as rest, but rest drawn out in an orderly series.[45] In drawings comprising Leonardo da Vinci's study of the movement of the body it seems that he actually drew rest. This was rest represented in an orderly series. Time - the present drawn out; movement - rest drawn out; quantity - unity drawn out; in the light of this sort of imaginative visualization we ought to think about Leonardo's praise of the painter as the philosopher who could freeze time and who could arrest motion. This vision of actuality prior to potentiality, this mode of seeing stability in change is the truly divine seeing power of the painter. Leonardo saw nothing as foremost in nature because time in essence was the present; and because form in essence was the point. Here is his source of inspiration:

> There is one point, not more; and that one point is infinite unity itself, for infinite unity, whilst it contains within itself the line and the quantity, is the point which is their term, perfection and entirety; and its first development is in the line, in which there is nothing to be found but the point.[46]

Thus the confirmation of the reality of nature is from God. The Cusan type of Christian Platonist sees everything in God and God limited within the parts, in all of the parts and in the whole. Thinking of Leonardo in this light can explain both his modernity and his strange remoteness. He is modern in so far as he relies on experience as his teacher and he is remote because without spirits or magic, everything within his experience actually belongs to another world.

The taste of wisdom

The descriptive phrase, a taste of wisdom, is really a metaphor taken from the experience of the senses and applied to the understanding. The Cusan taste of wisdom refers to an apprehension that men never really taste. Instead, they only mysteriously grasp the notion that beyond whatever ideas of truth or goodness they can attain, there is still an infinitely truer truth that is *the truth*, and a better goodness that is *the good*. They grasp this in the same way that they grasp the point, even though there is no physical point. What the intellect really gives is an 'untastable foretaste' of wisdom.

This is a sensibility that is not really of the senses, a kind of intellectual sensitivity.

The knowing power of the mind is such a sensitivity and this desire, or taste, is a kind of will of the mind. This will is excited by the way that the mind receives and interprets the experience that really does originate with the senses. In this vein Cusa continues:

> For as the odour multiplied from the thing that is odorable. . . allures us to the race, to run to the ointment in the smell of the ointments (to God); so the eternal and infinite wisdom shining in all things, invites us, by a certain foretaste of its effects, to be carried to it by a wonderful desire . . .[47]

Men long for the point of origin. The desire to understand the first principle is like a longing that is aroused by a sweet taste. The more that knowledge is tasted, the more the desire increases. Knowledge is in wisdom, and when men pursue knowledge, they pursue Him.

We can summarize by recalling that theology had fixed upon images of space and time in order to contrast worldly experience with God. Here it is in Boethius:

> . . .The changing course of Fate is to the simple stability of Providence as reasoning is to intellect, as that which is generated is to that which is, as time is to eternity, as a circle to its centre.[48]

These are now familiar contrasts of diversity with identity, evoked here to show the true goodness of Providence despite the shifts (motions) of Fate. Cusanus would also make such an application of these contrasts; but look what he also does with his learned ignorance:

> The ancient philosophers . . . lacked learned ignorance. It is now evident that this earth really moves though to us it seems stationary. In fact, it is only by reference to something fixed that we detect the movement of anything. How would a person know that a ship was in movement if, from the ship in the middle of the river, the banks were invisible to him and he was ignorant of the fact that water flows? Therein we have the reason why every man, whether he be on the earth, in the sun or on another planet, always has the impression that all other things are in movement whilst he himself is in a sort of immovable centre; *he will certainly always choose poles which will vary accordingly as his place of existence is the Sun, the earth, the moon, Mars, etc.* In consequence, there will be a machina mundi whose centre, so to speak, is everywhere, whose circumference is nowhere, for God is its circumference, and centre and He is everywhere and nowhere.[49]

Cusa reads his idea of God as non-being without form, or nothing, into philosophical conclusions about nature and the cosmos. From an essentially early Christian consideration of the impossibility of knowing God, Cusanus moves to a Renaissance position in the question of knowledge. By this he confirmed the unlimited knowability of the parts of the world as these parts could be compared and contrasted with each other. He confirmed the orderliness of the universe, and its homogeneity, while at the same time he saw that its order was not the order of perfection.

Nicholas of Cusa said that he conceived of learned ignorance and had a vision of the coincidence of opposites on a journey from Constantinople. Perhaps we can imagine him on a misty day, somewhere on the Danube between Constantinople and Vienna. From his boat he cannot see the shore. His mind is filled with his theological and philosophical speculations about the question of knowing, and suddenly he realizes that he cannot perceive that the boat is moving. If he didn't already know that water flows, he would think that the boat was absolutely still.

Cusanus radically modified the tenets of classical Neo-Platonism by doing away with the archetypes. Here is a more orthodox view expressed by Boethius:

> Therefore, whether Fate is carried out by *divine spirits* in the service of Providence, or by a *soul,* or by the whole activity of

nature, by the heavenly motions of the stars, by angelic virtue or diabolical cleverness, or by some or all of these *agents*, one thing is certain: Providence is the immovable and simple form of all things which come into being, while Fate is the moving connection and temporal order of all things which the divine simplicity has decided to bring into being.[50]

For Cusanus Fate expressed itself directly in the parts of nature. No intermediate agency conveyed the will of Providence to Fate.

Without archetypes above nature and the universe there is no reason to posit innate ideas in the mind. Innate ideas of what? Cusanus did away with the innate ideas and substituted a power of knowing. In the book about the mind, the third book of the *Idiot,* Cusa presents a dialogue wherein an Idiot explains the knowing power to a philosopher.

> Philosopher -
> ...We plainly find a spirit in our mind speaking and judging this good, that just, the other true, and reprehending us, if we decline from the just; which speech and judgement it (the mind) learned not and therefore it is connate or concreate.

The admonition by the spirit of the mind, as has been noted, is a characteristic of Leon Battista Alberti's version of the judging power. The Idiot continues:

> Idiot -
> By this we prove that the mind is that power which though it wants all notional form (it lacks ideas), yet being stirred up (by examples in nature), can assimilate itself to every form, and makes notions of all things: Like, after a manner to a sound eye which is in darkness and never saw the light, for it wants all notion of visible things; yet coming into the light, and being stirred up, it assimilates itself to the thing visible, that it may make a notion.[51]

Evidently, the mind no more possesses the ideas than an eye in the dark possesses the images of the things couched within the dark. But turn the light on, stir the power, and the eye sees the images. The mind has a grander seeing power than that of the eye. The mind can approach the essence of the image.

This is very like the idea that Leon Battista Alberti had when he saw honour telling-off the person for failing to perfect his own honour.[52] Cusanus also put forward a positive role for the human body in the light of man's quest for knowledge. His view contradicts traditional Christian Platonism; as St. Augustine put it, *'For, ever the soul is weighted down by a mortal body.'*[53]

The body can hardly be seen to serve the mind if it is only viewed as the material element that clouds mental processes. By contrast, Cusa praises the body and feels that it is vital to thought. Certainly, if physical desires alone are given free rein they can foster their own illusions. However, the body and mind together form the whole instrument of knowing for the soul. In fact, while in the body, the soul and the mind are the same, just as in the eye the sensitive part and the seeing part are just one power.[54] In and above this, the immortal soul can also exist outside of the body. The following is Cusanus on the subject of body and soul, and of the ideas and the knowing power:

> Philosopher -
> Aristotle said, there was no notion concrete (made with) with the mind or soul, because he likened it to a smooth and shaven table: but Plato saith, there were notions concreated with it, yet that for the . . . weights of the body, the soul forgot them; what do'st thou think to be true?
> Idiot -
> Undoubtedly our mind was, by God, put into this body to the profit and advantage thereof; and therefore it must needs have from God, all that, without which it could not acquire that profit and advantage, it is not therefore creditable, that there were notions concreated with the soul, which it lost in the body; but because it hath need of a body that the concreated power may proceed to act. As the seeing power of the soul cannot see actually, except it be stirred up by the object; and that cannot be, but by the representing of multiplied species by means of the organ, and so it hath need of the eye. Even so the power of the mind, which is the comprehensive . . . power, cannot proceed to its operations, except it be stirred up by sensible things, which it cannot be but by the mediation of sensible phantasms. Therefore it hath need of an organical body . . . in this, therefore, Aristotle seems to have thought aright, that there are no notions of the soul concreated from the beginning, which it lost by being incorporated. But because it cannot profit, it it want all judgement, as a deaf man can never profit to become a lutenist, because he hath in himself no judgement of harmony, by which he may discerne whether he do profit, *therefore our soul hath a concreated judgement without which it could not profit. This judging power is naturally concreated with the mind, by which, of itself it judgeth whether discourses be weak, strong, or concluding.* Which *power* if Plato called a concreated notion, he was not out of the way at all.[55]

By means of the instrument of the body the mind perceives, yet, the mind knows because it has an additional purely mental capacity. It judges and perfects the images. During this period of time comparable theories of vision taught that the eye

saw, first, because it was sensitive to light, and then because it
contained a specific seeing power. This power was thought of
as projecting on to or drawing from, objects in light. Sometimes it was seen in the form of rays going from the eye, sometimes, as a concentrated potency within the eye. Cusanus formulates his knowing power by analogy with this supposed concentrated potency of the eye. But there is also a substantial difference; for, the eye has the power of sight, but the mind, of
insight.[56] The perfecting of the images is entirely mental but it
could not begin without the body. Without the body, the soul is
without the forms of things.

The seed

In the first chapter I remarked that Alberti referred to the
judging power of the mind as a seed.[57] On the surface it can be
seen to be like a seed as it is innate, implanted in the mind. But
the meaning of the image of a seed can and must go deeper
than this. Alberti could be implying some sort of comparison
between the function of a seed and the actual character of the
knowing power.

In itself, the seed holds the potential for the whole plant that
eventually grows from that seed. In itself, the judging power
holds the potential to evaluate experience and make notions
or ideas. The fruits of this potency are continually perfectible.
As a parallel this does seem to be a bit awkward. But, it is possible to explore its terms for a clearer explanation.

In order to imagine this possibility of another view of the
analogy between a seed and a judging power in the mind it is
necessary to observe how Nicholas of Cusa used the image of
the seed.

In *De visione dei* Cusanus compares the generative power of
the point, meaning the indivisible point, to the generative
power of the seed of a nut tree. We are already aware that this
point is non-being or nothing; yet, the seed of a nut tree must
surely be something. As Cusa took forms and geometrical figures, such as circles, and projected them toward infinity, where
they could not possibly remain circles; then perhaps he also
took a known thing, a seed, and contracted it back to its term
or limit in infinity. This would be the point were it would no
longer be a seed. Now why perform this exercise? A review of
the power of the point suggests a solution; for, it is the point
that is being compared with the generative power of the seed.
The teachings of Cusa's *Idiot* shed light on this:

Philosopher (to the Idiot)
Thou agreest well with Boethius, saying, if thou add a point to a
point, thou doest no more than if you add nothing to nothing.[58]

Line, plane, surface, and the body in its vesture of planes, the
solid, all of these abstractions and things are generated from
the point. And by comparison, all of the ramifications of a
plant are generated from its tiny seed. Metaphorically, the
plant may be seen to be combined and contracted within its
seed and protracted and unfolded in the growing plant. Thus,
the seed-plant is a symbol for the universe that is in the divine
complicatio and *explicatio*, in the point and in physical reality. In
another similar parallel Cusa compares the universe to a rose
tree that is potential in winter and is developed and matured in
summer.[59] We know that God is beyond the seasons, thus the
universe is not potential but actual in him and it develops in
time and physical reality while it is real within the divine present.

All this makes clear how the seed can serve as a metaphor for
the universe. But how can it symbolize the knowing power in
the mind? Is there a conceptual relationship between Cusanus'
seed and the seed in the thoughts of Alberti? It is possible to
make such a relationship visible, but to do this generation has
to be made to work inwardly. For, the notions or ideas of the
mind are the unique fruits of this particular plant.

The eye sees images, reason compares and contrasts them,
and the intellect judges them. This happens both instantly in
the case of a new sense impression, and over time, in so far as
the mind stores images in memory. Men judge, and they can
also ponder and judge further. Over time, the intellect continually makes perfected images and forms ideal and simple
notions. The mathematical sciences are among the highest of
these notions. And, for example, the perceived beauties of
nature can become expressed in a purely mental idea of beauty. The idea of the artist cultivating his seeing is not alien to
this. God made the mind able to recognize, but recognition is a
practice within the all-embracing practice of learned ignorance.

All in all the intellect is the knowing power that has the
innate potency for generating the fruits or notions. This happens naturally. But cultivation of the practices of recognition,
of judgement, and of learned ignorance, all stages of one real
contemplative practice—all this itensifies and ripens the innate
capacities of the intellect. Men all can see beauty but some men
perfect their seeing far more than others. This was Leonardo's
drive, this open-ended possibility for reasoned knowing and
for seeing with insight. Hence, the mental seed relies upon the

body and the world to activate its process of generation. Similarly, a physical seed relies upon light and water. Only the seed as it is in God stirs itself by itself.

> Because the mind . . . in itself, (is) abstracted from matter, (and) makes these assimilations (notions), therefore it assimilates itself to abstract forms. And according to this power it . . . puts forth certain mathematical sciences . . .[60]

In the same way, Alberti's seed in the mind brings forth its fruits or assimilations. As a Pythagorean, Alberti certainly saw the mathematical sciences as foremost among these. These are fruits that are essential and necessary to the painter, sculptor, and architect.

There is no death

Leonardo da Vinci was particularly fascinated with the *Metamorphoses* of Ovid. Two of his own attitudes to life are expressed in these tales. First, there is his attraction to images involving continuance through change. It is a kind of continuity where beings do not pass away but are transmuted. This image reflects Leonardo's appreciation of the dynamics of nature. His second attitude is one of personal identification with an individual caught within the shifting panorama. The next chapter will show how this second attitude was entirely characteristic of Leonardo. He cried out even at the destruction of creatures such as bees. Nature is inevitably magnified by change but change often brings great individual suffering. This eventually became a point of reference for mechanical and moral philosophers of the Enlightenment. But Leonardo found this expressed in Ovid's work.

> Even as a tree, Phoebus loved her. He placed his hand against the trunk, and felt her heart still beating under the new bark.[61]

The changing pattern predominates in nature as a whole. Her variety and strength must be admired. In Cusan terms this is the infinite possibility of the divine *explicatio*. Leonardo was both impressed and overawed by this infinite variety of nature. Like Cusanus, he was inclined to think of death not as death but as change. Even on the physical level dying is only real in relative or entirely personal terms. On the spiritual level the soul is immortal and there is no death. This may be another

reason why Leonardo admired Nicholas of Cusa; because Cusa
did not recognize physical death.

> ...An individual may sometimes fall away into its constituent
> elements so that one or other mode of existence disap-
> pears; ...therefore it were better to regard corruption as differ-
> ent modes of being, and to pronounce with Virgil that there is
> no room for death anywhere. For death would appear to be no
> more than the resolution of a composite into its elements. And
> who shall say that such resolution occurs only upon this earth?'[62]

When knowledge was in wisdom

Nicholas of Cusa lived in an opportune moment in time, and
his seizure of this moment brought thought to one of its pinna-
cles. His mentality, together with his position in human events,
made him able to see and describe experiences that few have
been able to see so clearly or describe so well, and with such
evocative images. He left a legacy that was especially recognized
by a few of his contemporaries. They used it and bequeathed it
to further generations in the forms that their own contributions took and in which they modified and coloured Cusa's
original vision. For, he saw how apparent opposites might also
come together when and if they were placed against the background of the presumed consequences of absolute infinity. The
many could be one, the everything the all, and knowledge
could be in wisdom as long as men did not forget that the one,
and the all, and the wisdom would always also be primarily in
and beyond the many, beyond everything, beyond knowledge.
Now men still grope for that closeness portrayed by means of
Cusanus' gifts. This heritage was certainly developed with greater conviction by Leonardo and his age than it is by us.

What is seeing and what is knowing? What is the character of
the intellectual process and how, if in any way, does this relate
to wisdom, or to a spiritual understanding, or to men's experience
of revelation? In the fifteenth century the faculties of mind-
soul were seen to be both temporal and eternal. Among all the
others Alberti spoke of this, and now some contemporary
psychologists find deep holes in human psyches because the
eternal area has either been rejected or forgotten. Here I am
not concerned with making observations either on grounds of
faith or of science that this eternal area does indeed exist, but
rather, with making a historian's observation about the sympathetic character of times when it was seen to exist. In Cusa's

age it was just possible to follow the roads of reason while also travelling on wider spiritual planes of reality. Leonardo found the trips and transference more difficult. His involvement with individuals sometimes made evil seem more real than it ought to have been. Later minds tended to confine their empirical tripping to the sciences and their spiritual trips to churches, or to specific theologies and philosophies. Splits like these encompass a wide region in historical time. It was only in the late nineteenth century that most thinkers actually forgot to try for the earlier association of knowledge within the grander realm of wisdom. If knowledge pursued by reason and by empirical practices had not been so closely associated with the idea of wisdom in the western Platonic tradition, then there is good historical reason to believe that the potting might have been left to the potters and that the great doctors would have been overwhelmingly attracted to introspective processes of contemplation. Great forces in the whole development of western civilization undoubtedly pressed for the higher status of the increasingly desired practical knowledge, but these pressures had had their original chance for expression within the Platonic conviction confirming the reality of the world, and in the belief in the significance of Christ, and in Renaissance crystallizations placing knowledge in wisdom as a smaller brother, and placing art in reality as a grandchild. If it is assumed that the area of the human mind is both temporal and eternal, and if men know that on the temporal plane experience must be partial and fragmented, how can the exploration of any of these fragments tell men real truths? How can this turning towards time and the experience in time be accomplished without loss of the awareness that piecemeal time, time that is only known by means of a metaphor derived from motion, that this fragment, time, and all physical experience must really belong to a larger and all-encompassing but presently incomprehensible reality? It is no wonder that human beings have always been suspicious, and that they eventually placed meditation and contemplation at the opposite pole from study and science. Each mental process carried a fear of loss in terms of the other. If Cusa's ingenuity had got round this fear, we must now admit that any retention of his view of wholeness is almost impossible to keep in one's own mind all at once, or even to comprehend without looking again at some of his metaphors. Yet at one time practical mathematicians explored his views and were greatly reassured by them.

As men cultivate either one or the other end of the spectrum of understanding, human knowledge involves great loss as well as some gain. Those whose concerns have been entirely spiritual have not tampered with physical conditions much, and their personal enlightenment cannot be fully conveyed to any other person. Men can record and reproduce experiments, but most men will admit that we are at a loss when recording something as individual as spiritual rapture. Cusanus' vision of the coincidence of opposites was just such a spiritual and intellectual vision; intellectual, because it was conceived in wholly mental terms, and vision, because he said he experienced it all of a piece, and that it transcended a purely temporal context. Yet even his record of it is written, and sequential. It is the personal record of an experience, rather than the experience itself. Transcendental minds at most make maps and can act as guides. It seems that wisdom has to be experienced individually and alone, like birth, sleep, and death.

Now we live in a society that has trained many minds to reject or push aside that which cannot be recorded, confirmed, and reproduced. We really do not know if we should believe in such things. When we see the records of the personal spiritual or psychic experiences of others, their details make them seem remote, and we cannot distinguish dream and mere delusion from important information that we have not learned how to interpret or evaluate. But people were not always this way. Sometimes they were far less worried about delusions, and they compounded ragbags of ideas, perhaps containing greater truths than we now know, together with outrageous lies that we now won't let ourselves consciously imagine. Leonardo certainly wanted to sort the truth from the lie, but he would not throw away eternity because it wasn't graspable. Study and science were not a waste of time for him in the light of eternity. Cusa had said that the soul was magnified through the experiences of birth, growth and death in the body, and that the corporeal world had been made to be known. Knowing nature and revering God were related activities.

Presently, the spectrum seems to be especially polarized. Is knowledge of this world a waste of time in the light of eternity? The spiritual extreme seems foolish; for health is required for men to experience anything. At the same time, passionate engrossment with current fads in the world of learning sometimes appears to rob men of their identities, or their souls, and many show behaviour that manifests a sense of deep and irreparable loss. When Cusa said, in the *Idiota,* that in the universe things were the *explicatio* of God but that men were the image of God, he may have been psychologically more sensitive in making his ontological distinction between things and their activities, and men and their mentalities, than many subsequent thinkers have been.[63] Here we must shake off our indoctrination about progress and at least consider that early modern philosophy might have been on the brink of something rather more sophisticated than a great deal of psychological thought that has developed since those times.

Yet how can we question study and science when these methods have produced so many solid benefits in our under-standing, as well as great mastery over physical reality? Certain-ly, even current debates still circulate around these questions. In the civilization that has enabled more men to live in better health but with the inescapable aura of total destruction, that has produced a viable physics and a wider cosmology, but also great insanity, at least as great as in the past, and people who experience a deep sense of spiritual loss and yet find it difficult to discover any acceptable guidance - what can we say of this polarization of knowledge and wisdom *now* in contrast with their interwoven position during the Renaissance? It is impos-sible to know if man could have discovered nature in the way that he did without some loss of appreciation of macro-nature and eventually even of God and of eternity.

As it is now, many parts of the world or human groups that have great claims to spiritual wisdom depend upon foreign teach-ing and aid to improve their public health and material progress. Some good things come their way, many horrible; and the hor-rors that men put upon other men and upon nature have always seemed even more of a betrayal than the given horrors of nature. Still, even these horrors of nature worried Leonar-do, as we shall see below. Knowledgeable men were supposed to have controlled them to a large extent; for this was the lord-ship and power that God had given to men. Is it too soon in historical time, or really too late, in so far as men have made the sword that hangs above all of our heads? If life can be good, if accomplishment can be good, and if wisdom is the best good, how do we avoid either getting lost in time and in narrow knowledge, or getting lost in eternity, leaving other men and temporal experience behind in a great wasteland? Surely, crea-tion cannot really hold such a wasteland, and the conceptual fault in seeing it in this way must be our own. But for Cusa these were not such acute problems; for he could see know-ledge within wisdom in a way that we cannot. And, at least for a time, others followed him in his unique intellectual and trans-cendental conception of knowing.

Notes to Chapter Three

1. Cf. Paul Lawrence Rose, 'Humanist Culture and Renaissance Mathematics: The Italian Libraries of the Quatrocento', *Studies in The Renaissance*, XX, 1973, pp. 52, 59-65, 67, 80-82.
2. My own views do not rest heavily on prophecy. I find it sufficiently interesting that Cusa disregarded Aristotelian physics and conventional concepts of motion and space. Historians can see that some of the intellectual environment of the fifteenth century provided the opening and the possibility for the reform of ideas in this area.
3. Nicholas Cusanus, — *Of Learned Ignorance*, Book I, chap. xi, (New Haven, Yale University Press, 1954), p. 25. The modern tone of expression is present in Cusa's language:

> Quando autem ex imagine inquisitio fit, necesse est nihil dubii apud imaginem esse, in cuius transsumptiva proportione incognitum investigatur, cum via ad incerta non nisi per praesupposita et certa esse possit. Sunt autem omnia sensibilia in quadam continua instabilitate propter possibilitatem materialem in ipsis habundantem. Abstractoria autem istis, ubi de rebus consideratio habetur, - non ut appendiciis materialibus, sine quibus imaginari nequeunt, penitus careant neque penitus possibilitati fluctuanti subsint - firmissima videmus atque nobis certissima, ut sunt ipsa mathematicalia.

De docta ignorantia, ed E. Hoffman and R. Klibansky, Leipzig, 1932. pp. 22-3.

4. Francis Bacon, *The New Organon*, Book II, vii.
5. Cusanus, *Of Learned Ignorance*, (London 1954), Book II, chap. ix, p.101.
6. Meister Eckhart, *Eckhart*, tr. R. B. Blakney, (New York, 1941), sermon 25, 'Get Beyond Time', pp. 212-217.
7. Max Jammer, *Concepts of Space* (Harvard University Press, 1969) pp. 59-61.
8. Eckhart, *Op. cit.* p. 214.
9. Cusa, *Of Learned Ignorance.*, Book II, chap i, pp. 67-68.
10. Cusanus, *Of Learned Ignorance*, Book II, chap. xi, p. 109:

> Historians of astronomy still tend to think that Cusa believed in the spheres and that his vision of the relativity of motion in the universe was an abortive one. However, I think we must puzzle out what Cusa means within Cusan terms. Without any physical centre or circumference, and with no fixed points in the cosmos, we have to think hard about his meaning when he uses the word *spheres*. Cusanus draws great distinctions between appearances and reality. By comparing and contrasting appearances in our mind we arrive at an approximative knowledge of things. We know that only God can be absolutely equal, and thus, no movement can be the equal of another even if they appear to be

the same. Place a man on the pole, and to him it will look as if he's on a fixed centre. In this way the heavens seem sphere-like to an observer. However, if we leave out the part about the equality of things in God, the reality of the whole universe in God, we are still left with a real universe limited within time. This reality is quite apart from any individual's perception of it. Therefore, are the spheres limited in time? Does the word spheres describe the approximative relations between heavenly bodies? There isn't a simple answer to this. But I think if we consider a passage *(Ibid.:* Book 11, chap. xiii, p. 120) where Cusa says that in each star (planet) God adjusts the proportions of the parts to each other to secure the whole, and that the heavy parts (relative to others) move downward to the (approximative) centre and the lighter parts move upward toward the surface, and that they all participate in a constant motion around that (approximative) centre, so that men *perceive* each star to move only through its orbit, if we reflect about this statement we can arrive at some conclusions. First, in the universe movements are conducted so that the whole and its parts, and all lesser wholes and their parts maintain a regular relation to each other. Second, although there are no absolute forms above or within the universe, the limited forms of things apparently do relate to each other in coherent patterns. Those principles or patterns describe the universe as it is in time. What we are left with is that men can understand that the universe is real and that it is a rational order both in the parts and in the whole. The pattern of the whole is coherent but men cannot fully perceive or know the whole. This is because it is unified only in God. Hence, we know that the heavens seem sphere-like, stars going round the earth, and the earth is also heavier than other combinations of elements within other celestial bodies. However, we also know that there is no true sphere without a true centre, that stars cannot be fixed, and that, although the earth seems central, it cannot be a true centre. In all honesty, I do not think that Cusanus takes us much further than this. He tells us what God cannot be less than, and in terms of that, what the universe is not; but he does not formulate a complete new cosmology and originate a scientific description of what the whole universe is. Theoretically, the mind could over-extend specific appearances and create such a description. He saw this task to be worth doing and historians have wrongly blamed him for what amounts to his not being a sixteenth-century person.

11. Cusanus, *Of Learned Ignorance,* Book II, chap. xi, p. 109.
12. E. Garin, *La Cultura Filosofica del Rinascimento Italiano,* 'Paolo Toscanelli', (Florence, 1969), passim.
13. Vol II (Paris, 1955), chap. xi, pp. 97-279.
14. Some of Cusa's works were 1450, *Idiota,* iv, De staticis experimentis.

Transmutationes geometricas
Arithmeticum complementum
1458, *De mathematica perfectione*
1463, *De ludo globi*

15. Cusanus, *Idiota*, Book III, tr. London 1650, Sutro Branch of Calif. State library, reprint series 19, San Francisco, (May 1940) p. 28.
16. Cusanus, *Of learned ignorance*, Book II, xiii, p. 120.
17. *Ibid*. p. 121.
18. Cusanus, *Idiota*, Book III, chap. vi, p. 41.
19. Cusanus, *Idiota*, Book III, chap. v, p. 39.
20. Cusa used another mirror metaphor to explain knowing. The mind was like the indivisible point of a diamond, a living diamond. Without any surface the diamond reflects all perceived forms, all imagined forms, and all the reasoning of the mind about all of these forms. Then in its own indivisible unity the knowing power understands the essence of all created things. It perfects notions of honour, beauty, wisdom, justice, etc. This was truly a matching process between images, and now not innate ideas, but a power to recognise truth from the mind's own unity.
21. Vitruvius was known to Cusa and is cited frequently in the fourth book of the *Idiot*, 'Concerning Static Experiments'.
22. Cusanus, *Of learned ignorance*, Book II, chap. xiii, p. 118.
    Nevertheless, God arranged that there should be part transmutation of the elements. When this takes place successively a new thing is brought into existence. This endures in being as long as the agreement of the elements remains.
23. *Ibid*. p. 119.
24. Book IX, chap. vi, (247).
25. Cusanus, *Of learned ignorance*, Book II, chap. xiii, p.120.
26. *Ibid*. p.119. See also Chapter two, p. 58.
27. Cusanus, *Of learned ignorance*, Book I, chap. 1, p. 7.
28. Cusanus, *Of learned ignorance*, Book II, chap. ix, p. 102.
29. Pico della Mirandola, Heptaplus, 2nd. proem, tr. D. Carmichel, (N.Y. 1965), 75-6.
30. Cusanus, *Of learned ignorance*, Book II, chapt. ix, pp. 102-3.
31. Cusanus, *Of learned ignorance*, Book I, chapt. xi, p. 27.
32. Notional parallels and even possible meetings between Alberti and Cusanus have been considered, cf. J. Gadol, *Alberti*, note 68, pp. 196-7; However I think that the mutual radical innovations of rejecting the archetypes while maintaining nature as the model of the maker's idea, and substituting a knowing power for innate ideas reinforce the case for, at least, conceptual contact and influence.
33. Cusanus, *Of learned ignorance*, Book II, chap. xiii, p. 121.
34. Eckhart, *Meister Eckhart*, tr. R. B. Blakney (New York 1941) sermon 26, 'Like a morning star, God shines', p. 219, my italics.
35. Eckhart, *Meister Eckhart*, p. 218.
36. Cf. above, chapter two, pp. 79-84.

37. Eckhart, *Meister Eckhart,* p. 219.
38. Cusanus, *Of learned ignorance,* (London 1954), Book II, chap. iii, p.78, my italics.
39. Cf. above chapter two, p. 75.
40. Cf. above, chapter two, p. 82.
41. Apparently Leonardo both heard and read some teachings of Cusanus but exactly what works, and when, seems to be a matter for the debate of experts. He is even thought to have read some Cusa in manuscript. There were three printings of Cusa's works during Leonardo's lifetime. The first edition is undated and there is no clue to it from the type, but scholars seem to think it was printed before 1500. The next edition was in 1502 from Corte Maggiore near Milan. It seems to have been commissioned by Roland Marquis Pallavicini and dedicated to Cardinal Georges d'Amboise. Leonardo had contact with the Pallavicini of Lombardy. There was a Paris edition in 1514. Other points of contact for Leonardo were Paolo Toscanelli, both his teachings and the *De transmutationibus geometricis,* and later with F. Luca Pacioli, another distinguished mathematician inspired by Cusan ideas. Cf. Duham, *Études,* v. 2 pp. 101-104 and R. Klibansky, 'Copernic et Nicolus De Cues,' *Leonardo De Vinci* (Paris 1952), pp. 225-235.
42. Edward McCurdy, *The Mind of Leonardo da Vinci* (New York, 1928) quoted from Leonardo, CA. 273 rb.
43. St. Augustine, *Confessions,* Book XI, 15, trans. P.S. Pine-Coffin, (Harmondsworth, Eng. 1961), p. 266.
44. Cusanus, *Of leanred ignorance,* Book II, chap. ii, p. 76.
45. Cusanus, *Of learned ignorance,* Book II, chap. ii, p.76.
46. Cusanus, *Of learned ignorance,* Book II, chap. ii, p. 76.
47. Cusanus, *Idiota,* De sapientia I, p. 6.
48. Boethius, *Consolation,* Book IV, prose 6, p. 92.
49. Cusanus, *Of learned ignorance,* Book II, chap. xii. As far as I know, Cusanus was the first *modern* to make an imaginative transference of man, to the sun or to another planet. It seems necessary to get rid of Aristotelian cosmological categories before one can do this; how can a being from the impure earth transfer himself to a higher and purer sphere? The literary voyages of the seventeenth century were inspired by Kepler's *Somnium.*
50. Boethius, *Consolation,* Book IV, prose 6, p. 92. My italics.
51. Cusanus, *Idiota,* Book III, chap. iv, pp. 35-6.
52. Cf. above chap. i, p.26.
53. St. Augustine, *Confessions,* Book VII, 17, p. 151, his itals.
54. Cusanus, *Idiota,* Book III, chap. i, p.27.
55. Cusanus, *Idiota,* Book III, chap. iv, p. 35; my italics.
56. Kemp, Martin., 'Il concetto dell'anima in Leonardo's early skull studies', *J. Warburg and Courtauld Institutes,* vol. XXXIV, 1971, 115-135. The Cusan vision of mind-body relationship may be the same as that of Leonardo. The skull studies show perceptions going straight to the intellectual centres of the brain. This began with optic nerves and included other senses in the

later drawings. The soul's great function was the comprehension of the natural world. In this the body was the vital servant of the soul (p. 129). All this supports, and can be seen within the context of, the practice of learned ignorance.
57. Above, chapter I, pp. 19, 24.
58. Cusanus, *Idiota*, Book III, chap. ix, p. 52. Only surfaces can be constructed from the point. But on the metaphysical plane materials like wood or stone also have their origin in God. They are even mathematical in so far as they were thought to have been brought about through proportioning the elements. In God they are nothing, the original indivisible point. Here the seed is like wood or stone in so far as they are formless in Him. Thus the term of the seed is not knowable and could be represented by nothing, by the zero, by the point.
59. Cusanus, *Of learned ignorance*, Book II, chap. vii, p. 92.
60. Cusanus, *Idiota*, Book III, p. 46.
61. Book I, (tr. M. M. Innes, England, 1955), p. 43.
62. Cusanus, *Of learned ignorance*, Book II, chap. xii, p. 116.
63. The psychologist-philosopher R. D. Laing has protested the frequent confusion between things and beings that do not experience ('it-beings'), and those that do, ('human-beings'). (Cf. *The Politics of Experience* (Penguin Books, 1967, p. 53)). On the surface, this protest appears to contradict Susanne K. Langer's approach wherein she regards feeling and consciousness as phases of physiological processes rather than as products of them. (Cf. *Mind: An Essay on Human Feelings*, Baltimore, vol. I, 1967, p. 23). This apparent contradiction appears to me to be entirely superficial to the question, 'What is the significance of conscious thought and feeling; what does it mean?' Of course, men must break with the old body-mind dualism; but, if the result is mechanical behaviourism then the earlier mis-conception is still more descriptive of human minds than recent behaviourists' solutions. At present, the break should not be made between physiology and psychology, or in the older framework, between body and mind. The real jump comes between unknowing-experience and unconsciousness, and the actual awareness of experience and conscious behaviour. When the mind experiences this awareness of the world and itself these feelings may not be different entities from the rest of the biological experiences of the organism, but they do represent a unique state. No psychologist or philosopher should diminish the value of that state. It generally increases the flexibility of any animal capable of supporting it. Awareness of experience is highest in the human being, the most flexible animal known. This human flexibility of expression so far exceeds the known possibilities of specific-it-beings that it lays claim to special value. At the same time, men should remain clear about its physiological wholeness, about the possibility that aware-states must be part and parcel of physiological-states that are not consciously experienced in all of their phases.

4

THE ANTITHESIS OF HARMONY AND THE PRE-CONDITION OF MAGIC IN THE SIXTEENTH CENTURY

> Before I die I'll leave such an account of myself that the whole world will be dumbfounded.
>
> Benvenuto Cellini

An ambivalent attitude to nature

Reflecting for a moment on the word 'antithesis' it is necessary to say quickly that I am shifting my ground. The following discussion is an attempt to display the emotional colours of Leonardo da Vinci's mind and to explore the possible historical meanings of that state of mind. I have no desire to imply an intellectual shift in Leonardo's basic assumptions about man, nature and God. Instead I am proposing that this ardent believer in universal harmony was not himself gifted with a harmonious temperament; further, that his pessimistic emotional tendency, although personal, was not entirely personal. It was also part of a wider historical shift in styles of self-consciousness and perception.

Generally, just as the purely classical figures of painting could not possibly remain within their early Raphaelesque niches, and just as the balanced sweetness of Michelangelo's 'Pieta' could not be reproduced in his later works, so the burden of Leonardo's desire for universality in the knowledge of nature inevitably introduced dissonance in the psychic picture. Leonardo turned inward to confront what he recognized as helplessness and inadequacy. He never resolved this confrontation. But some of his contemporaries and later thinkers thought that they had found a solution. This was Magic.

In the past Nicholas of Cusa could still maintain his faith in the ultimate goodness of apparent evil in so far as God was the coincidence of opposites. Cusa turned to nature to heighten his own and the general human apprehension of God. However, any benefits for man's capacity to manoeuvre natural things and to work within nature were, in some measure, gratuitous and ancillary to Cusa's ultimate quest. The fundamental desire of the originator of learned ignorance was for an

apprehension of God and for salvation. However, the knowledge of nature was not excluded from higher levels of the
enactment of this desire. These were levels of thought and of
contemplation. Cusa stands as a Renaissance man among thinkers because of his strong advocacy of the knowledge of nature
and experience within the wider question of reality. In contrast
to him, the position of Leonardo was substantially different,
different in time, different in terms of the secular economic
arena, and also in both training and vocation. Despite these
obvious differences, Cusa's practice of learned ignorance certainly ripened Leonardo's sense of the spiritual character of
nature and of all reality, and it supported and justified his
activities and works. However, Leonardo da Vinci's personal
desire for effectiveness and worldly reputation both complemented and was the equal of his intellectual and spiritual
longing. He was a maker and doer of things, a scientific artist
and genius who was subject to all of the accumulated social and
economic pressures of Renaissance society. He was commissioned for design and invention first, not for philosophy and
theology. But historically this does not represent a simple shift
of point of view wholly based on where the money was. Rather,
Leonardo da Vinci made a most intimate and heightened
response to the general culture of his area and time. Although
the expression of his vocation was entirely secular and his reputation depended upon what, in fact, he could do or accomplish,
Leonardo devoted more energy to the development of his own
understanding than he did to specific jobs. This is one reason
why theories based on overt economic shifts cannot do as full
explanations of Leonardo's cast of mind. He grew up in the
Florentine workshop atmosphere where he developed his skills
and techniques. However, he used these skills on an intellectual
quest that far exceeded the economic exigencies of the day. His
own personal understanding of nature became his vocation.
And it can be seen to be psychologically comparable to the calling of the Renaissance Magus.

Men like these desired understanding in order to achieve
control. In this view, man was not cast as the purely passive
microcosm but as the being gifted to create after the divine
creator. Magic was not, however, Leonardo's method. He
primarily relied on observation and reason, and on mathematical operations, those of number, weight and measure. Furthermore, his mystical vision of the human intellect as soul
unified his intellectual with his spiritual quest.

In this sense, Leonardo da Vinci set himself the goal of personal universality and it was conceived of in the imagery of
man the maker in partial and finite analogy with God the

creator. His ambition relates to his faith in this way. But it was also conceived of within the specific terms of his works, his science, and his desire to predict, manoeuvre, manipulate and control nature. However, nature was indefinite in size as it was also impersonal and relentless in its order and workings. This realization was the root and cause of Leonardo's creeping despair. He suffered not merely the agony of his own predicament, but a real dawning of the helplessness of the human condition and of the dilemma of all creaturehood. Man was God-like among creatures but creature-like before inexorable nature. Still man had grown more forward in his ambitions. The sin of pride was ripe for a new manifestation in history and an archetypal figure was formulated to represent this particular posture in human psychology.[1] The figure is that of a Faust. No one of sense would try to maintain that Leonardo da Vinci was completely like Faust; but, it is an interesting experiment in historical speculation to see how Leonardo was, in fact, Faust-like.

One conclusion arising from these observations should be that an exclusive consideration of analogies described in preceding chapters must leave a limited and, in some ways, misleading impression of Leonardo. It would be wrong to think of him as having a mentality rather like Alberti's, only with wider interests and scope, a mind with a straightforward classical frame of reference that positively affirmed an orderly harmonic universe. While it is true that the orderly part of the cosmology remains and is even reaffirmed, Leonardo's personal attitude toward nature underwent some startling alterations. Truth began to loom larger than beauty and the harmonious universe was beginning to be seen to encompass some surprising dissonance. A broader base of examples from Leonardo's work, either of his paintings, his drawings, or his notebooks, reveals him as a man who was preoccupied with visions of strife. However, this was not strife as opposed to ultimate natural harmony, but strife in so far as individual happiness was still almost impossible to achieve, and to maintain.[2] There is a deeply romantic cast to Leonardo's thoughts. Therefore, in order to place the examples of analogies in wider perspective and develop a more precise view of what they say about Leonardo's personality and its relation to his work, and his times, we must consider elements of his world view that are not always obvious in the analogies.

A clue that foreshadows strife, as it is expressed in Leonardo's thinking, was uncovered when I pointed out an element of hybris in some of Leonardo's reflections about the status of the painter. Recall how he praised the ability of the painter to make permanent that which nature could not. Actually, this point of praise was a rejoicing in the creative powers of the artist's mind. Nature could only run on relentlessly whereas mind could recall, anticipate and abstract from experience. But at least one more important emotion is revealed in this particular praise of painting, in Leonardo's desire to 'freeze time'. It shows that he saw the individual ego being abused by nature's incessant mutability. Nature's pattern of cause and effect is ruthless and yet admirable at the same time. Nature's law of continual growth, decay, and renewal does not, on one plane of thought, contradict the concept of nature as harmonious; but the conscious individual, aware of his own subjection to this law, has often tended to read it in different terms, and to find in it discomfort rather than inspiration. He may well end by feeling that he and all other living beings are doomed to live, not in personal harmony but in inevitable and hopeless strife with nature. Short of this his view of nature may waver between these two conceptions and he will be at odds with himself in his attitude towards the natural order. One of Leonardo's most typical comments describes the negative end of this ambivalent view of nature. After Ovid he writes:

> O time, consumer of all things! O envious age! Thou dost destroy all things and devour all things with the hard teeth of years, little by little in a slow death . . .[3]

The desire to give permanence to individuals and to individual things is illustrated by his frequent recommendation to men not to devote themselves to projects that will die with them:

> . . . Miserable life should not pass without leaving some memory of ourselves in the minds of mortals . . . .[4]

And:

> . . .We do not lack ways and means to divide and measure these our miserable days which it should be our pleasure not to spend and pass away in vain and without praise, and without leaving record of themselves in the minds of mortals. . . .[5]

The unashamed and unqualified declaration of this desire for worldly reputation is something of a Renaissance innovation. Not that this sentiment was unknown. Certainly it had always been part of western psychology. However, the very rapid development of urban and secular culture in the fourteenth and fifteenth centuries reinforced this yearning. Before, there had been strong moral opposition to this cast of mind, opposition in the values put forward by the church and in the recommendations of philosophy as well. For example, Leonardo's declaration of this desire contradicts the traditional and well known advice of Lady Philosophy to Boethius. Inspired by high ambitions imbibed from the values of Roman public life, Boethius desired worldly reputation. But Lady Philosophy ticks him off even on his rather worthy perch. Notice the terms that she uses to cure him of his failed ambition:

> You know from astrological computation that the whole circumference of the earth is no more than a pin point when contrasted to the space of the heavens; in fact, if the two are compared, the earth may be considered to have no size at all. . . . Do you, therefore, aspire to spread your fame and enhance your reputation when you are confined to this insignificant area on a tiny earth? How can glory be great that is severely limited by such narrow boundaries?[6]

In the light of advice like this, Leonardo still emphasized the pursuit of a 'lasting name'. This was not because he was entirely indifferent to other-worldly values. Furthermore, we are aware that he had additional reasons strictly to attend to the smallness of the place of man relative to the size of the cosmos.

It may seem curious that one who influenced Leonardo, Nicholas of Cusa, was also the first modern to propose an increase in the size of the physical universe, making it infinite for all rational purposes. Should this not have reduced the legitimacy of all subsequent human claims to fame? Or, if not Cusa, should not the later combined impact of Copernicus, Tycho Brahe, Kepler and Galileo have quieted these sorts of personal ambitions, the hopes of very small beings in an infinite universe?

A crucial thing to realize about the psychology of early modern thinking is that neither the hypothesis of the indefinite size of the universe, nor the scientific acceptance of its vast or even infinite size - that none of these points really substantially impaired man's ever growing ambitions. This applies to social ambitions, and, even more, to ambitions having to do with knowledge and with works, ambitions of the kind that Leonardo had.

While the size of the earth was diminishing relative to that of the heavens, the range of the human mind was seen to be increasing and growing ever larger. This increase is subtle; and, if we think of the period of time from about 1440 to 1640, it is not that thinkers did not appreciate the mystery of the absolute infinity of God, nor that they did not realize that the cosmos was vast; but rather, that some of them also believed that nature was homogeneous and was the proper, even the providential, ob-

ject of human knowledge. Men had been especially gifted to realize and appreciate God's works. Medieval Theology had
emphasized the soul and God as the proper subjects for human
enquiry. This does not mean that they were considered objects
in the way that things might be objects. They were mysterious
and inspiring goals. Frequently, thinkers by-passed or moved
through physical nature quite quickly, looking for signs and
gleanings but only inwardly for substance. Naturally, I do not
mean all philosophers; for I am referring to very general tendencies in the learned world. What many educated men
thought they should be doing had more to do with contemplative knowledge than with worldly knowledge. But strangely, as
the presumed size of the physical cosmos grew, the value of
knowing it also seems to have grown. By the seventeenth century Francis Bacon wrote of achieving a model of the universe
in the mind. This knowledge was also a form of devotion, or, at
least, many saw it in this way. Despite sceptics, man's discovery
of the universe was seen to be providential. Some, for example,
Robert Boyle, were prepared to make this a moral duty.

Now the earlier Cusan formulation that suggested a special
judging power of the mind and that also emphasized the universe as the primary object of this judging power, makes real
sense of Leonardo's extraordinary efforts towards universality.
Nature was the legitimate object of human knowledge both
because of the creation and because of God's mysterious joint
immanence and transcendence. It does not matter that Cusa
himself still subjected progress by reason to a superior practice
of learned ignorance. He saw reason as an innate gift that man
was intended to use. He saw that nature, not God, was its
proper object. He saw God lurking invisibly at its limits. So,
these limits had to be reached. Intellectual procedures were
encompassed in a contemplative practice. It was not possible to
turn to God while turning away from his creation. This early
philosophical reassurance took place both in and above the
diverse pressures of Renaissance society. Society, culture and
thought all seemed to be confirming a desire for efficacy
through knowledge. And these pressures that confirmed pursuits in natural philosophy also confirmed the outrageous
ambitions of the magician. In the human mind, within the very
image of God where Cusa had placed knowledge as an instrument in the process of revelation, the devil also saw and took
his own chances. It is not surprising that the Magus, Giordano
Bruno, was the one who most took up and publicised Cusan
ideas. These ideas raised the importance of nature and confirmed the judging power of the human mind. It did not take
many further steps to nurture all kinds of worldly ambitions

and to reinforce the dream of power of a magician.

Of course, the tone of Cusa's dramatic imagery was not entirely exceptional. The general development of humanism, and the whole social and economic character of Renaissance cities also formed the ground upon which both pride in the powers of the human mind and worldly ambitions grew. This occurred in many forms and formulations and was received at different times in different ways. However, Cusa was the first to both raise the human mind and also increase the size of the universe. And this, I think, was the spirit in which Leonardo da Vinci took up his own works. Here was both the challenge and the source of his optimism. In the wake of such a spirit, he struggled for results. A 'lasting name' was the desired prize. The power of human understanding and the significance of human works came to mean much to Leonardo and to other Renaissance men. In the face of this recently ripened desire for results and for control, the order of nature, then, in its turn, gradually came to be seen as impersonal, driving and even relentless. And this is the way that the wheel turned from early Renaissance optimism and ambition to anxiety and frustration.

Then, in Leonardo's comments, men and their works are likely to appear very much otherwise than in the thoughts of Alberti. They no longer comfortably fit into proper places wherein something of the self was easily subjected to the proper order and good of the whole. In Leonardo, the path of time, and the processes of development and decay in nature, often appear as threats to the individual. The phrase, harmonious nature, quite suddenly acquires an irony that almost foreshadows the impact of Pangloss' 'this is the best of all possible worlds.' While for Alberti the order and rational harmony of nature necessarily included beauty and potential happiness, for Leonardo, this same admired and aesthetically satisfying harmony sometimes became negative, almost mockery.[7] In such a state of mind he writes:

> Why did nature not ordain that one animal should not live by the death of another? Nature, being inconstant and taking pleasure in creating and making constantly new lives and forms, because she knows that her terrestrial materials become thereby augmented, is more ready and more swift in her creating than time in his destruction; and so she has ordained that many animals shall be food for others. Nay, this not satisfying her desire to the same end, she frequently sends forth certain poisonous and pestilential vapours and frequent plagues upon the vast increase and congregation of animals; and most of all upon men, who increase vastly because other animals do not feed

upon them; and, the causes being removed, the effects would cease. This earth therefore seeks to lose its life, desiring only continual reproduction as you bring forward and demonstrate by argument; like effects always follow like causes, animals are a type of the life of the world.[8]

A similar attitude is expressed when he writes about the fossil of a sea creature:

... Now destroyed by time thou liest patiently in this confined space with bones stripped and bare, serving as a support and prop for the mountain placed above thee.[9]

Even his recognition of the wonder of the soul's return to God does not always seem to give emotional compensation for the fact of the destruction of the living creature. Leonardo shows a mixture of attitudes towards the body-soul relationship. He reflects that it is perfectly natural for the soul to wish to fly from the body and join its maker. On the other hand, he also says, 'The spirit desires to remain with its body, because without the organic instruments of that body, it can neither act nor feel anything.'[10] An example of ambivalent reflections follows:

Now you see that the hope and desire of returning to the first state of chaos is like the moth to the light, and that the man who with constant longing awaits with joy each new springtime, each new summer, each new month and new year... deeming that the things he longs for are ever too late in coming ... does not perceive that he is longing for his own destruction....[11]

As if in answer to these thoughts he also says:

But this desire is the ....quintessence, the spirit of the elements, which finding itself imprisoned with the soul is ever longing to return from the human body to its giver.... This same longing is that quintessence, inseparable from nature, and .... man is the image of the world.[12]

Once again, we have his reiteration of the familiar organic theme in the cosmic analogy, and here in a context that reveals his mingled emotional reactions to this pattern.

The dual nature of the emotion that he attached to his world view is evident in several aspects of his life and work. An exploration of some of these will fill out the picture of the historical significance of Leonardo's assumptions about nature.

Self-esteem is possible for Leonardo solely on the basis of work, and, like Alberti, he frowned misanthropically on those who did not pursue some job of work. He went so far as to

describe some of his more indolent fellow men as only passages
for food and fillers of privies.[13] Because he applied it to himself, his idea of work as the basis of self-esteem appears to have
had deep psychological consequences. He seems to have found
it extremely difficult to satisfy himself by the only means by
which he would accept that satisfaction could justifiably be
gained. Notice the cumulative impression received from the
following group of statements. He writes:

> The natural desire of all good men is knowledge.[14]

And,

> Thou, O God, dost sell unto us all good things at the price of
> labour.[15]

But,

> There is no perfect gift without great suffering.[16]

And so,

> ...The foundation of pleasure is labour with pain ....[17]

Finally the man who does not accept this painful burden of
labour and who has 'frittered life away':

> ... leaves no more trace of himself upon the earth than smoke
> does in the air or foam on the water.[18]

This awareness and concentration on the pain that accom-
panies labour, and on the short-lived nature of satisfaction is
continually evident in Leonardo's comments: 'Cosa bella mortal
passà e non dura.'
   By comparison a Magus could look forward to satisfaction,
albeit after great effort, but most important, by being able to
summon and draw upon forces beyond his own mental powers.
In all instances of magic there is an attempt to contact agencies
outside the self and outside the magician's understanding. In
Renaissance natural magic the purpose is close to what we
might recognize as a scientific purpose, but the methods are
not. Just as a man may wish to tap an underground well, the
practitioner of natural magic wanted to tap some natural agency,
for example, Solar or Jovial influence. He might or might not
have been superstitious in his belief in the nature of that influence. This is not what matters here. What the magician was
doing was attempting to use what he saw to be some natural

force or energy, either for his own purposes or for wider social purposes. Among other forms of magic, this is what Bruno and Campanella did. In terms of their desires then, the essence is comparable with scientific motives.

By contrast a natural philosopher uses his own mental resources and those of other men. He will also use instruments that extend perception and the possibilities of manipulation. However, he relies on his knowledge which he equates with his power, or with the power of the human mind; he does not attempt to summon unknown and mysterious powers. How does this compare with the activity of a Renaissance Magus who may have wanted to tap an archangel or even a demon?

A few contemporary mystical theologians have described angels as specific forms of energy rather than spiritual analogues to minds or personalities. Certainly there is no agreement about either the existence of or the nature of these sorts of energy. They are not proven sources. And the very impossibility of identifying or proving them leads men to doubt them in a way that they do not doubt solar energy, even when they do not understand it.

So, by contrast to a Renaissance Magus, a natural philosopher like Leonardo endeavoured to work by power of intellect alone. Pythagorean inspirations and his studio experience led him to trust empirical and rational methods of understanding, while on the other hand, the Magus did not limit himself to these methods. He not only held a mystical view of reality but he also addressed himself to mysterious sources and used magical methods of verification. But when Leonardo wished to tap nature his aims and methods were scientific in the terms of his time. He did not try calling upon archangels to tell him about aerodynamics.

If, however, we consider the tremendous accentuation of purpose alone as characteristic of the intellectual life of the early modern era, this purpose, the manipulation and control of nature and human destiny, was common to both the magician and the philosopher. This longing for the mastery of nature on a grand scale was as important, or perhaps was even more important for the seventeenth-century scientific revolution than the frequently noted refinement of methods.

By the early sixteenth century the strength of this purpose, the desire to know and to control or, in the case of the magician, to know how to summon in order to control, this aim could enjoin almost super human efforts on the part of some individuals. In the future, the turnings taken attracted men either to cooperative efforts within natural philosophy or to the intensification of magical practices. Inevitably some thinkers were involved with both of these occupations.

Leonardo stands at a pinnacle and near to the end of the attempt, by a single individual, to encompass a universal knowledge of nature. After his lifetime, the historian must discriminate between individuality as a social phenomenon, and the self-conscious limits of the individual natural philosopher. Francis Bacon makes a good example in so far as he shows pronounced individuality and yet he was the one to prescribe the limits of the single mind and to advocate cooperative science. Certainly western European society continued, and still continues, to foster and promote individuality; however, almost no individual confronts the universal knowledge of nature, head-on, in the almost solitary style of Leonardo. While this is not surprising in the present, the shift can be marked from the early part of the sixteenth century. Undoubtably personal universality went on, but almost no single thinker was quite as aloof as Leonardo was. And even more important than this, other forms of the universal ambition begin to be expressed in academies, in societies, and even eventually in the cooperative efforts of the encyclopaedia.

Leonardo da Vinci wanted to achieve an unachievable self-satisfaction. The foreknowledge that it really was unachievable was almost conscious in him; and in this, his veiled consciousness, Leonardo resembles the Faustian archetype.

Thus, the Faust of the old German puppet play repeats the same desire that Leonardo did, the desire to live on through his effects, or his works. The puppet Faust says, '. . . all of us bear within our breasts the goad that drives us on towards a higher point than that whereon we stand . . .'; he continues saying that his own goal is an 'imperishable name'.[19] Once again in a modern version of Faust, by Thomas Mann, the Faust, composer Adrian Leverkühn, is also tempted with the same desire: he is offered a way of living on by means of his works. The devil says to Leverkühn:

> We pledge you the success of that which with our help you will accomplish. You will lead the way, you will strike up the march of the future, the lads will swear by your name . . . Do you understand? Not only will you break through the paralysing difficulties of the time . . . you will break through time itself . . .[20]

This metaphor of Faust for Leonardo may yield explanations that can relate his personal discomfort and pessimism to his analogically conceived and harmonious cosmology. Aspects of his personality, like the perfectionism that so annoyed Vasari, can perhaps show something more than his personal foibles if they are examined from a Faustian point of view.

Faustian elements in the personality of Leonardo

Yea, to this thought I cling, with virtue rife
Wisdom's last fruit profoundly true;
Freedom alone he earns as well as life,
Who day by day must conquer them anew . . . [21]

This idea, expressed at the conclusion of Goethe's 'Fasut', brings us close to the attitude of Leonardo in his relentless and laborious pursuit of knowledge by means of experience and reason, and in his creation of works of art as one expression of that knowledge. Another similarity, Nature, only allows man to reach some pinnacle of self-esteem to deal him a more shattering blow.[22] We can compare these kinds of emotions with the following thought from Goethe's 'Faust'. Faust says 'Accursed be the lofty opinion in which the mind wraps itself! . . . Accursed, the dreams that lie to us, the delusion of glory and of a lasting name!'[23] The contrast is that Leonardo's cynicism, unlike Faust's, is accompanied always by his contradictory affirmation that there is satisfaction in the study and contemplation of nature, in other words, in his work. Faust despairs of this, and, at least in Goethe, at last finds comfort and salvation in it only at the end of his life. Marlowe and Mann never even let their Fausts arrive at this point. The former Faust is dragged off to damnation by devils, the latter finally goes mad. Leonardo, however, is not as consistent in his emotions about the self-satisfaction derived from work as he is about his conviction that work is the only true source of this satisfaction. There is still overwhelming evidence that the natural harmony and order which theoretically let the human ego exist in close analogy with nature, the harmony, the contemplation of which provided him with his most intense aesthetic and intellectual inspiration, failed at the same time to ease the burden of his self-consciousness, failed in the same way to allow him to believe consistently in it as a source of self-esteem.

Faustian elements in Leonardo's personality illustrate the many overlapping characteristics of his pessimism. Some of the relevant components of this personality are more apparent from observations of Leonardo's behaviour than they are from the content of any of his comments in the notebooks. For instance, it has been noted, that for one who was so universally talented, and who placed such high expectations upon himself, Leonardo was at times surprisingly inefficient. Like a Faust, he took up projects with great emotional intensity, and then gave them up, uncompleted. Our explanations for the respective behaviour may be different, but the pattern of this behaviour is the same. Kenneth Clark has repeatedly mentioned instances of Leonardo's most important projects that failed either through incompletion, because of some unforeseen and catastrophic circumstances, or because the conception was both grandiose and yet in some essential respects impractical and impracticable. Clark describes this behaviour of Leonardo's as a kind of 'romantic unreality.'[24]

A case in point is the casting of the Sforza Monument. In 1476 Ludovico Sforza decided to resume the design of an equestrian monument in honour of Francesco, his father. The project became Leonardo's. He took sixteen years to achieve the making of a model, and he (although we do not know if it was his fault) never completed the monument. His failure was only in small part technical. The difficulty appears to have arisen both from the extreme grandiosity of his conception of it in the first place, and from other aspects of his perfectionism. These difficulties are clues to his attempt to bring the work to a climax. Leonardo's first conception of the design was grandiose in that he tried to represent the horse as prancing. Clark tells us that at that date no equestrian statue of a prancing horse was known. He describes Leonardo's ambition as being far ahead of his experience.[25] However, after 1490 Leonardo seems to have reconciled himself to the traditional pose of a walking horse. He made some extremely beautiful drawings of horses in silverpoint, and in 1493 we find him still taking notes on horses. In the autumn he constructed a full-scale model in clay, but the casting in bronze never took place. In 1494 Ludovico Sforza was forced to send the bronze set aside for the monument to his brother-in-law, Duke Ercole d'Este, for the casting of cannons. Imagine the frustration of this final impasse.

On the other hand, Leonardo's drawings of the proportions of the horse were known to his contemporaries. In these he employed the canons of proportional perfection; Clark adds that twenty years later, when he was involved with a similar project, the casting of a monument for Marshal Trivulzio, one can follow through a larger series of drawings the 'calculations by which he strove for perfection'.[27] A model of this monument was destroyed and the actual casting also did not take place.

This is not the only project that shows Leonardo's perfectionism together with his ambitious imagination acting as an inefficient combination. Variations on this type of failure are numerous.

His well known disregard for media of execution is apparent

in the Last Supper, which began to fade from the walls of Santa Maria delle Grazie in his own lifetime. In the project for the canalization of the Arno, where he specified that he would cut through mountains, there is no apparent attempt to devise a real method of doing so. The big painting of the battle of Anghiari was also never completed because of a terrible storm. Perhaps his extreme reluctance to make generalizations in his writings might be added to the list of similar behaviour. He appears to have needed more and still more knowledge before he could accept the commitment of making a statement about the world, either by making generalizations, or by carrying through to completion his inventions, and works of art. Perhaps his self-image as a second creator, together with his equally strong feeling that the individual ego must submit to the pattern of a marvellous and yet terrifyingly indifferent nature, provide important sources from which we can understand his personal discord in a harmonious universe.

Thus the idea of man, especially of the artist as a creator after the divine creator, both confronts and is complicated by Leonardo's continually growing realization of the terribly impersonal character of the natural order. Can such an ambitious man face reality with its constraints of time and chance and not long to manoeuvre it, to mould it to the human will and advantage? This is the real conflict between an active or a passive self-image in relation to the whole of nature. Leonardo's difficulty in his attempt to balance the active and passive roles within himself does not simply illustrate a personal problem. This dilemma is symptomatic of some of the prevalent psychological postures in European society at the time of the Reformation. After all, what was the gift of faith given only by the grace of God, but a vision of passive man in the face of divine will. Belief in pre-destination is an extreme of this view. On the other hand, look at the pride involved in removing oneself from the possible mediation of the mother church. This is the active role, a form of extreme individuality that encompassed the desire for some control over one's own ultimate spiritual position. Men took the Bible into their own hands, or, at least, many saw it in this way.

By the time of the Faustian conception of Christopher Marlowe both the desire for mastery through knowledge and power, and the contrasting feeling of smallness in the face of divine omnipotence and impersonal forces, have become crucial attitudes. Marlowe's Faust deplores the futility of knowledge without efficacy so he bargains his soul for a few years, not merely of riches and fame, he bargains his soul for a period of guaranteed effectiveness. Later this same Faust exhibits the

contrasting attitude when he doubts whether he can call upon
the mercy of God. Apparently God honours his contracts even
with the devil. Thus, Faust's position is inevitable. At least this
is the interpretation of Mephostophilis; and neither Faust, nor
even his supposedly faithful scholar friends can contradict him.
So in the wake of causes the relentless effects must take place.
Not only is nature blind but God also does not contradict his
providential order. The striving for mastery and the consequent anxiety of the ego up against it, both co-exist in the same
temperament. So at the end of the century this Faust is something of a descendent and psychological extreme of the
Leonardo-Faust at the beginning.

Leonardo showed these symptoms but he did not try the particular cure of Magic. In a way, his universality was his magic.
The other rational cure, that of cooperation in the advancement of learning, was not yet truly launched. Leonardo stood
fixed in a curious position; for he showed the maximum of
personal dissonance for a passionate believer in the harmony of
nature.

Leonardo, once again like Faust, was fascinated with grandiose projects; for example, Faust, in this instance in Marlowe's
play, dreams of what he might do with his newly acquired
power:

> I'll ... make a bridge through the moving air
> to pass the ocean with a band of men:
> I'll join the hills that bind the Afric Shore
> And make that country continent to Spain. ...[29]

These lines call to mind Leonardo's project for canalization of
the Arno, and even more in spirit, his elaborate studies and
attempts to understand the flight of birds in order to devise a
flying machine. The appeal of Faust rests, after all, on a certain
archetypal way of perceiving the human dilemma. Leonardo
often manifests this kind of perception. Both Leonardo and
Faust are the men who would be supermen or demi-gods.[30]
Although Leonardo never despairs to the same point that Faust
does (to the point of attempting a methodological shortcut to
knowledge, either through the inspiration of a satanic source
or by the practice of magic), there is still a great deal of evidence of how he felt the weight of this superman standard,
weight that seems to be indicated in the facial expression of his
God-like self-portrait.[31] Leonardo, like Faust, eschewed the
intimate company of other men. To the artist Leonardo writes,
'While you are alone you are entirely your own and if you have
one companion you are but half your own, and the less so in
proportion to the indiscretion of his behaviour.'[32] This alone-

ness is characteristic of a Faustian type: it is illustrated by the
devil's command to Faust, here Adrian Leverkühn, that 'Thou
must not love', 'A general chilling of your life and your
relations to men lies in the nature of things . . . rather it lies
already in your nature.'[33] Goethe's Faust explains how he was
tempted to sin by this characteristic aloneness; he says, 'To solitude I fled, to wilds forlorn and not in utter loneliness to live,
Myself at last did to the Devil give!'[34] I cannot prove that for
Leonardo solitude meant loneliness. There is no statement as
clearcut as that of Michelangelo, who said that experience
could only be won in isolation, and isolation spells agony.[35]
However, it is the state of solitude that delineates the Faustian
character, and in Leonardo's wishes and behaviour this role is
borne out.

Solitude on a Faustian-da Vincian scale may be one of the
many manifestations of Leonardo's personal stoicism. The
whole problem of control tends to appear within his stoic
moods. Although there are many specific types of stoicism, all
those who have a kind of stoic awareness share the common
characteristic of an overpowering realization that the only
things that they can control are their own attitudes. In the light
of this awareness the stoic tends to inwardly qualify his enjoy-
ment of goods which he sees as inevitably uncertain and temporary. Leonardo makes this kind of stoic observation of relations between men. He writes, that those who never put their
trust in any man will never be deceived. His most overwhelmingly negative view of human relations is found in a frequently
quoted letter to one of his brothers on the birth of a son. He
wrote, ' . . . you are pleased at having created an enemy intent
on his liberty, which he will not have before your death.'[36]

Then true pleasure and the best good must come entirely
from the self, from the inner rewards of one's own work,
thoughts, and virtuous life. But, are even these recognized
sources of personal gratification reliable ones for Leonardo?
When he writes things like, 'supreme happiness will be the
source of greatest misery,' or the 'perfection of wisdom is the
occasion of folly,' it does make you wonder about the nature
and personal significance of the emotions that he was describing. Once again statements like this one have a Faustian twang,
a suggestion of a belief in the illusory nature of any pleasure;
even of theoretically justified self-satisfaction and the pleasure
derived from knowledge itself. It is in this spirit that Goethe's
Faust struck his bargain with Mephostophilis. Thus Faust says:

> If you can ever flatteringly delude me into being pleased with
> myself, if you can cheat me with enjoyment, be that day my
> last! . . .[37]

If knowledge is raised as the supreme standard of self-satisfaction, as it is by the would-be superman, can there ever be enough knowledge to sustain that satisfaction? Faust wished to learn what held the world together at its core; his cry was, 'Where shall I seize you, infinite nature?'[38] Does Leonardo's awareness of the limitations of the human mind sometimes also represent an echo of the cry of Faust? 'Mind ranges over the universe,' writes Leonardo, 'but being finite it does not extend to infinity.'[34] The immensity of his self-designated enterprise may have made him insatiable. Perhaps this is why happiness (in work) could, for him, also be the greatest cause of misery.

All this is very suggestive and admittedly no more than that since the personality of Leonardo has eluded scholars involved in far more comprehensive studies. Part of this elusiveness is in the nature of the evidence, because the notebooks are a mass of unconnected material. The other is in the personal complexity of Leonardo. Certainly, he did not walk about beating his breast in the manner of Marlowe's Faust all the time. Thus, the actual strength of his pessimism reveals itself more in the sorts of preoccupations he had, and in the observations he made, than it does in the wringing of hands and weeping. He wrote of the terrified fish and of the unhatched chickens in the eggs we eat. Put together these sentiments with many other similar phrases and an idea of the magnitude of Leonardo's passion emerges. The strength of his feeling can be appreciated, but not its kind. For though I believe that Leonardo experienced the emotions of loneliness, fear, and at times even despair, I do not believe that he registered them, or better still that they registered with him, in the most usual way. I suspect that Leonardo had a faculty to make his imagination quickly transcend from his subjective to a more objective view of nature. In his objective moods he played the demi-god. And this ability made it possible for him to decry the ruthlessness of nature in one breath, and to admire its continuity in the next. Because of it, it was possible for him to praise God in one instance because of God's power to be partial, and to praise him again, in another instance, because of his glorious impartiality. He says:

> I obey thee, Lord, first for the love I ought in all reason to bear thee; secondly for that thou canst shorten or prolong the lives of men.[40]

But also;

> Oh admirable impartiality of Thine, Thou first mover; thou hast not permitted that any force should fail of the order or quantity of its necessary effects.[41]

The same switch from a more subjective to an objective mood is evident in how Leonardo speaks about time. First in Ovid's terms: '. . .Helen, when she looked in her mirror and saw the withered wrinkles which old age had made in her face, wept, and wondered to herself why ever she had twice been carried away . . . Oh time, thou that consumest all things.'[42] But also he reflects: 'Wrongfully do men lament the flight of time, accusing it of being too swift, and not perceiving that its period is yet sufficient . . . '[43]

Leonardo's admiration of the processes of cause and effect in nature is emotionally counterbalanced, so to speak, by his personal melancholia. However, the melancholic mood is not as evident in the gnashing of teeth as it is in his behaviour and in his general attitudes. Among these are his cynical attitudes towards men together with all their effects, and also his more than normal preoccupations with fear, death, universal destruction, and the very horrible and very ugly.

In spite of these attitudes Leonardo was never as subjectively emotional as Faust. Faust who, when confronted with a Helen who did not age in time, cried out, '. . .beyond time's limits . . . happiness . . . how rare!'[44] Leonardo would never have really wished to stop time. So by contrast to him we see the Faustian Mephostophilis who does not recommend the observation of nature from an objective point of view. Thus he judges against nature and God with his proud pronouncement that since subjectively all good things end anyway, better nothing.

> There, now 'tis past 'tis past . . .what may it mean?
> It is as good as if it ne'er had been,
> And yet as if it being did possess,
> Still in a circle it doth ceaseless press:
> I should prefer the Eternal Emptiness.[45]

The artist is the artist's model

Some historians and psychologists have been tempted to seek explanations for Leonardo's divergent attitudes, and to assess their effects on his work. Most of these views are extremely personal. Although Freud's impressive essay is said to have missed its mark, modern psychologists have not been discouraged from attempts to describe Leonardo's elusive personality. In a comparatively recent study, K. R. Eissler, *Leonardo da Vinci* (psychoanalytic notes on the enigma)[46], posits an interesting thesis. Briefly, it is that Leonardo was more than usually vulnerable to traumata, or simply that he was very easily frightened. This leads Eissler to conclude that the overwhelming desire of Leonardo's life was to attain control over natural events by the accumulation of knowledge.

As a historian concerned with psychological shifts, I have a different reaction from that of the professional psychologist. I see Leonardo's quest for control of nature through knowledge as one part of a general historical movement in which many men sought parallel or similar effectiveness. I also tend to think that Leonardo's fears indicate a heightened expression of far more general tensions. These tensions were to a large extent, brought about by a ripening of Renaissance individuality to the point of super-human ambition in some, and to an inimitable pride. Certainly this extreme was not exhibited in every group or case; but, as I have mentioned, some of the general tensions of the Reformation and the scientific revolution can be viewed profitably from this point. The throwing off of the mother church, the burning of the books by Paracelsus, and the casting off of past philosophies by Descartes and Bacon, all of these acts show that individual personalities felt that they had to come to newly formed ideas of reality and, frequently, to teach these new ideas to others. Whereas waves of optimism gave thinkers courage, periods of sharp anxiety also assailed them; else, why the very general association between genius and melancholy, and why the passionate denial of any personal control over one's salvation in the Calvinist belief in pre-destination? The efficacy of man, both the intensified hunger for it and the pessimistic doubt of it, is a central theme of early modern cultural life.

If the subject matter of many of Leonardo's scientific studies is thought to be medieval, the state of mind with which he confronted the world must assuredly be seen to be modern, modern in the Renaissance sense. The scale of his ambition to master nature is just not easily thinkable in pre-Renaissance terms.

Now I am not only talking about individuals, but about the widespread quest for a reform of learning and of the reassessment of man's roles, both wordly and spiritual that was evident in the Renaissance and afterwards. And the deluge and disaster nightmares, these too are not exclusive to Leonardo. Although the ways that he drew these things are unique, and his emotional intensity also is unique, the specific preoccupations were typical of Renaissance pessimism.

Faust was a popular invention. A man who could be tempted to bargain his soul for power and effectiveness was easily recognized by all. His sin of pride was quickly grasped and understood. So now it is possible to understand the genius who shifted about between desire and anxiety. The desire was for more and more certain knowledge; and the anxiety was because no knowledge could shelter him, or any other creature, from the indifference of nature and from its relentless rhythms. These impersonal rhythms were regarded with mixed fear, awe and wonder. And the more he learned about their details, the more he was both amazed and tormented.

Eissler has an interesting point to make about Leonardo's painting, The Last Supper. In it Leonardo chose to represent the moment Christ revealed that he knew about his coming betrayal, instead of representing the more usual moment of the institution of the Eucharist. In this choice Eissler sees Leonardo's preoccupation with moments of horror.[47] He notes, as does Kenneth Clark, the apparent awkwardness of the extant sketches for the painting, and Eissler goes on to suggest that this unusual awkwardness might have been caused by the intensity of Leonardo's own personal emotional involvement with his chosen subject. Here, we cannot fail to observe that Leonardo did choose to represent a moment when each apostle experienced his own subjective emotional reaction, rather than another possible moment when they were all spiritually unified. The earlier point made about Leonardo's carelessness in choosing the media of execution may add weight to Eissler's idea. It reveals another possible manifestation of anxiety with regard to the subject of the painting. However, the most interesting supporting idea comes from the work of another author with a psychoanalytic approach, Ernst Kris.[48] Kris brings to our attention the remarkable originality of Leonardo's advice to the artist, that the artist should not make his represented figures too similar to himself in appearance; he must be aware of, and resist the natural tendency to substitute his own bodily experience for that of the model he wants to depict.[49] Something must be said about Leonardo's awareness and rationalization of this tendency because it could be that the tendency to portray the artist's own self in the body also indicates a tendency to portray that self in the mind and in the emotions. Leonardo's familiar statement about his intention to show what was in men's minds by the way that he represented their figures makes this plausible.

Representation in art is limited to what the artist can portray on a surface. In representing men, when in almost all instances both physical and psychical things are being portrayed together, the body and the face form the centres from which the artist must project both the physical actions and the inner emotions.[50] Leonardo widened the means by which he either conveyed or commented on these emotions. His very original use of background forms, and of light and shade, are some of his methods. I am thinking, for example, of the unusual rocky wilderness backgrounds in both versions of the Madonna of the Rocks, and the deeply sombre and shadowy backgrounds of the Bacchus and of the St. John. Leonardo was primarily concerned to portray the passions of the soul.[51]

If we accepted Eissler's views with regard to the Last Supper this would not mean that each apostle was supposed to have reproduced Leonardo's own fear, shock, awe, etc., but only that Leonardo made a personal identification with each of their emotional reactions. Since his choice was to represent a moment of shock, or horror, the choice and its manner of presentation may possibly be revealing about Leonardo's own emotions on the subject of awful moments. On the other hand, certain of the drawings appear to go further in that they suggest a direct representation of Leonardo's state of mind. One, the depiction of an old man looking sadly into the distance, is described by Clark as a caricature of himself or a simplified expression of Leonardo's essential character.[52] This image of the old and bitter sage recurs in Leonardo's works and in it there is always some suggestion of the face in the self-portrait. However, Leonardo's expression of subjective or personal attitudes in the drawings and paintings actually involves more than just a discussion about the ways in which he may have revealed his anxiety. These expressions are evidence of Leonardo's ideas about man, or any other creature which might be personified or shown in circumstances consciously felt to be outside the control of the subject. When someone finds himself in this position, Leonardo always portrays the resulting emotions as negative. However, Leonardo's depictions present us with far wider ranges of emotions than those singled out by Eissler in The Last Supper; for, he does not exclusively represent creatures as being confronted by overwhelming circumstances. A real contrast can be seen between his representations of beings involved in some struggle between the self and circumstances, and his depictions of beings in less self-conscious circumstances.

If, in The Last Supper, he identified himself with the shock of each apostle, could we not also find meaning in his possible identification with the unselfconscious serenity of the Madonna and Child shown in most of his Madonna drawings? In these the Madonna is usually totally absorbed in the actions of the Child, and the Child in some small animal. These figures are always made into a visually and emotionally harmonious composition. Leonardo may also have identified with his mysterious St. John who appears to be smiling at some secret revealed knowledge, and who is at the same time totally unselfconscious. It appears to be the thought of struggle between the individual ego and circumstances that causes Leonardo bitter reflections. This was an extremely important theme in his works but others also show him as having a wide range of sensitivities. A group of depictions indicate his awareness of both strife and serenity. A particularly pertinent instance is his drawing of a confrontation between youth and old age. The old man is shown as very embittered, thus suggesting the results of his struggle with life's experiences. The youth, on the other hand, is serene to the point of blankness. Perhaps Leonardo suggests that the youth's experiences have as yet been insufficient to cause him to believe in an inevitable disharmony between his own subjective feelings and circumstances. Other indications of this kind of emotional dichotomy appear in paintings which show the figures as unselfconscious and serene but contrasted with an ominous even almost menacing background. I am thinking of The Madonna of the Rocks, where the background foretells the crucifixion. In this kind of painting the dramatic situation is the representational equivalent to situations we often find in opera when it is possible for the orchestra, or part of it, to comment independently on the action.

These remarks about Leonardo's representations, like previous comparisons between his written statements, show his ability to universalize or, better still, his inability not to universalize. He had to envision man's circumstances both from subjective and objective points of view. His emotions register both a superman-like satisfaction with the rational organization of nature together with a human-like struggle to accept the consequences. Leonardo's emotions are, at least in part, circumscribed in the categories set by the concept of man as a microcosm. There is an analogy between man and God insofar as man participates in spiritual and mental qualities that are seen as divine. The human soul is immortal, and the human mind has both intellectual vision and reason. At the same time, man is a microcosm by virtue of his place in the physical order of nature. Because he is described by mental and spiritual qualities, God can be said to occupy the philosophical position of subject (the conscious element). Then, in this scheme, all of nature is the object. However, man fulfils both roles. He is the subject and can see himself as the object.

Thus when microcosmism is combined with the image of the creator after the divine creator a definite tension is set up between man's awareness of his visive and creative capacities and the vision that he must also have of himself as an object acted upon by forces outside his consciousness. Man, the subject and the object, may employ and embody the same harmony of nature, but this circumstance does not affect the vulnerability of the ego in its position as object of overwhelming and perhaps unfortunate circumstances. Here is where Boethian values differ from those of the Renaissance. In *The Consolation* Lady Philosophy points to the futility of ambition and achievement, but Renaissance culture recommends them. The path of Leonardo's emotional dichotomy then is evident in this type of cosmism when it is expressed in a Renaissance culture. It is not really surprising to find that the terms of this imagery were continually reformulated in the sixteenth and seventeenth centuries.

Notes to Chapter Four

1. Johann Faust was supposed to have been a magician who lived in Germany from about 1488 to 1541. Legends of his doings were recorded in the 'Faustbuch', the 'Historia von D. Johann Fausten' published in Frankfurt-am-Main in 1587. Christopher Marlowe took his material from an English translation that appeared in 1588. Thus the state of mind to be connected with the figure of Faust originates in about the early sixteenth century. And the popularity of the figure continues throughout that century and afterwards.
2. K. Clark, *Leonardo da Vinci*, pp. 66-87. Martin Johnson, *Art and Scientific Thought* (London, 1956), pp. 133-181. K. R. Eissler, *Leonardo da Vinci* (Psychoanalytic notes on the enigma) (London, 1962), pp. 152-158. All of these authors remark on and explore aspects of Leonardo's unharmonious temperament.
3. Leonardo da Vinci, *Literary Works*, ed. Richter (1162).
4. *Ibid.* (1169).
5. *Ibid.* (1165A).
6. Boethius, *The Consolation of Philosophy*, tr. R. Green, (New York, 1962), Book II, prose 7, p.37.
7. André Chastel, 'Leonardo et la culture', *Leonardo da Vinci* (et l'expérience scientifique au seizième siècle) (Paris, 1952), pp. 250-263, cf. p. 255.
8. Leonardo da Vinci, *Literary Works*, ed. Richter (1219).
9. *Ibid.* (1217).
10. *Ibid.* (1142).
11. *Ibid.* (1162).
12. *Ibid.* (1162), also see, A. Chastel, *Léonard*, p.258.

13. Leonardo da Vinci, *Literary Works,* ed. Richter (1179).
14. E. MacCurdy, ed., *The Notebooks of Leonardo da Vinci,* vols. I and II (London, 1956), p. 83, Quaderni V24 r.
15. *Ibid.* p. 85, C.A. 119 v.a.
16. *Ibid.* p. 83, Windsor Drawings 12349 v.
17. E. MacCurdy ed., *The Notebooks,* vol. II, p. 444, Oxford Drawings Part ii, no. 7.
18. *Ibid.* vol. I. p.83, Windsor Drawings 12349 v.
19. *Dr. Faust,* trans. T. Hedderwick (London, 1887).
20. Thomas Mann, *Doctor Faustus,* trans. H.T. Lowe-Porter (New York, 1948), p. 243.
21. Goethe, *'Faust',* part II, trans. A. Swanwick (London, 1902), p. 263 (870).
22. K. Clark, *Leonardo da Vinci,* p. 69.
23. Goethe, *Faust,* part I, trans. F.G. Schmidt (New York, 1935), p. 50.
24. K. Clark, *Leonardo da Vinci,* pp. 14-16, 86-89; and 'Leonardo da Vinci, a note on the relation between his science and his art', *History Today,* 11 (May, 1952) pp. 301-313.
25. K. Clark, *Leonardo da Vinci,* p. 87.
26. Leonardo da Vinci, *Codex Madrid,* 'the two unpublished manuscripts of Leonardo da Vinci in the Biblioteca Nacional of Madrid,' ed. Ladislao Reti, *The Burlington Magazine,* (I. Jan. 1968, II, Febr. 1968) I, p.21.
27. K. Clark, *Leonardo da Vinci,* p. 89.
28. Leonardo da Vinci, *Codex Madrid,* p. 18.
29. Christopher Marlowe, *The tragical history of the life and death of Doctor Faustus,* reconstructed by W.W. Greg (Oxford, 1950), I, iii, 100-110.
30. C. Marlowe, *Faust,* 60, 'A sound magician is a demi-God'.
31. Rudolf and Margot Wittkower, *Born under Saturn* (London, 1963), see the caption of Fig. 11, and p. 82.
32. Leonardo da Vinci, *Literary Works,* ed. Richter (494).
33. T. Mann, *Doctor Faustus,* pp. 248-249.
34. Goethe, *Faust,* part II, p. 220.
35. R. and M. Wittkower, *Saturn,* p. 74.
36. Leonardo da Vinci, *Literary Works,* ed. Richter (1357A).
37. Goethe, *Faust,* part II, p. 53.
38. Goethe, *Faust,* part II, p. 15.
39. Leonardo da Vinci, *Notebooks,* ed. MacCurdy, vol. I, p. 69, H. 67 (19) r.
40. Leonardo da Vinci, *Literary Works,* ed. Richter (1132).
41. *Ibid.* (1134).
42. Leonardo da Vinci, *Notebooks,* ed. MacCurdy, p. 60, C.A. 71r.A. Also cf. André Chastel, *Léonardo et la culture,* pp. 254, 255.

43. *Ibid.* p.60, C.A. 71v A.
44. Goethe, *Faust,* part II, p. 263 (870).
45. *Ibid.* p. 401 (560).
46. London, 1962.
47. K. Eissler, *Leonardo da Vinci,* p. 158.
48. Ernst Kris, *Psychoanalytic Explorations in Art* (London, 1953). Kris was not purposefully trying to support Eissler.
49. *Ibid.* p. 113; Kris writes that Leonardo was the first artist to remark so perceptively upon the relationship between artist and model.
50. This was especially true in a period when the style was still basically naturalistic. The face, the figure, and specific iconographical symbols were the language of representation, even of the representation of highly abstract mental or spiritual states of mind.
51. K. Clark, *Leonardo da Vinci,* p. 95.
52. *Ibid.* p. 148.

5

HARMONY AND NATURALISM IN MUSIC

Through music's power you happily venture through death's dark night.

The Magic Flute

The hierarchy

The idea of good proportion and its setting in a wider assumption of natural harmony is now familiar. This familiarity has been developed from sources that are far removed both in time and spirit from the original conceptions of such a world order. The idea of universal harmony originated in Pythagorean and Platonic philosophy where the cosmic order was one based on geometric and musical principles.[1] This scheme was adopted and revitalized by Neo-Platonists and some Renaissance humanists.

Several examples of conceptions of harmony in theories of art and architecture, and also in suppositions about nature and reality have been brought forward. Up to now it has been my point to stress how comparatively little emphasis was placed on the hierarchical content of the examples. However, concepts with a pronounced hierarchical content are to be found within both classical and medieval expressions of this idea. At this point, I want to call attention to the hierarchical strain in the tradition, and to emphasize that any application of ideal proportions in man-made works was generally believed to be an application far removed from the creator's use of proportions in the design of the universe. When the creator devised an imitation or replica of his concept, in making the universe, he already was seen to be making his imitation different from his plan. For example, it was necessary for the reproduction to possess materiality.[2] All further applications of the ideas, insofar as men recognize them, either from their analogues in experience and/or from innate foreknowledge, all of these analogies generally are seen to be even more removed from the parental ideas. Human works devised in the light of divine ideas are partially analogous to them, but also different and inferior. Here is St. Augustine's view of this kind of distinction:

But there is as great a difference between the wisdom which
creates and the wisdom which is created as between the Light
which enlightens and the light which receives its brilliance by
reflection, or between the Justice which brings justification and
justice which results from it.[3]

According to St. Augustine, 'Wisdom is the first of all created
things.'[4] After this characteristic was placed by God in the universe, the many individual manifestations of it follow. In terrestrial nature, it is situated in the mind of man. However, each
manifestation of wisdom is less than wisdom as it is in the universe. So each example of it is essentially different from the
first created wisdom, and even more, from wisdom as it is in
the divine source.

Thus, the fact that there are material embodiments or
replicas of eternal ideas can lead to confusion. For instance,
what is the true relation of *The Ideas* or God's plan to the principles of geometry or music, and further, what is their relation to the end products in which these sciences are applied?
How does geometry stand with relation to building, town planning, or painting; and, how does theory of music stand with
relation to composition, singing, or to the playing of instruments, when both the theories and the products involve different levels of replication of the parental conception? The per-
plexity caused by these various levels of reproduction can be
traced back to Plato's *Timaeus*.

The most perfect thing here is the plan. The universe is the
initial replica of the plan, and it is brought about by the
maker's intermingling of material elements with soul or spirit.
Historically the hierarchical emphasis in this classical model
was advanced in a long tradition of interpretation by early
Christian thinkers, themselves exceedingly preoccupied with
distinctions between matter and spirit. And also, in the course
of time, Plato's original qualitative distinction was reinforced
by a different, but overlapping set of hierarchical ideas. These
were developed from Aristotelian physics and philosophy
where distinctions of rank or degree were seen to be gradu-
ated both within the physical universe and in all being. Base
and high, corrupt and pure, mutable and immutable are all
terms that indicate the kinds of distinction drawn between
things in the Aristotelian tradition. These terms were applied
to the cosmos where all matter between its centre, the earth,
and the moon was looked on as inferior to the material of the
other planets and stars. Aristotle's model of ever dininishing
excellence, from the unmoved mover to the most humble existing
thing, became incorporated in Neo-Platonism and in medieval
Christian philosophy.

The Platonic emphasis in Neo-Platonism placed a somewhat different accent and vocabulary within this long tradition. The maker's designs, the archetypes, or, most often, The Ideas, were, as we have seen, unchanging and eternal and above the universe. The further products of the initial blend of material and spirit in the phsyical universe were products of the mind, for example mathematics and music, and then works. These works were of compositions or designed objects made with the guidance of the concepts of the mind. The vocabulary of this set of distinctions hinges on the initial separation of spirit and body. Thus, finite and infinite, other and same, partial and absolute, mortal and immortal are all expressions belonging to Neo-Platonic thinking. It goes without saying that these two related hierarchies mixed and intermingled over and over in varying degrees and in the course of time.[5] We have had an example of this in Cusa's efforts to purge Aristotelian ideas and modify the Platonic scheme while still preserving the distinction that he thought essential, that is, that of quality between God and all that descends from Him.

We are also aware that neither Alberti nor Leonardo accentuated a many-levelled hierarchy. Taking their cues, among others, from a Cusan view of knowledge, they formed an idea of direct recognition. Once more, briefly, this was a supposition about the ability of the trained intellect to see and recognize absolutely good proportions and the principles and causes of things within the many examples of nature. What did this do to the hierarchies? In the first place it pushed aside many of the Aristotelian distinctions, especially Aristotle's evaluation of space in terms of its proximity to bodies. As these Renaissance artists handled and viewed space geometrically within their own work they also determined that this geometrical view represented the real principles of things in the universe. Bodies gave space dimensions but not qualities. Space must be described geometrically, just as forms are. In this way they did not so much confront the Aristotelian categories as move away from them through their emphasis on mathematics. In the light of this emphasis, the very low status that Aristotle gave to human works was not satisfactory. Certainly, Alberti and Leonardo both contradicted this low evaluation for any number of obvious reasons. However, it was Cusa who actually did the philosophical work of showing why Aristotelian physics was incorrect in its description of the cosmos. There was no clear imperative for the artistic community to approach the task in this way. Rather, the fifteenth-century scientific artists formed a receiving ground for Pythagorean, Platonic, Boethian, Vitruvian and, sometimes, Cusan ideas. They associated this background with the thoughts of some of the Roman rhetoricians who had also contradicted Aristotle's low opinion of human works. In later chapters I will say more about this Roman background. I think that the Cusan view of knowledge was especially appealing to the artist. For one thing, it elevated the status of the mind in terms of the mind's ability to develop and employ mathematical disciplines; and, perhaps most important, it revealed the refinement and perfection of the mind's predictive and comprehensive powers as coming from a constant dialogue with experience.

By contrast, Cusa's own mentor, St. Augustine, saw experience as something like a pinprick that stirred the mind. Once stirred, the mind drew into its own inner territory, drawing back from the 'confusion of images' pressing upon it. When Cusanus created this vision of the development of knowledge as the result of a constant exchange between the mind and experience, but with the important addition of learned ignorance, or a leap to contemplation that always began where experience ended, he was not outwardly contradicting his own source in Augustine. Instead Cusa was shifting emphasis from St. Augustine's largely contemplative process to a process of illumination that truly involved experience. However, it did not even stop at that because Cusa also talked of the place where the mind could still ask but experience could not answer. Intellectual desire oversteps the reasoned analysis of experience. A visual example of this sort of relationship between experience, reason and desire, might be seen in Leonardo's St. John. Real in the depiction of flesh, bone and muscle, in the textures and forms of the image, the figure, John, points upwards towards nothing and secretly smiles. The picture shows nature naturalistically, as men see it; the picture, as a product, is also the embodiment of its maker's understanding, of the idea in the artist's mind. But beyond this, the depicted attitude of St. John indicates something that cannot really be symbolized. Here Leonardo suggests a limit of the symbols of experience in the attempt to indicate qualities like wisdom and spirit. Leonardo does not turn from experience but yearns beyond it, for wholeness, unity and rest.

Perhaps for Leonardo, and for Cusa, before him, the sciences of men's minds made up the human understanding of the incorporation of God's concept, in the whole, and in the parts of nature. Apart from this, only God is the origin and source. So, insofar as God's plan can be understood at all, it must be approached from the sciences of the mind.

The incorporation of the divine concept in the universe was seen to have happened in a manner and on a scale beyond human comprehension. However, although human science, for example, mathematics, only reflected God's unity in its own harmonies, and although that science had to be understood in a piecemeal fashion, still, in the variety of its forms and the proportions between numbers, mathematics could describe the reality of examples in nature. This is not a direct knowledge of God, but it promises a very real knowledge of his works.

These lines of thinking actually do limit the traditional hierarchies to the most overt distinctions; first, between God as God is, and God as he limits himself within the forms of created things, and second, within man, between spirit, soul and intellect, on the one hand, and the body. Although no one can claim that these are not hierarchical notions, the overall line of thought does place the human understanding and human works much closer to their origin, reality and end.

In this spirit Leonardo's arguments, that were intended to dignify and elevate painting, stressed the geometry of painting to contradict those who regarded it as a purely manual skill. It was a science not just a technique. As the science of vision, perspective had long had the status of a branch of mathematics. Music held a similar status, but less in terms of what was actually written and heard than in terms of its being established in the quadrivium, established as number in sound.

By the sixteenth century many composers and musicians wanted to clarify the issue and base the status of music upon the practice of music.

But, for the moment, returning to the example of Leonardo, he was aware that painting was as much the study of colour, light and shade, and life, as it was of perspective and form. However, he himself esteemed the mathematical basis as a natural reason. Even purely physical things like the elements could be reduced to a mathematical essence.

An awareness of the situation of music in the sixteenth century can be built upon this example from Leonardo and upon the general discussion of traditional hierarchies. For example, one way to make sense of the superior status that traditional theory accorded to vocal music above instrumental music, is by grasping the implications of hierarchical distinctions. Vocal music was regarded as an activity of the mind. Music was conceived and understood in the mind as it was sung. Instrument players, however, were thought to be technicians. They used the facilities of their objects, the instruments. So, in theory at least, sixteenth-century musicians were often classed down, just as painters had been over a century before.

Consequently, even in 1517, in the *Micrologus* of

Ornithoparchus published in Leipzig, the category of *Organical Music* was defined as music made by artificial instruments. The voice was called a natural instrument. Musicians using artificial instruments were not supposed to have been engaging in the intellectual part of music, although it was admitted that they might be aware of that part as well.

From the present point of view, a treatise like the *Micrologus* seems to face backwards, its inspirations came from medieval traditions of idealistic music theory. Much of the substance of such traditions had been formulated in Boethius' *De Musica* where he set out the Pythagorean idea of music for subsequent generations. This was the source that thinkers had in order to tell them about Pythagorean musical ideas.

Boethius ascribed a wide variety of powers to music. He repeated Platonic and Aristotelian views of its moral and educative potential. He also believed in special powers that music was supposed to have had, powers to affect the emotions. Rightly used, music could soothe anger and calm violent states of mind. Important categories like *musica mundana* (the harmony of the spheres) and *musica humana* (the seasons and the elements) are found in Boethius. *Musica humana,* though less exalted than that of the spheres, was an important and complex category, for among other things, it involved the harmony of the human body, its health. This was seen in the balance of the humours, and also in a psycho-spiritual harmony, the harmony of body, spirit, and soul. While in the body, the soul itself was actively involved in balancing reason and instinct.[6]

The guiding aesthetic of Boethius is expressed in the, now familiar, analogical form. Men can easily recognize a triangle when they see one, but, at the same time, they cannot know the properties of a triangle *a priori*. They must learn arithmetic and geometry to understand these properties. In the same way men have to study the mathematical sciences to know what they hear; for, human beings appreciate music by use of reason, not by the ear alone.[7] Although consonance and dissonance are initially perceived, they are not understood until men comprehend them through the science of number. Boethius calls consonant intervals natural. They reflect the harmony of the universe.[8] This harmony was seen to be based on the proportional relationships between things, and within things. For example, between macrocosm and microcosm, and within the microcosm, between the humours, etc. Any number of examples could be given where balance or harmony is stressed, rather than the physical qualities of the things. The four seasons are not made out of the same physical stuff that music is made out of, but the order of the seasons is seen as a harmony corresponding to rightly ordered music. Beyond this, there is an implied mathematical reductionism. Things that appear different, bodies, sounds, smells, etc. can all be reduced to a mathematical essence. The view of proportion and order is true to the source in Plato's *Timaeus* where harmony is expressed in terms of a series of proportions and blends that make up the universe on the physical level and the soul of the world on the spiritual level. In this mood Boethius' conceptions are also strictly hierarchical. Harmonies played out on instruments do express the harmony of nature, but at a very low level. As concepts are not material, the understanding of harmony is superior. However, concepts are still partial and form a limited understanding of universal harmony. Thus, this tradition placed the harmony of the spheres above these other levels. Here, the intrusion of medieval Aristotelian thinking is clear. Not only were the spheres made of superior stuff, but the celestial music was the music that was directly descended from the creation.

At the beginning of the sixteenth century, the philosophical and idealistic part of music theory, as distinguished from the practical part, was generally formulated in these traditional hierarchical terms. However, a radical change took place during this century. It took the form of a very real abatement of emphasis on this hierarchy. This shift resembles earlier changes in the visual arts, and man's view of his understanding of nature.

The new theory moved actual music-making near to its presumed natural principles. From exalted theory and bastard practice, we move to a practice that is seen as a living demonstration of the ideal. The terms in which this was done are not the same as those that have been shown in the Cusan view of knowledge; although they were still substantially Neo-Platonic in character. Certainly, men continued to believe that music could educate, and that it had powers to embody the harmony of nature. However, this notion, the idea of harmony itself was revised and was newly conceived of in terms far broader than those of traditional theory. The old relation between sweet sounds and harmonious numbers survived, but only as one manifestation of the grander harmony of nature and of its presentation in music. Discord and dissonance were as much a part of this newly conceived harmony as was beauty.

Consonance

One of the central issues of sixteenth-century theory was the treatment of consonance and dissonance in music. The position of consonant sound as it related to the more general concept of natural harmony was being examined. Consonance is the pleasing effect of the simultaneous sounding of a pair of, or several, concordant notes. This effect is the result of the ratios of the vibrations between the notes concerned. Simple ratios (those between small numbers) were observed to produce sounds that were concordant. Ratios between higher numbers resulted in increasingly discordant sounds.[9] Here is a list of the combinations that were traditionally accepted as consonant: Unison, 1:1, Octave, 2:1, Fifth, 3:2, Fourth, 4:3, these were considered the perfect consonances. The Major Third, 5:4, Minor Third, 6:5, Major Sixth, 5:3, Minor Sixth, 8:5, and the Major Second, 9:8 were also accepted but as having imperfect consonance. Perfect consonance, imperfect consonance, and indeed dissonance, were used in polyphonic music but, in the sixteenth century, the imperfect ratios were still felt to require philosophical justification. On the other hand, the current view, that concordance is more the result of the placement of specific harmonies within a whole composition rather than the result of complementary ratios already began to make its appearance.

If ratios between the first four numbers, and gradually between the first six numbers, were considered consonant, almost all other combinations were considered dissonant.[10] These preferences hark back to the views that were attributed to Pythagoras. He was supposed to have discovered that ratios between small numbers characterized concordant sounds and thence he concluded eventually that all nature consisted of a harmony which arose out of number.[11] We recognize that this came to be the Boethian point of view.

These theories are recognizably similar to some features of Leon Battista Alberti's ideas, especially about architecture. The similarity is not surprising, for Vitruvius, Alberti's main source of inspiration, was himself inspired by the Boethian scheme. However, architectural theory was not the only discipline to assimilate Boethian harmonic ratios in the Renaissance. The work of Alberti himself testifies to the common fact that the dividing line between architect and painter could be a faint one. Thus, the architect who envisaged the imitation of nature on the basis of harmony and proportion, and the painter who began to talk of the imitation of nature both in mathematical terms, and in terms of naturalistic design, were often the same person.

Two complementary goals were concurrent; one, to make a replica in a work that was based on mathematical proportions and geometrical forms, the other, to make a replica in a work that so resembled nature, either in its appearance or in its effects, that it recreated the truth of experience for the audience. It is evident that the second goal might be seen to be the inevitable consequence of the first. Certainly, both goals were intermingled in the minds of many artists and theoreticians of music. In the fifteenth and early sixteenth centuries some of the theoreticians were really philosophers more than musicians. This tradition continues, as will be illustrated in the course of this chapter. Mersenne is a fine example of it. But in the sixteenth century a lot of composer-theorists were popular too. These musicians tended to think more about producing effects than about the pure beauty of numbers. Thus there is a point in the history of the theory of music where these goals began to part company. For although Alberti had never tested the numbers he took to be harmonious, among them, the ratios of consonance, sixteenth-century music theorists were sometimes moved to make tests and acoustical experiments. The results of these experiments somewhat confused the status formerly granted to the consonant ratios. Perhaps other elements in music were even more important in the production of the natural powers of music. Acoustical tests and a whole world of other cultural pressures, having to do with the changing desires of composers and of the tastes of the musical public, eventually shifted the analogy between music and nature from one of proportion and numbers to one based on *imitazione* in the wider sense. In the end, this rather more obscure goal was the one that superseded the older traditional one based primarily on truly beautiful numbers.[12]

Traditional ideals applied to music in the fifteenth and sixteenth centuries

I allude to a world of other pressures but, in order to illustrate changing patterns in the role of music and its analogy with nature, it is best to begin with the theories that show the influence of Boethius. The gradual development of a modern analogy between music and nature can be best understood by beginning at this final point of medieval philosophical traditions.

An older contemporary of Alberti's, Ugolino of Orvieto (c. 1380- after 1457), is describing as having been rector of San Antonio di Rivaldini, but as having occupied himself principally as both a composer and theoretician of music. Ugolino had ideas that illustrate the traditional cosmology which conceptualized music as the portrayer of number in sound. He indicates one way in which the conception of harmony was expressed in musical theory at the beginning of the fifteenth century.[13] His ideas represent a traditional handling of theory based on Boethian inspiration. For example, he reiterates the mistrust of the senses regarding music, a discipline that was only truly comprehended in the mind and by powers of reason.[14] On the basis of this type of supposition he drew an analogy between speculation, in which he includes the understanding of music, and ethics. Because these two are complementary, throughout all the ages the beauty of good proportion in sound will inevitably delight men's souls in the same way as reason and propriety in thought and behaviour. This analogy, which we recall as one of Alberti's views, contains a general assumption of complementarity between the whole and all the parts of nature. Proportion or harmony is the uniting feature, and it is interesting to see that mathematically based proportions are considered as parallel to a kind of social decorum.

Men recognize harmony by means of the faculty of reason and their sensitivity to harmony is innate, implanted in the character of their minds and souls. The harmonious scheme prevails both inside men and throughout nature. Thus, it is written in the *Micrologus*:

> What other power doth sober and glue that spiritual strength, which is imbued with an intellect to a mortal and earthly frame, than that music which every man that descends into himself finds in himself? . . .Hence it is that we loathe and abhor discords and are delighted when we hear harmonical concords, because we know there is in ourselves the like concord.

The tradition is also evident in the kinds of categories used in the *Micrologus. Harmonical* music is described as a weighing of the differences between high and low sounds by the senses and by reason. In fact, it is 'a cunning bringing forth' of music with the voice accompanied by instruments, together with the judging of all those sounds.[15] He distinguished various categories of music. *Inspective* and *Active* music involve judgement and the use of reason; these are in contrast to the category *Organical* music, which means purely instrumental music.

The music or harmony which is imprinted in the soul is not simply the result of any pleasing group of sounds. Thought, and the kind of contemplation that involves a searching within the self must also be involved in the judgement of the good or beautiful in music. This then is the good that is truly pleasing and uplifting. In all this the senses remain unglorified. Ornithoparchus speaks of men 'pondering sounds', and by contrast, of hearing as 'a decision of the ears, whose judgement is dull'. It seems clear that Ornithoparchus was by no means contending for a closer complementarity between perception by the senses and by reason, a complementarity that clearly emerges in the earlier artistic theories of Alberti or in the contemporary thought of Leonardo. Knowing this, it is startling to find that John Dowland translated Ornithoparchus' work into English as late as 1609 when the effect of empiricism on music theory was supposed to have made assumptions like these outmoded.

Getting back to the traditional conception of music as sound in number, number was involved with music in three absolutely basic ways. First, music is measured (rhythm). Second, each tone has a numerical equivalent in the frequency of vibrations required to produce that particular tone (pitch). Third, there is the involvement of number in the intervals made by combinations of two or more notes (harmony).[16] The last of these, involving the intervals between the notes, their consonance or dissonance, eventually became one issue around which much theoretical discussion hinged. Traditionally oriented theorists still gave absolute endorsement to ratios between the first four numbers. However, these old boundaries had already been disregarded by earlier practitioners.

The musical cosmology that had been inherited from Boethius had distinguished three different levels of music in nature. These were the *mundana*, the *humana*, and instrumental music, and they were arranged in a descending order on a hierarchical scale. Often, medieval descriptions of such a scale were far more elaborate. This tendency to elaborate the hierarchy is still apparent in the fifteenth century. Ugolino provides examples of this.

Of primary importance is the *Musica Caelestis*. This is the plan itself. It is the foundation of nature and the beginning of music at the same time, and its essence is expressed by number. The replica which immediately follows in this hierarchy is the *Musica Mundana*. This is the harmony which is associated particularly with the orbits of celestial bodies but also with the connections that exist between the elements, and the changes of the seasons.[17] *Musica Mundana* receives harmonic proportions through the agency of *Musica Caelestis*.[18] Evidently the proportions of the *Mundana* approximate those of the *Caelestis* and Harmony is introduced into this replica by emanation from the more exalted *Caelestis*. The following description of the 'Harmony of the Spheres' gives an example of the traditional music theorists' belief in the essential connection between musical harmony and physical nature.

> When God . . . had devised to make this world movable, it was
> necessary that he should govern it by some acute and moving
> power . . . now that motion, i.e. the motion of celestial bodies
> (because it is the swiftest of all other and most regular) is not
> without sound: for it must needs be that a sound be made of the
> very wheeling of the orbs . . . the like said Boethius, how can this
> quick moving frame of the world whirl about with a dumb and
> silent motion? From this tuning of the heaven there cannot be
> removed a certain order of Harmony . . . This harmony hath
> been observed out of the consent of the heavens, the knitting
> together of the elements and the variety of times . . . The world is
> God's Organ . . . We cannot hear this sound . . . (and this) is
> because the greatness of the sound doth exceed the sense of our
> ears. But whether we admit this Harmonical sound of the
> Heavens or no . . . certain it is, that the grand Work-Master of
> this *Mundane Fabrick* made all things in number, weight, and
> measure, wherein principally Mundane Music doth consist.[19]

The reference to God as one who works or plays, and to nature
as the instrument which is played, illustrates once more a distinction between harmony in the form of ideas in the mind and
harmony as it is reproduced in things. As was said, this distinction was implicit in the original conception of analogy between
the whole and the parts of nature. Spirit and intellect together
form the receptacle of innate principles of harmony which are
then imparted to harmonious works. Mathematics and music
are the disciplines which typify these principles in the most
abstract forms accessible to men's reason. However, nature has
mysteries that reason cannot fully comprehend. Man depends
upon intellectual apprehension and on revelation for his vision
of the divine mystery.

The theories of music of sixteenth-century humanists were
developed along lines that extended classical traditions.
Emphasis shifted somewhat from cosmology to Plato's views
on education, and to the decorum of Horace's *Ars Poetica*. Music
was seen to be both emotive and educative. Musical humanists
intended it to be employed as a vehicle to awaken men to harmony, both the inner harmony of the soul, and the harmony
that was being perfected in human experience. As historians
approach the seventeenth century the language of this movement often changes. Thinkers refer to the harmonious character of divine providence and its lawful disposition.

Despite the continuance of traditional values in music theory,
there was also a definite and passionate search for the terms
with which to express the newer vision of harmony. A renewed
desire to exploit the presumed powers of music involved the
musical humanists in a massive reappraisal of traditional

sources, and simultaneously, in the formulation of new styles of composition, new aesthetic theories, and, in some cases, in the scientific exploration of the physical nature of music.

In later generations, these acoustic interests were further enlarged, and they eventually came to involve studies of the nature of hearing and the physics of sound.

Thus, the sixteenth century marks the beginning of absolutely fundamental changes in the philosophy of music, the explanation of music's meanings. While changes in the actual music had already been going on. However, I am concentrating upon the evolution of ideas that supported music and that gave it its status in the cultural world. Harmony that had once been envisaged as the natural relations between numbers, came to be formulated on a broader, but far more ambiguous basis.[20] This basis emphasized new complementarities, for instance, between human hearing and consonant or dissonant tones, or, on a more general level, between the psychological make-up of men, the emotions or passions, and the overall experience of good music. In an instance like this it was argued that men appreciated the artistic use of dissonance, despite the unpleasing sounds, precisely because those sounds might be adding to the emotional dimensions and dramatic representation within the music. Other new parallels were beginning to be made between human emotions, actions, attitudes and events in the natural world, and the imitation of all of these by music. From music, as a reproduction in sound of a formal ideal of proportion expressed in number, the analogy is extended to envisage music as an imitation or reproduction of the human experience of nature. It is assumed that the perceptive equipment of man, the hearing, the mind, the sensitivities of the soul, are devised in such a way that true music can evoke not only the experience of pleasure through sound, but true meanings, conveyed and stimulated by good music. Music has the power to reproduce or recreate natural experience; therefore between music and nature there was an analogy based on replication. Some aspects of the development of this broader view of the harmony of nature as it is expressed in music is the subject of this and of parts of the following chapters.

A theoretical upheaval

At the beginning of the sixteenth century in Italy the philosophical position of music was still described in much the same terms that illustrations from Ugolino of Orvieto have indicated to us. This body of theory was not related to actual

practice. Already, in the ninth century, the development of
heterophony, and later of counterpoint, had led to violation of
the ideal ratios of consonance. A situation developed in which
the status of music as a discipline was still maintained and
argued for in terms of Pythagorean number theory, but, at the
same time, actual musical practice, and even the theory relating
directly to that practice, did not conform to the Pythagorean
ideals.

This discrepancy between the theory and practice of music-
making on the one hand, and the ideals which had traditionally
supported the elevated status of music on the other, did not
become painfully apparent until Renaissance humanists
became seriously interested in rediscovering and reviving the
music of the ancients. At this point, the Boethian type of
arguments which often prefaced treatises on music within
which their precepts were violated, became visible in an entirely
new way. The new visibility was partly caused by the long-term
weakening of a rigidly hierarchical structure. There had been a
weakening of the mode of thinking which permitted a
philosophical theory of music to be *real* and *true* on one level,
while practical music developed in its own way on another,
inferior, level. However, an even stronger reason for the
humanists' discomfort was their knowledge that Boethius was
supposed to have known the theories of the Greeks. Thus, as a
result of their interest in classical antiquity, humanists sought
somehow to apply those supposedly Greek ideals to current
practices. On the other hand, musicians who were sometimes
also humanists were imposed upon by the restrictions of the
traditional theories of music in the light of the musical inventions of the later Middle Ages and early Renaissance. The two
pressures, one from humanist scholars, who began to ask why
the effects were not being accomplished, the other, from musicians who wanted both freedom for their composition and also
the status that had been maintained by traditional theory -
these pressures together produced a theoretical upheaval.

The question arose as to whether the traditional ideals of
music might not be taken at face value and applied in the practice of music. In their attempt to answer this question the sixteenth-century theorists tried to reapply traditional theory to
practice and, at the same time, to perfect their knowledge of
such theory in order to refine its application to practice. Also,
at the same time, they were determined to preserve features of
modern music that they valued, especially the treasured invention of polyphonic and harmonic techniques. Frequently these
desires led to conflicts and contradictions in values, both between different theorists and even in the mind of a single man.

Inevitably, all this involved them in reinterpretations of theory and continual revaluations of current practices in the light of differing trends within that reinterpretation.

A lag between practice and the theoretical endorsement of it is exemplified many times over in sixteenth-century theory. For instance, Pietro Aron's (1495-1545) arguments justifying simultaneous composition for all voices appeared in the 1520s, long after the practice of simultaneous composition had been developed.[21] Similarly, in the latter half of the century, Gioseffo Zarlino (1517-1590) belatedly furnished theoretical recognition for use of ratios outside the first four numbers. The major and minor thirds and sixths that had been accorded practical recognition as consonant intervals within medieval polphony were only then given ideological justification.[22] These examples can give the impression that theorists were simply endorsing all current practices and disregarding the tenets of classical theory. But, this impression is misleading. The arguments that were devised to justify the new practices were most generally formulated with great care and attention to traditional philosophy. This was not primarily because a firm authority induced all theorists to do this. The whole justification of new practices and the simultaneous recall of old principles, both of these apparently opposing attitudes, bear witness to the same thing. They both express a renewed concern with the philosophy of music.

The arguments to justify practices that were already flourishing were, in fact, put forward because of a new mentality in the artistic world. Many composers and musicians were influenced by Renaissance humanism and Neo-Platonism, by the revival of the classics, by the reaffirmation of the special powers of music. Suddenly the interpretation of present music in the light of past philosophy became a compelling task. Those who did this were motivated by definite and insistent pressures within their contemporary culture.

Similarly, the philosophers who deplored all forms of support for the new styles were reacting to the same pressures. However, in these individuals this showed as a deep concern for the truth of traditional sources. With a few noted exceptions, they thought that practice had long since strayed from the true Boethian path. Now it was to be set right again. Many churchmen thought on these lines. For, in the late medieval musical world practical musicians had ignored the traditional rules, while they also took the status of music in the quadrivium for granted. However, the effects of the literary and artistic Renaissance gradually penetrated musical circles. Where theorists had once been lax, they progressively became zealous.

Theory was taken seriously once more.

It is best to clarify the use of terms like humanism and Neo-Platonism as these apply to sixteenth-century musical ideas. Early modernists frequently think of humanism as a definite and largely literary tradition, one that is not really synonymous with Renaissance Platonism, though clearly, they sometimes overlapped. As familiar examples, they certainly mingled in the mentalities of Cusa and Alberti. This sort of mingling of traditions applies to the whole field of music, and briefly, it worked in the following way.

The actual search for a new theory and practice of music in the sixteenth century had largely been inspired by the long established recovery of the culture of the ancient world. Stylistic trends within music were both forceful and important; but, the concurrent desire to recover and recreate the effective music of the ancients shows how the wider learned and artistic world was generally influencing thinking in this field. Shortly this will become clearer from an example of the views of the musical humanist Girolamo Mei. From him it will also be possible to show that other cultural realities were also part of this story. For one thing, there was no escape from the fact of the actual content of classical theory. A lot of this content was Platonic in its inspirations. So, the historians who enjoy separating and streaming things can certainly distinguish between humanist and Platonist influences, but they ought not to sever them. In and above the heritage from the Platonism of the late ancient world, music also received the attention of Ficino and the Florentine Platonists. From a variety of sources and traditions these academicians publicized the efficacy of music, its mental, medical and even magical powers. And these diverse roots mingled with the humanists' view of art, now musical art, art seen as the imitation of life.

Ancient sources, literary, philosophical and rhetorical, Greek and Roman, all of these captured the attention of humanist theorists. At the same time as they sought confirmation of what they felt was of value in recent practice, they also considered the possibility of making radical changes in that practice. These changes were to be devised in accordance with their reinterpretations of traditional literature. An example of one of the most radical of these proposed changes was the development of a body of opinion wanting to reinstate strict monody.

The concern and awareness of some Renaissance philosophers for current violation of the classical tenets is shown in the opinions of G. M. Artusi (1540-1613). Artusi was one of those who did not approve of the new styles of interpreting music as the imitation or replica of actual human experience. His bias against the histrionic interpretation of songs is clear:

> They (new masters) think only of satisfying the sense, caring lit-
> tle that the reason should enter here to judge their composi-
> tions. If such as these had read the ninth chapter of the first
> book of Boethius, and the first chapter of his fifth book, and the
> first chapter of the first book of Ptolemy, they would no doubt
> be of a different mind. They do not even think of looking at the
> volumes of Boethius . . . they are content to know how to string
> their notes together after their fashion and to teach the singers
> to sing their compositions, accompanying themselves with many
> movements of the body, and in the end they let themselves go to
> such an extent that they seem to be actually dying . . . this is the
> perfection of their music. (Second discourse, on the dawn of the
> seventeenth day)[23]

Artusi's concern manifests itself in an appeal to philosophical tradition. However, theorists and musicians who wished to accommodate new trends, both in composition and style of per- formance, also used the inspiration of the supposedly ideal music of the Greeks to justify their own revived interpretations of the essential relationship between music and nature. The whole later Renaissance idea of music as an imitation of experi- ence depended upon assumptions which posited a special rela- tionship between true music and the human mind and soul. And, as we have said, these assumptions had long been carried on in past traditions together with the ruling assumptions involving music and numbers. As an example, Giovanni di Bardi (1534-1612), the patron of the Florentine *Camerata*, an important group of humanist music theorists that included the father of Galileo, Vincenzo Galilei, used the same body of cita- tion to develop his modern arguments. He wrote, or had pub- lished in his name, an affirmation of the primary importance of the complementarity between words and music. This type of complementarity was thought of as essential to the production of a catharsis similar to that produced by Greek tragedy.

> . . . Just as the soul is nobler than the body, so the words are
> nobler than the counterpoint. . . .

A belief in ideal proportion and natural harmony lies at the back of this opinion:

> . . . Would it not seem ridiculous if, walking in the public square,
> you saw a servant followed by his master and commanding him,
> or a boy who wanted to instruct his father or his tutor? The
> divine Cipriano [Cipriano de Rore] towards the end of his life.

was well aware how very grave an error this was in the counterpoint of his day. For this reason, straining every fibre of his
genius, he devoted himself to making the verse and the sound
of the words thoroughly intelligible in his madrigals . . .For this
great man told me himself, in Venice, that this was the true
manner of composing and a different one. . .he would in my
opinion have restored the music combining several melodies to a
degree of perfection from which others might easily have
returned it little by little to that true and perfect music so highly
praised by the ancients.[24]

Bardi's concept of harmony as a just proportion between text
and music in which the text prevails in and above the music is
recognizable and similar to the many other ideas of decorum
which have been cited. The appropriate relation between
words and sounds is not just in the interest of good taste. This
idea also contains assumptions of philosophical value. For, in
addition to just tastefulness in music there is the 'true' or 'perfect' music.

The ideals of Bardi and the Camerata are also illustrated in
the thoughts of Giulio Caccini (1550-1610). Caccini became
famous for his compositions and performances for solo voice in
monodic style. He expressed his own debt of gratitude to the
Bardi circle:

> I can truly say that I learned more than I learned in thirty years'
> study of counterpoint from the wise discussions I heard when
> there flourished in Florence the brilliant Camerata of the illus-
> trious Giovanni di Bardi, count of Vernio, which I frequented, and
> where there gathered not only a great part of the nobility, but
> also the best musicians and men of genius, poets and
> philosophers of the city. These learned gentlemen always
> encouraged me, and with clear reasoning persuaded me not to
> adhere to that type of music which, not permitting the words to
> be clearly understood, distorts the idea and the line (prosody),
> now lengthening, now shortening the syllables in order to make
> them fit the counterpoint, that destroyer of poetry. They urged
> me to adhere instead to that style so highly lauded by Plato and
> other philosophers who maintained that music is nothing if not
> words and rhythm first, and sound last, and not to the contrary.
> For if one is to penetrate other people's minds and produce
> those wonderful effects admired by the writers, it cannot be
> achieved by counterpoint in modern [15th and 16th century]
> music . . . .[15]

The idea of music as a vehicle of ideas, composed with the
purpose of penetrating the minds of men and producing the
renowned effects, seems to have been the central topic in the
Bardi circle. This idea of music was not exclusive to that group.

The same idea is apparent within the following citation of a treatise written earlier in the century. Glarean(us) (1488-1563) reveals his own enthusiasm for the absolute nature of harmony described in classical theory of music by the way in which he praises (though not unreservedly) the great contemporary composer Josquin des Prés. By contrast to Artusi, Glarean already shows sympathy to the idea of music as the imitator and inciter of human experience and passion. His sympathy expresses his concern with both the refinement of current practice and the reinterpretation of classical theory. Thus he was interested in tonality and the proper use of the modes. Glarean criticizes Josquin in the light of his own interests. 'If this man (Josquin des Prés) ... had had an understanding of the twelve modes and of the truth of musical theory, Nature could have brought forth nothing more majestic and magnificent in this art. ...' Glarean proceeds, remarking on the unbridled temperament of Josquin but concludes his appreciation with the high compliment of a comparison between Josquin and Virgil. Both have a feeling for the good proportion of the appropriate metre and rhythm to the passion which is described in the text. This awareness enables Josquin to write soul-inciting music.

> No one has more effectively expressed the passions of the soul in music than this symphonist ... for just as Maro, with his natural facility, was accustomed to adapt his poem to his subject so as to set weighty matters before the eyes of his readers with close-packed spondees, fleeting ones [matters], with unmixed dactyls ... to use words suited to his every subject, in short, to undertake nothing inappropriately; as Flaccus says of Homer, so our Josquin, where his matter requires it, now advances with impetuous and precipitate notes, now intones his subject in long-drawn tones, and, to sum up, has brought forth nothing that was not delightful to the ear, and approved as ingenious by the learned . . . . [26]

This quest for an appropriate balance between metre, rhythm, and mood continued right into the seventeenth century. The desire is illustrated in Claudio Monteverdi's (1567-1643) description of his invention of a style of composition that expressed angry moods, the *agitato* style. He also clearly states that his inspiration was from Plato and Boethius. Notice that it is Boethius' general idea about the effect of music on men, and not a theory of consonance and dissonance that is cited. Monteverdi begins his description by approving the idea of the 'best philosophers' that anger, serenity, and humility are the principal passions of the soul. He also agrees that these passions are imitated in the nature of the human voice. The passions have their analogues in vocal sounds. Although he managed to find past compositions in the soft and moderate styles he found no example of an agitated style. The following is a description of Monteverdi's attempt to recreate that style:

> Plato describes the first in the third book of his *Rhetoric* in these words: 'Take that harmony which would fittingly imitate the brave man going to war' [*Republic*, 399 A]. Knowing that contrasts are what move our souls, and that such is the aim of all good music . . . as Boethius asserts: 'Music is a part of us, and either ennobles or degrades our behaviour.' . . . I set myself with no little study and zeal to rediscover this style. . . .[27]

The best philosophers, he continued, advised pyrrhic or fast tempos for agitated and warlike dances and slow spondaic tempos for their opposites. Hence he thought of whole notes and proposed that each whole note (semibreve) correspond to a spondee. Then he reduced these to sixteenth notes (sixteen semichromes) struck one after another and joined with words that expressed anger and scorn. Then he turned to the 'divine Tasso' as the poet who best expressed in words all the emotions that he was depicting. In this way Monteverdi decided to set the combat of Tancred and Clorinda to music. He says that he made this selection in order to be able to portray the contrasting passions that are aroused by war, prayer and death.

So, briefly, the situation of music theory and practice in the Renaissance was one of revival and reinterpretation going on at the same time. Restrictions imposed by Pythagorean concepts had only been restrictions of abstract theory until the time when humanists took the application of that theory absolutely seriously. Then they began to reform it, in terms of the sources, and also of contemporary standards of good practice. As a consequence they invented new goals for composition. One aspect of this process was to provoke a real scientific and aesthetic examination of the relationship between pleasure in sound and meaning in music. They also developed the broader concept of natural harmony in music. In it, number still had importance, especially in the area of rhythm and metre, but the idea that music had one or another of a variety of means by which it could imitate and reproduce experience engulfed the narrower traditional issue of natural numbers. As far as the aesthetics of music went, the whole question of consonance and dissonance was eventually resolved in terms of broader conceptions of harmony. Discord was accepted because it could provide dramatic effects. Stylistically this might be comparable to the acceptance of formally discordant relationships in Mannerist painting. Discordance added scope to the panorama of meanings that could be signified in compositions; by enlightened use of it, created works could imitate and even embody the whole range of human experience. Here the simply formally beautiful and the true have parted company.

This distinction is particularly pertinent to the arts. However, because natural philosophy is also part of this cultural configuration, note that the shift in stress away from numbers in the aesthetics of music, does not hold for acoustics or for general scientific fields. Galileo himself asserted the primary reality of only form, movement and number. These things altered material and affected the senses, and then the senses reported to men in odours, tastes and sounds, etc.

Even in music, although the stress shifted away from the issue of consonance, this did not always mean a break with the assumption that numbers were the basis of reality. All the attempts to match rhythm in music with poetic metre belong to this company of ideas. Our emotions or the animal spirits or something in our make-up was seen to have natural rhythm, or a natural attunement to the created rhythms of the artist. In all this, ugliness could be appropriate; for by this time, harmony connoted the artist's unravelling of all facets of nature and reality. Art did not just present sweetness; it was, in fact, the agent that raised all experience so that the mind and soul of man could be awakened to harmony. Thus, men came to speak of the wonderful variety of nature, and of how this could move the soul by means of the presentation of shades, moods and contrasts. Zarlino shows this view:

> Thus, the ancient musicians judged that they should admit in composition not only the consonances which they called perfect and those which they called imperfect, but dissonances also, knowing that their compositions would thus attain to greater beauty and elegance than they would without them.

True beauty then, or true elegance, consisted of a great deal more than adherence to consonant ratios:

> For they knew very well that harmony can arise only from things that are among themselves diverse, discordant and contrary, and not from things that are in complete agreement.[28]

The idea of ancient music as inspiration

When the word modern is applied to theorists like Zarlino, or those of the Camerata, it raises some problems. It can easily be confused with Vincenzo Galilei's use of the expression, 'the moderns', by which he meant the contrapuntalists of the previous one hundred and fifty years. He regarded these as indifferent to classical sources. Humanists criticized the so-called moderns who composed in the style of the fifteenth and early sixteenth centuries. This type of criticism was offered by Vincenzo Galilei (1533-1591):

> For all the height of excellence of the practical music of the moderns, there is not heard or seen today the slightest sign of its accomplishing what ancient music accomplished, nor do we read that it accomplished it fifty or a hundred years ago when it was not so common and familiar to men. Thus neither its novelty nor its excellence has even had the power, with our modern musicians, of producing any of the virtuous, infinitely beneficial and comforting effects that ancient music produced. From this it is a necessary conclusion that either music or human nature had changed from its original state. . . .[29]

Clearly, it was music that had changed. Many innovations in style and practice were made in the spirit of this attempted restoration of the music of the ancients. The results however were entirely novel and had little, if anything, to do with ancient music. An obvious example is the development of opera which was the result of attempts to recreate Greek theatre. In this matter of assessing modern elements in Renaissance theory of music, over-great distinctions have been drawn between the figures of Zarlino and Vincenzo Galilei, to the extent of representing Zarlino as one who delighted in Platonic number theory, in contrast to Galilei who was empirical, and therefore modern and scientific in his approach.[30] A contrast like this can obscure the fact that Zarlino and Galilei both were involved in the general humanistic reform of the theory and practice of music. Galilei himself refers to the fact that he and Zarlino both were participants in this reinterpretation and reform while he still reserves room for the great differences between them. Galilei envisages this reform in typical humanist style, as an attempt to free music from what he sees as the misinterpretations of it made in the dark ages.

> . . .The Romans had a knowledge of music, obtaining it from the Greeks, but they practised chiefly that part appropriate to the theatres where tragedy and comedy were performed, without much prizing the part which is connected with speculation . . . .

Galilei continues with an account of the Barbarian Invasions and of the loss of all sciences as a consequence of them.

> ...Until first Garfurius and after him Glarean and later Zarlino began to investigate what music was and to seek to rescue it from the darkness in which it had been buried.[31]

Thus, he acknowledges the trend of a desire to restore into practice 'the part (of music) which is concerned with speculation'. All differences between Zarlino and Galilei[32] must be seen with relation to this common desire, a desire which depends on the assumption that there once had been a significant relationship between music and speculation and also that it was indeed possible to recreate that relationship.

Unlike the artists and architects of the Renaissance who were similarly convinced that the ancients had understood how to replicate the analogy between nature and the human sciences and arts, the musical humanists had no actual examples of the ancient forms of their art (music) before them. Their attempted reconstruction had to be based exclusively on classical literature which they combined with their own imagination and musical experience.

On a much wider scale this situation in music is reminiscent of the position of Alberti when he wished to prescribe good and true proportions for statues although the ancient prescriptions for such proportions were assumed to have been part of a lost knowledge of the ancients. Thus, Alberti tried to re-establish these proportions by relying on reason and the sensitivities of the artist's mind. This is what the musical humanists also saw themselves as doing, but with no real examples from the ancients. At least, Alberti had had some classical statues and also live human models to refer to. It looks like gaps in information about the ancient world could actually be stimulating. Originality was brought about by the combination of pressure to change, in the light of the ancients, with the actual changes, representing contemporary styles, skills and values. In visual arts this combination led to Renaissance naturalism; while in sixteenth-century music it led to a theoretical preoccupation with the dramatic musical forms, with poetry and music, song, music-drama, and eventually, with opera. In all this both nature and experience were seen to pass through the medium of the senses. Thus, the view that the senses must be used to complement the understanding generally gained currency, while the opposite view, that the senses were wholly bad and misleading, mostly receded.

Does all this represent an advancement of attitudes with art

rivalling nature and with the experience of art refining and
educating men? It can look this way when it is understood that
it was accepted that the mind interpreted the real meanings
contained in the reports of the senses. These conceptual
meanings did not necessarily resemble the messages of the
senses. For example, the combination of certain words,
rhythms, and beats might present anger, hatred and war, but
the meaning raised in the mind might open whole ethical
questions. The painted moon might be made to resemble the
moon through Galileo's telescope, but the meanings raised in
the minds of viewers might encompass a whole contradiction of
Aristotelian cosmology.

One thing is certain, the largely medieval idea of withdraw-
ing from the senses into an inner spiritual reality was reformed
in most, but not all, aesthetic ideas of the Renaissance. But this
is not to say that the late Renaissance did not have its own versions of spiritual value. The poetry or late sculpture of
Michelangelo was certainly filled with the life of the spirit; but
behind this there was a real regard for physical reality, for what
feelings actually felt like, and for what men experienced in the
world. The mind drew, and drew hard, from a possibly infinite
field of sense impressions. However, it drew systematically, and
this pattern of activity might be seen to have advanced developing empiricism. But the mind also made its own conclusions, in
and above the reports of the senses, as in Galilean physics. The
point is, that there was room for both of these sorts of reaction
to the proposed relation between mind and senses within the
theoretical frameworks of Renaissance art and later, music.
Generally it came to look as if the analytical powers of reason
were both more accurate and comprehensive than the information of immediate sense impressions, but, at the same time, the
mind necessarily and consistently drew from experience. Effective music was supposed to have been moving, and naturally so.
No one was supposed to have to sit there and listen to it out of
a conviction that it was good for him.

The absence of examples of ancient music appears to have
stimulated the artist's desire for confirmation of the quality of
the music by his moving the audience profoundly. The senses
needed to be awakened, the passions stirred and then resolved
for the mind and soul to be moved. The senses did not dictate
to the mind but the mind responded to the universal idea presented in art. From normal experience this theory claimed a
heightened experience and mostly, all for the good education
of mind and spirit. Theoreticians urged a complete experience
of music, rather than an unheard and purely intellectual
experience. Thus, the route of art to the mind changed from

the pressing of correct buttons, the natural ratios, to the immersion of the whole being in the experience.

The desire to recover the effective music of the ancients also opened the question of what it was in music that made music affective. Here the particular collapse of traditional reliance on consonance shows; for, Renaissance theorists could not completely agree with each other about the essential stuff of music, about modes, or rhythms, or proportion between words and music, that was to bring about specific moods. More important than this, however, is that they did agree about the aesthetic aims of music, about its presumed place in human thought. True music was, at first, speculation in sound, and later it became an experience in sound that gave rise to speculation. It presented the model of the essence of nature and experience, or it presented the model of the passions and whipped up feelings; and by direct route or not, music moved the mind.

Now all this did not come about simply because of an absence of classical examples, but this did act as a trigger. The general trends in sixteenth-century music, trends of style and of expression, all reinforced the view of complementarity between ear and mind. Most theoreticians were no longer theologians or philosophers but practitioners, composers or their patrons. Naturally, these kinds of men fell easily into the view that music should be a total experience; from the ear, and from the eye too, as great value was placed on the visual and histrionic aspects of performance. Thus, by means of the senses, music moved the minds and souls of the participants. As once the eye had been directed to the outward world, now the ear and all the senses followed. But with regard to the development of empiricism, there are some differences between music and the visual arts. Renaissance painters included the order and functions of physical nature among their portrayed subject matter. The reality of personal experience rather than of physical nature, despite Jannequin's birds, was more appropriate to poetry and music. Not that painters did not do this too. However, poetry, music, and music-drama worked though feelings and the idea of the truth of feeling. The relation of this to sciences like botany or anatomy or geography is real only in the sense that the awakened mind and spirit will be attuned to all aspects of the harmony of nature.

We know that a positive attitude towards the role of the senses had always been available within Platonic traditions. Although the senses were never considered without an expression of their serious limitations, when they were weighed by the mind, they were significantly judged as the starting points on the road to knowledge. This qualified though positive treatment of the role of the senses can be found in Aristotle, Plotinus, and later in St. Augustine and St. Bonaventura. Naturally this does not resemble the interpretations of Renaissance men who gave the senses a completely new importance, and who, at the same time, held Platonic assumptions about nature. The past treatment of the senses as starting points on the road to knowledge nevertheless gave these Renaissance men the edge that they needed, both to contradict traditional assumptions, and yet still to maintain an active belief that the purpose of art was to exploit its analogies with nature.

The ancients' positive view of the senses had often been minimized. Medieval music theorists especially decried the senses in favour of pure understanding. The following example shows how unremitting this type of attitude was.

> Whatever is delightful in song brought about by number through the proportioned dimensions of sounds; whatever is excellent in rhythms, or in songs, or in any rhythmic movements you will, is effected wholly by number. Sounds pass quickly away, but numbers, which are obscured by the corporeal elements in sounds and movements, remain.[33]

Contrast this with St. Bonaventura (1221-74) who, though he was no advocate of a comprehensive attainment of knowledge from dialogue with the senses, did admit them, as he also admitted the external human body and the corporeal world as the necessary starting points on the road up a series of levels to ultimate truth in God.

> That we may arrive at an understanding of the first principle, which is most spiritual and eternal and above us, we ought to proceed through the traces which are corporeal and temporal and outside us; and this is to be led into the way of God.[34]

Bonaventura's six stages of ascension are: sense, imagination, reason, intellect, intelligence, and the illumination of conscience.[35]

This basically positive but submerged attitude to the senses was, of course, singled out and elaborated by Renaissance thinkers. It influenced many, either directly through classical and medieval philosophy, or indirectly through literature (especially Dante).[36]

In summary, then, the real result of the attempted revival of ancient music in the Renaissance was the development of a new theory of music and, for the most part, a totally new music. In this theory, and behind some of the new musical forms, like the new poetry and music, or opera, there rested a new and broader assumption of natural harmony. Harmony that had once been confined to absolute relationships between numbers, came to be interpreted as a harmony demonstrable through the whole of experience, and through art, whose business it was to imitate and even replicate that experience. By the middle of the sixteenth century, we find musical theorists struggling to make sense of the differences that existed between contemporary practice and those concepts that had had the support of tradition and theory.

One important issue around which some of this theoretical revision circulated was the practice of tempering. Since the eighteenth century, tuners of keyboard instruments have divided the octaves into twelve intervals, none of which is quite true in terms of the ratios of their frequencies of vibration. Even before this time, tuners practised an unequal type of temperament. The key of C major was tuned true, but then all the other tones of the keyboard were forced to conform to this tuning. This conforming was in terms of the pleasingness of the sounds produced and was not in strict accord with mathematical theory. The situation arose because the theoretically proper tuning for the commonly used modes (scales) could not, for mathematical reasons, be valid for the whole gamut of the board.[37] By the sixteenth century, some composers had begun to use harmonic chromaticism (excursions from the modal norms) much more freely than ever before. In order to make these sound well, it became necessary for tuners to abandon all attempts at absolute mathematical certainty. The ear, and not number, was guiding the tuner.[38] As we are already aware, in sixteenth-century polyphony, the accepted consonances which functioned ideally in purely monodic music became harsh-sounding unless they were tempered by the ear. This was one among several reasons why theoreticians, like Vincenzo Galilei and Girolamo Mei, thought of instituting the strict use of monody and reinstating the use of consonant intervals. Clearly, for men who were concerned to increase the powers of music by restoring a purity that they thought the ancients had accomplished, this discrepancy between theory and practice, and the fact that in polyphonic music the practice produced pleasing sounds, was provoking questions about the actual nature of sound and the pleasingness of musical sound. Why and how did some numerical ratios produce pleasing sensory experiences while others did not?[39] Questions like these involved theorists in a long series of scientific studies which began in Italy in about the 1540s and continued there, as well as in the rest of Europe.[40] This type of musical theory was inseparable from natural science. The same international community of people were involved with both.

As we have said, some of the first theoretical arguments to justify the acceptance of ratios outside the first four numbers were basically metaphysical. At times this was how Gioseffo Zarlino argued. He justified consonant ratios between the first six numbers by maintaining that the properties of the number 6 were as sacred asthose of number 4. The fact that numbers 1, 2 and 3, when added or multiplied with each other produced 6 was testimony to the special position of 6 within the harmonic scheme. This theory argued the acceptance of the major third (5:4), the minor third (6:5), and the major sixth (5:3). Zarlino also accepted the minor sixth as consonant, although one of its terms (8:5) falls outside the first six numbers.[41] Although this type of argument certainly seems basically idealistic, it is really an attempt to widen theory in order to encompass current practice. Zarlino, who succeeded Cipriano de Rore as chief organist of St. Mark's in Venice, in 1565, wanted music theory to be significant for current practices. Also, as I have said, he wanted these practices to conform to theory. He was willing to bend and reshape both of these things. Still, it was his pupil and sometimes adversary, Vincenzo Galilei, who devised tests and experiments which took the issue of number from the idealistic sphere into an experimental one.

Galilei's early stand on the issue of tuning exemplifies his earlier accord with his teacher Zarlino. Zarlino had objected to the assumptions of many musicians that the basis of their composition and singing was a specific type of Pythagorean tuning (diatonic ditonation). When this tuning was strictly applied in polyphonic music the thirds and sixths sounded false. Galilei held that the tuning and singing was a Ptolemaic one, and he admitted that the instrumentalists tempered this tuning. Galilei argued that because all natural things were expressed in degrees, the good, the better, and the best, it was justifiable to play with an artificially tuned instrument but to sing the natural ratios: people should not sing the way that they play because then the consonances would only exist potentially and would not be of utility in nature, in that they would never be allowed to happen.[42]

Still, Galilei does not appear to have remained satisfied with this type of argument. He wanted to find out more about ancient music within which theory and practice were assumed to have been complementary.[43] In this spirit he began a long and learned correspondence with the historian and theorist of ancient music, Girolamo Mei (1519-1594). From about 1572 Mei's influence made Galilei change his views.

Mei, a humanist scholar who was also influenced by Renaissance Neo-Platonism, found the analogy between music and poetry and rhetoric even more important than the analogy between music and cosmology.[44] He felt that the parallels between number and music, and number and nature, were more applicable or relevant to natural philosophy than to musical practice, a practice that was more comparable to the other arts. The arts resembled nature because they could evoke similar feelings. And this is not as straightforward as it might at first appear because all the arts, and especially the combination of poetry and music, were envisaged as having special moral and emotive effects, both on the performers and on the audience. The right performance had the power to play upon the harmony of the human soul. The thoughts of Mei and Galilei form a central part of this humanist trend that emphasized the moral powers of music. Mei advocated composing in monody, rather than in polyphony. Monodic music was appropriate for the natural ratios of consonance and dissonance, and Mei believed that the ancients composed in monody. This was the form with which the special effects of music had been accomplished. Galilei was sympathetic to this view, but he, and many other theorists and composers who also wished to reproduce the effects of ancient music, did not find that it suited them to give up all modern harmony in order to do so. After the deaths of the composers Palestrina and Orlandus Lassus, in the 1590s, there was a swing in popular taste towards monody.[45] The natural scientist, philosopher and theorist, Père Mersenne (1583-1648) who was influenced by earlier efforts of French composers and theorists to produce the effects of ancient music, thought, at least at one point, that monody was superior to polyphony, superior in terms of efficacy. He expressed the view that polyphonic music demanded too much of the mind and the ear at the same time.[46] He like his predecessors in French musical theory, speaks of the ear and the mind in a spirit of mutual confirmation. This type of spirit marks, once again, the gradual and frequently on-and-off trend of regarding the judgement of the senses in music in a far less suspicious light than medieval theorists had done.

A little more attention should be given to the French musical humanists whom Mersenne later praised so highly. Sixteenth-century French musical humanists were inspired by earlier Italian academies, principally Ficino's Florentine Academy and Bardi's Camerata.[47] The French groups, the Pléiade, and then Baïf's academy of poetry and music, both reflect and reinforce the trends that we have noticed developing in sixteenth-century music theory. These groups wanted to revive the musical arts of the ancients, to reproduce the profound effects of music on the human soul, to accomplish a marriage between words and music, and to make music a mirror of nature, and of the actions and attitudes of men. Ronsard (1524-1585) led the Pléiade; he often wrote poetry that was especially designed for musical setting.[48] Most of the new French music was not monodic, as was the music most highly recommended by the Italian Camerata; rather, the polyphony was arranged in such a way that the words were clear and the verse complemented the rhythm of the music.[49] The humanist and composer friend of Ronsard, Antoine de Bertrand, set the poet's 'Amours de Marie' to music in 1578[50] The poems had been published since 1552. Bertrand's settings were devised with the effects of music in mind. Bertrand not only says this, but he uses some of the methods which, at the time, were acceptable for the production of the effects. One of these was his use of chromatic genera, a use of halftones attributed to the Greeks.[51] Another was his repeated juxtaposition of contrasting emotions with appropriate music. Juxtapositioning and other means, such as the marriage of words and music, the reform of intonation, and the proper use of modes, all were popular methods.

Baïf's academy of poetry and music (1571-3) also devoted itself to the recreation of the effects of ancient music, as well as to the universal education of its members.[52] This latter was to be accomplished by the provision of courses in all of the arts and sciences. The two great aims were interconnected because the music was to have been designed to be used as a moral educator in the true Platonic sense. The integration of all types of activities under the power of love, Platonic love, is illustrated in Baïf's poem 'Les Amours'.[53] This thought is reminiscent of Leon Battista Alberti's idea of vocation not simply as a practical choice of trade but in the Platonic and Christian sense of this word. Work through love, and the moral elevation of spirits, these things depended upon the individual's attunement to them: hence the educative function of the academy.

Baïf was more rigid than Ronsard had been in his attempt to complement the verse with musical rhythm. In order to achieve the closest possible relationship between words and music Baïf adopted a new form of French phonetic spelling. He tried to reproduce the sounds of spoken language more accurately in order to distinguish the long syllables from the short and to match these to the notes.[54]

In general, the necessity of the marriage of words and music, and the identification of poetic with musical rhythms were assumed by French and Italian musical humanists to be self-evident truths.[55] The appropriate use of the modes was also thought necessary for the accomplishment of the effects. But the modes posed a difficult problem. Modes were coordinated with the depiction of specific moods, for instance the Lydian mode was grave. This matching of a given mode with a given mood was almost universally accepted, but the tonal components of any given mode varied with the interpretations of different scholars. Thus, all agreed that the Lydian mode was grave but there were different versions of the Lydian and also of other modes. Glarean, Zarlino, and Galilei with Mei each had their own systems.[56] Despite this disturbing ambiguity the identification of modes for the portrayal of specific emotions was so firmly accepted that later seventeenth-century composers attributed emotional characters to all the major and minor keys.

The sixteenth-century attempt at musical depiction, often called musical naturalism, has its more amusing aspects. For instance, a composer of this school, Clément Jannequin, wrote bird concerts, music portraying specific battles, hunting scenes, street scenes, and musical imitations of gossiping women.[57] However, most of the works portrayed complex states of mind and emotions, as in the compositions of Nicola Vincentino, Antoine de Bertrand, and Jaques Mauduit. Mauduit composed Ronsard's funeral Mass. This work is preserved in Pére Mersenne's 'Harmonie Universelle'.[58] Mersenne praised not only the work, but the whole intention and dedication of Baïf's Academy. And as before, we know that Mersenne supported the use of monody that had been voiced earlier in the Camerata and by Galilei and Mei. Thus, Mersenne was sympathetic to Galilei's eventual aesthetic: and further, he thought it was impossible to conceive of a meaning that was just purely musical. If music abandoned the balance between sound and verbal meaning of the text, it was not more than pleasant noise.[59] This was an extreme humanist position. The tradition of number and meaning in music also continued. Perhaps Leibniz was its outstanding philosophical spokesman.

The empirical approach

Having said that Mei's ideas and line of argument did not represent an isolated trend in Renaissance music theory we can return to his effect on Vincenzo Galilei. Mei, convinced that the ideal intervals could never be adhered to in practice, suggested that Galilei test the quality of intervals actually being sung against the accepted consonant intervals. Galilei eventually expanded this empirical line of approach, using tests and demonstrations in order to refine his own interpretation of theory.

Another Italian philosopher who pursued an empirical approach and made discoveries which contradicted classical views of consonance and dissonance was Giovanni Benedetti (1530-1590). He was especially interested in instrument tuning and, when experimenting with vibrating strings, he discovered two basic principles of string vibration. The first, that when the tension of the strings is equal then the ratio of their frequencies of vibration varies inversely with their length. The second, that the concord of specific intervals depends on the coincidence of the terminations of their vibration cycles.

Vincenzo Galilei also used experimental methods to determine the question of whether the numerical relationships that were usually associated with musical intervals on the basis of string division were actually related to the physical cause of the intervals. Galilei tested weights on strings, glasses and bells, in order to produce the same consonant intervals and he found that these required different numerical ratios from the ratios arrived at from the lengths of strings.[60] Thereby he demonstrated that there were no ratios more natural than others.

At least, this is what we can now conclude. Other experiments performed by theorists at about the same time had similar implications with regard to the assumed relationships between small numbers and consonance. As early as 1546, another Italian, Girolamo Fracastoro, discovered the sympathetic vibration of strings. He had done so by demonstrating that two strings of equal lengths and with the same tension are susceptible to each other's vibrations. A hundred years later, Mersenne added to this idea of the sympathetic vibration of strings by demonstrating that the time period of the vibration of strings was proportional to the square root of the weight of the string. He demonstrated this by using different strings which had the same length and tension. Mersenne also worked on a theory of the plurality of tones in a single string, that is, that each note contains a fundamental tone plus upper partials. Aristotle had noted that a musical note always contained its octave. Mersenne was surprised that Aristotle had not heard more; he observed that Aristotle was ignorant of the fact that each string produces five or more different sounds at the same instant. Mersenne named the strongest sound, that is the one that is primarily characterized by the fundamental tone, the natural sound. Above this sounded its octave, twelfth, fifteenth, and the major seventeenth and twenty-third. The English scientist John Wallis (1616-1703) put Fracastoro's observations together with Mersenne. He discovered that every vibrating string held points of no vibration, called nodes. A clear and multiple sound would occur only when the nodes were not disturbed by plucking.[61]

Clearly, these discoveries about sound had implications which could affect the traditional notions of consonance and dissonance. For instance, even an awareness of the existence of overtones could cast doubt on the supposed purity of the number-relationship between consonant notes. Certainly, beliefs in the particular virtue of relationships between small numbers could be, and were, shaken. If concord was not the result of a combination making ideal proportion in sound, then the whole idea that particular numbers had special significance in both nature and in music might become open to question. Eventually, Descartes, Mersenne, and Christian Huyghens all maintained that there was a relative, not an absolute, difference between consonance and dissonance. The premium that had once been placed on the analogy between music and nature on a basis of ideal numbers and consonant proportions developed into the assumption of a relationship based on both the physical and psychological side of hearing and of what is heard, the sympathetic relation between body, mind and music. In other words, the naturalness of certain consonant intervals was not doubted, but it came to be based on the physical or emotional nature of man, the auditor of music, instead of on the abstract virtues of numbers.

Still, in the seventeenth century, Huyghens argued that the augmented fourth (10:7) and the diminished fifth (7:5) could be justified as acceptable. He reasoned that just as thirds and fifths were not acceptable consonants in ancient times, so the augmented fourth and diminished fifth were not considered acceptable in contemporary times. In other words, his basis of acceptance is seen to be grounded in the musical experience of the audience. But Huyghens did not extend this line of argument to justify unlimited acceptance of any or all combinations.

Now all this might look like the end of the line for the relation between music and nature, but it was not. For, it is clear that natural numbers were only a minor element in the relationship as it was viewed by musical humanists. Once harmonious music had been thought to be speculative. It was assumed that the order of nature could be reduced to mathematical terms and music was a sonorous presentation of those terms; to appreciate it, you had to understand, and when it was understood, effects upon body, spirit and soul ensued. These points had been seen to follow one from the other. It is interesting that this theory, based on an implied mathematical reductionism, and that had justified music's place in the quadrivium, had adhered during the later middle ages when the prevailing ethos of natural philosophy was largely Aristotelian and anything but mathematical.

After the sixteenth century the emphasis on natural numbers became comparatively unimportant; the relation between music and nature was conceived of in rather vaguer terms of sympathy. I say vague because it was far from generally agreed as to what the actual basis of that sympathy was. Rhythms, the physiology of the ear and its response to certain times, harmonies or beats, unconscious counting, the power of art to create heightened experience through contrasts, key colours, and/or words with the appropriate musical settings, all of these and more ideas were put forward in place of those neat consonant ratios between the first six numbers. However, even if sympathy was a far less exact concept than the one inspired by Pythagorean harmony, the relation between these sympathetic theories of the arts and the characteristic tone of natural philosophy was actually far more tangible than in the later middle ages. Art imitated nature and experience. Experience was of the utmost importance. Men were educated and improved through experience.

We look at it narrowly when we look and only say things like, 'Zarlino was mistaken in imputing a universal harmony to nature.'[62] In the purely scientific sense he may have been, and so may have Leibniz, or later, Haydn, Mozart, Goethe, etc. The real relation between musical ideals and natural philosophy, meaning between the world-views of composers and theorists and those of the prevalent school of natural philosophers, had not depended on Pythagorean harmonies since about the thirteenth century. Those harmonies were part of the residue of a different cultural age, of the Platonism of late antiquity; and, although musical theorists evoked them, and philosophers accepted them, they largely accepted them on the basis of tradition. Actually, the majority of medieval natural philosophers, though not all, were not primarily concerned with number as a basis of nature and reality.

The Renaissance presents an entirely different situation. Among others, Vitruvius and Boethius are reread with new vigour, and several eras of theoreticians of the various arts mingle their ideas with those of Aristotle's *Poetics* and Horace's *Ars Poetica* and other Roman rhetoricians. Now while it is true that these diverse sources do not establish a claim to the analogy between music and natural philosophy in the precise way of Boethius, if we do not look at the claim, but at the actuality of any real parallel, with a few exceptions, we find the posture of the artistic world and the scientific world far closer than before. The hierarchies have become relatively unimportant. Efficacy is the keynote, whether it is for the power of art, or of knowledge. The arts are educative, they serve in the quest for knowledge, be it moral or natural. The mind is stirred by experience and the systematic evaluation of experience can bring both heightened artistic pleasure, on the one hand, and the apprehension of the true axioms of nature, on the other. These suggestions will become clearer in following chapters. However, perhaps one reason for the impact of Bacon's *Great Instauration* had to do with at least two hundred years of confirming the value of the senses, of mundane experience, and of viewing the mind as the interpreter of experience, within the world of the arts.

Notes to Chapter Five

1. Plato, *Timaeus*, VII. He explains that the material world is a concord arising out of the proportion between fire, air, earth and water. Although the elements are material the proportion between them is envisaged in mathematical terms. Cf. Jacques Handschin, 'The Timaeus Scale', *Musica Disciplina* (Rome, 1950), iv, Fasc. 1, 1-42. Cf. note 10 on pp. 107-108 of R.D. Archer-Hind, *The Timaeus of Plato* (London, 1888); see also A.E. Taylor, *A Commentary on Plato's Timaeus* (Oxford, 1929), pp. 137-8; and, F.M. Cornford, *Plato's Cosmology* (London, 1937), pp. 66-72.
2. Cf. Plato, *Timaeus*, X.
3. St. Augustine, *Confessions*, Book XII, 15, p.291.
4. *Ibid*. his ital., the primacy of wisdom continues in future epistemology; cf. Francis Bacon, *The Advancement of Learning*. 1st book, VI, 1-5.
5. Their basic kinship is a common background in Greek philosophy, and also a common emphasis on the difference in quality between the partial and changing and the eternal and unchanging.
6. H. Potiron, *Boèce: Théoricien de la Musique Grecque* (Paris, 1954), p.41.
7. *Ibid*. p.35.
8. See below for a description of consonant intervals; p.180.
9. Sir James Jeans, *Science and Music* (Cambridge, 1961, 1st edn., 1937), p.154. Cazden, Norman, 'Musical consonance and dissonance: a cultural criterion, *J. Aesthetics and Art Criticism*, vol.

4, 1945-6. 'Tone combinations taken in isolation can be said to present numerical ratios in the vibration frequency of their constituent tones. When these ratios are abstracted and considered as numbers, there is a certain correspondence between mathematical simplicity of ratios containing low numbers and musical consonance, and between mathematical complexity of ratios containing high or incommensurate numbers and musical dissonance.'

10. Briefly, dissonance is an unpleasing sound resulting from slight off-beats between the fundamental tones, the overtones, and the resultant tones, of two or of a number of notes when they are sounded together. Every note we hear is actually the result of a combination of sounds. This combination consists of a fundamental tone (one that gives the value of the note itself), and the overtones (often these are also called harmonics, or upper partials). The overtones sound together with the fundamental tone and they can only be heard as separate or distinct from it by a trained ear. The resultant ones, which also sound together with the simultaneous sounding of the fundamental tones, break up into two different types. One, the differential tone, is heard when two tones of considerable intensity are sounded together. It is a low tone whose pitch is equal to the difference between the frequencies of the fundamental tones. The second, called the summation tone, corresponds in its frequency to the sum of the frequencies of the fundamental or generating tones. For more detailed descriptions see: *Groves Dictionary of Music and Musicians*, 'acoustics' (London, 1954), v. 1, and also P. A. Scholes, *The Oxford Companion to Music*, 'acoustics' (London, 1950), 8th edn., v. 1.

11. J. Jeans, *Science and Music*, p. 154. It is generally surmised that he made this discovery by measuring the lengths of a string that were required to produce the different tones on a monochord with a movable bridge. See E. G. Bugg, 'A Criticism of Leibniz's Theory of Consonance'. *J. Aesthetics and Art Criticism*, vol. 21, p. 4.

12. Alfred Einstein, *The Italian Madrigal*, (Princeton, N.J., 1949), vol. 1, 'Music in Sixteenth-Century Aesthetics', pp. 212-245.

13. Albert Seay, 'Ugolino of Orvieto Theorist and Composer', *Musica Disciplina*, vol. IX, pp. 116-118.

14. *Ibid.* p. 146.

15. Ornithoparchus, *Micrologus*, trans. Dowland, p. 2.

16. Seay, 'Ugolino', *Musica Disciplina*, p. 150.

17. Leonardo also extended this to animal life both in the life span, birth, growth, decay, and death; and, also to metabolism, the rhythm of the breathing, the pulse, the ebb and flow of the blood.

18. A. Seay, 'Ugolino', *Musica Disciplina*, p. 146.
19. Ornithoparchus, *Micrologus*, trans. Dowland, p.1.
20. The ambiguity does not apply to the assumption that music is the vehicle for the expression of natural harmony, but to the concepts of definitions of what harmony is, and, of the way that music replicates it.
21. Chief work, *Toscanello in musica*, first edition 1523. In his comprehensive article on 'Music in the culture of the Renaissance', *Journal of the History of Ideas*, vol. XV, no. 4 (October, 1954), Professor E. Lowinsky enumerates simultaneous composition among Renaissance innovations but general opinion appears to confirm that the Renaissance saw both the intensification and theoretical justification of the (in fact) already established practice of simultaneous composition. Even the term simultaneous composition describes a change in thinking even more than a complete change in composition itself. Before people learned to think in harmonies and to compose in terms of this complete and simultaneous conception men used to compose by making a structure of successively erected layers. Cf. p. 529.
22. Zarlino's principal work is *Istituzioni Armoniche*, pub. 1558, reprinted in 1562 and 1573. Claude V. Palisca, 'Scientific Empiricism in Musical Thought', in Toulmin *et al.*, *Seventeenth Century Science and the Arts* (Princeton, N.J., 1961), p. 102.
23. Principal work, *L'Artusi, Ovvero, Delle Imperfezioni della Moderna Musica*, original ed., Venice, 1600, cited from O. Strunk, *Source Readings in Music History* (New York, 1950), p. 402.
24. Giovanni di' Bardi, 'Discourse on ancient music and good singing', pub. in G.B. Doni, *Lyra Barberina* (Florence, 1763), translated by O. Strunk, *Source Readings in Music History* (New York, 1950), p. 295.
25. From Giulio Caccini's preface to *Le Nuove Musiche* (1614), in *Composers on Music*, ed. S. Morgenstern (New York, 1956), p. 9; Count Bardi had addressed the Discourse (cited just above) to Caccini, called Romano.
26. 'Dodecachordon' (1547), book III, chap. 24, cited in O. Strunk, *Readings*, pp. 220, 221; cf. Smihers, A., 'Josquin Des Près, *Proceedings of the Musical Associations*' (London, 1926, 7), pp. 94-116. At about 1500 Josquin was universally praised by theorists with few reservations, for, if he tampered with classical doctrines and practised and taught the imperfect consonances he also satisfied the increasingly popular standard of composing in a style that was thought to be naturally appropriate to the subject and truly moving in the soul-inciting sense.
27. From Claudio Monteverdi's preface to the eighth book of madrigals. . .madrigali guerrieri ed amorosi 1638, in *Composers on Music*, ed. S. Morgenstern (New York, 1950), p. 22.

28. Gioseffo Zarlino, Le istitutioni harmoniche (Venetia, 1558), cap. 27, p.173, cap. 29, p.176, trans. O. Strunk in *Source Readings in Music History* (New York, 1950), pp. 232, 233. Zarlino calls the consonant ratios sonorous numbers which, I think, makes clear that he envisages harmony as a wider phenomenon than just making combinations of sweet sounding intervals; [but that] harmony also encompasses the intelligent use of dissonance.

29. Vincenzo Galilei, '*Dialogo Della Musica Antica e Della Moderna*', ed. Fabio Fano (Milano, 1947), p. 93, trans. O. Strunk, *Readings* (New York, 1950), p. 306.

30. Claude Palisca, 'Scientific Empiricism in Musical Thought,' in Toulmin *et al., Seventeenth Century Science and the Arts* (Princeton, N.J., 1961), pp. 102, 121; and *Letters on Ancient and Modern Music,* to Vincenzo Galilei and Giovanni Bardi (a study with annotated texts), American Institute of Musicology 1960, introduction. These texts imply this type of contrast but the distinction is not absolute because the overall comparison of Galilei with his teacher Zarlino is never completely drawn. Certainly they are contrasted with respect to the fact that Zarlino argued within the traditional Neo-Platonic and Pythagorean framework by just extending that framework to justify use of ratios within the first six numbers, whereas Galilei's ultimate position related the phenomena of consonance to the senses alone. However, it seems to me that it is not so easy to cast these personalities in the contrasting roles, idealist vs. practical empirical man. Palisca himself describes how Zarlino was prepared to accept the practices involved with equal temperament (this involved violation of the ratios) whereas, *at stages,* Galilei criticized any abuse of these ratios and considered use of strict monody as a way of conforming to the ratios in practice. In other words it seems that in this instance the Idealists, Galilei, and Girolamo Mei, used the empirical approach to debunk what they believed to be the false ideals of contemporary theory, whereas Zarlino was rather less inclined to worry because number theory was not borne out in practice. In this restricted sense, it was he who was less idealistic.

31. Vincenzo Galilei, *Dialogo della musica antica e della moderna,* ed. Fabio Fano (Milano, 1947), p. 45, trans. O. Strunk, *Readings* (New York, 1950), pp. 302-3.

32. Zarlino is generally considered first among the moderns, as can be seen from Rameau (1683-1764) in *Traité de l'harmonie.*

33. Scholia enchiriadis c. 900, cited in *Source Readings in Music History,* ed. O. Strunk (New York, 1950), pp. 137-138. The effectiveness of this concept of the transitory and impermanent nature of sound appears in Leonardo da Vinci's argument that

painting is superior to music because music can only be perceived in terms of the notes actually being played. Only memory and recollection can make it whole.

34. St. Bonaventura, *The Mind's Road to God*, trans. George Boas, (New York, 1953), ch. I, p.8.

35. *Ibid*. p. 9.

36. J. A. Mazzeo, 'The Augustinian Conception of Beauty and Dante's Convivio', *J. Aesthetics and Art Critism*, vol. XV, No. 4., pp. 446-47.

37. J. Jeans, *Science and Music*, pp. 166-172.

38. For a more complete and technical explanation of temperament see almost any work on musical acoustics. I have used C. Culver, *Musical Acoustics* (New York, 1956), pp. 123-40.

39. Until the sixteenth century there had been no attempt to find out how a numerical ratio became a pleasing sensory experience.

40. See Palisca, 'Scientific Empiricism,' pp. 93-100.

41. *Ibid*. pp. 102-3.

42. See Palisca, *Letters on Ancient and Modern Music*, 'The Problem of Tuning,' pp. 63-64.

43. Most of the following remarks about Galilei and Mei are based on the work of Claude Palisca.

44. D. P. Walker, 'Musical Humanism in the sixteenth and Early Seventeenth Centuries,' *Music Review* (Cambridge, England, 1941-2), vol. II, pp. 291, 297, 306-308. See Palisca, *Letters*, pp. 5, 34, 35, and 65.

45. Allen, *Philosophies of Music History*, (New York, 1962) p.6.

46. *Ibid*. p.10.

47. D. P. Walker, 'Musical Humanism,' pp. 7, 8. Frances Yates, *The French Academies of the Sixteenth Century* (London, 1947), pp. 4, 9. Edward E. Lowinsky, 'Music in the Culture of the Renaissance,' *J. Hist. Ideas*, vol. XV, no. 4 (October 1954), p. 515.

48. Henri Pruniéres, *L'Opéra Italien en France Avant Lulli* (Paris, 1913), p. xxi.

49. D. P. Walker, 'Musical Humanism,' pp. 306-307. Henri Prunières, *L'Opéra Italien*, p. 2. By the seventeenth century Roman composers were declaring that the Camerata had sacrificed the art of the madrigal.

50. Beverly J. Davis, 'Antoine de Bertrand: a view into the aesthetics of music in sixteenth century France,' *J. Aesthetics and Art Criticism* (Belmont, Calif.), vol. XXI, no. 2, pp. 189-200.

51. The chromatic and enharmonic genera were believed to be especially effective in playing upon the emotions. Cf. D. P. Walker, 'Musical Humanism,' p. 119.

52. D. P. Walker, 'The Aims of Baïfs Académie de Poésie et de Musique,' *J. Renaissance and Baroque Music* (Rome, 1946-7), vol.

I, F. Yates, *French Academies*, p. 35.
53. F. Yates, *French Academies*, p. 4.
54. *Ibid.* p. 50.
55. D. P. Walker, 'Musical Humanism,' p. 297.
56. *Ibid.* pp. 221-222.
57. E. Lowinsky, 'Music in the Culture of the Renaissance,' pp. 539-542.
58. F. Yates, *French Academies*, p. 177.
59. Walker, 'Musical Humanism,' pp. 66, 67.
60. Palisca, 'Scientific Empiricism', pp. 127-130.
61. Palisca, 'Scientific Empiricism', p. 99.
62. Palisca, 'Scientific Empiricism', p. 122.

6
UNIVERSALITY AND THE BRINGING TOGETHER OF DISCIPLINES

> We must not fancy that one kind of knowledge is more obscure than another since all knowledge is of the same nature throughout.
>
> René Descartes

Analogical assumptions and the bringing together of disciplines

A shift in stress in analogy making has been marked in the field of music, and, I believe, in the visual arts as well. Across the sixteenth century analogies between the arts and nature were formulated less upon the basis of Pythagorean assumptions and increasingly upon the basis of some notion of natural sympathy. In music, we have just seen that this sympathy could be conceived as one between the mind and/or emotions and the balance between the content of words and music, or alternatively, it could be seen between the human subject and the rather mechanical correspondence of rhythm and poetic metre. Awareness of this situation raises questions about the wider analogy. Did all analogy-making exhibit similar shifts? Were the ancient notions that characterized the objects of this world and their relations as essentially mathematical forgotten, finally pushed aside, or overcome? Some historians have described the fate of notions of harmony in these dramatic terms. However, we can expect to discover something more subtle.

By way of introduction we should recall that mathematical ideals with Pythagorean and Neo-Platonic inspirations did stimulate important natural philosophers and mathematicians in the seventeenth century, for example, Galileo and Kepler, and later, Newton and Leibniz. So these inspirations were not passé. But what about the arts, and what about those areas of natural philosophy that were more empirical than purely mathematical? Perhaps, as motives or goals changed within these areas of learning, the analogy was flexible enough to express itself, indeed, to be expressed, in the form that best supported the newer aims. For a general example from the seventeenth-century world of more communal efforts in science, the old Creator-artist analogy shifted to one between providence and mankind. Human minds were seen to be destined to understand the Creator's marks in nature. You might say, clearly, the analogy is just pushed around to suit the case. But remember, the ways that men describe themselves to themselves ought never to be automatically taken lightly. If they really mean it, the image can contribute to conceptions of great originality.

Leon Battista Alberti has given us a stunning demonstration of the concept of analogy between wholes and their parts both in nature and in the arts. The assembly of this concept was derived from Boethian-Vitruvian-Cusan antecedents and also from Ciceronian-humanist ones. His description of the relations between physical nature and the arts, indeed, all human works, supported his own integrated effort to set out the theory of geometrical space and to develop and refine naturalistic practices in painting and sculpture. This whole effort involves imaginative images derived from mathematics, from the observation of nature and mechanics, and all in connection with an assumed psychology of perception and aesthetic sensibilities. It makes little sense to separate the mathematical and mechanical from the empirically devised, and from aesthetic and/or epistemological images. This is a full bringing together of disciplines, with the artist-philosopher selecting and shaping diverse tools to conceive and express a new theory and practice. Leonardo exhibits this even more. For example, think of his studies of the dynamics of movement. These had observational, mathematical, empirical and rational phases. From the line of motion of a projectile to the physiology of man or beast in motion, all these approaches were sometimes blended. So, when Leonardo remarked on the kinetic infinity of the circular movement of the human arm he was not entirely detached from parallel studies of the workings of muscle, nerve and bone.

However, this closeness of the disciplines could not and did not remain static. Inevitably, as the terms of intellectual challenges shifted, the consequent associations between the disciplines also changed. For example, Descartes had thoughts pertaining to the arts but he approached the arts as a philosopher and mathematician. His involvement was not the first-hand practitioner's involvement of Leonardo; nor was Mersenne's with music if we compare him with Vincenzo Galilei. I do not want to draw too much from this point but, possibly an intimate universality, that of both conception and practice, might be somewhat distinguished from a more general sort of universality. This second sort can be described as a belief in basic associations between various fields of knowledge and a reflecting on fields that are really not one's own central area of practice and expression. Leibniz's writing on consonance might fall into this category. Certainly, this distinction is not always discrete. These modes of universality overlap both in individuals and in historical time. But there is also a detectable shift from the first to the second as the seventeenth century progresses.

As for the combination with abstract physics and mathematics, of the systematic observation of nature and empirical-experimental approaches, several early modern fields of scientific endeavour continued to exhibit the early Renaissance mingling of diverse approaches. Some of these are medicine, surveying, architectural planning, military science, cartography, navigation, and mining-engineering, not to speak of the broad study of natural history that was and still remains a highly interdisciplinary field. We should not simply think of the scientific revolution as one of physics, mathematics, and astronomy in the early seventeenth century, and of chemistry and related fields in the eighteenth. Granted, radical developments took place in these fields at these times, but there was also a large region of overlapping territory between the highly abstract sciences and the watching, recording, and brewing ones. Pertinent though this may be, it is not my specific point. For we can still see how Leonardo da Vinci might have been a Pythagorean in his view of nature while performing dissections. Was this particular form of the idea of harmony equally important to later empiricists? Did Bacon view things in this way? In music we have seen ideal number parallels give way to notions of sympathy. Some of these were mechanical, rhythms evoking passions; and some were more refined, signifying the effects evoked by looking like nature or by rousing thoughts and feelings akin to those raised by nature and by experience. All along there had been some notion of sympathy, because either recognition of or the recalling of ideal notions had to be stimulated, or sparked-off by some type of experience. Thus, the knowledge of first principles had always arisen, at the first stage, from the recognition of the reflections of these principles in nature.

This is the beginning point of all true knowledge in the philosophy of St. Bonaventura (1221-1274):

> For since relative to our life on earth, the world is itself a ladder ascending to God we find here certain traces (of His hand), certain images, some corporeal, some spiritual, some temporal, some aeviternal; consequently some outside us, some inside.[1]

Ancient Neo-Platonists had designated the sensible world as the first object of knowledge.[2] This is the significance of the sensible world in Plotinus:

> The excellence, the power, and the goodness of the intelligible realm is revealed in what is most excellent in the realm of sense, for the realms are linked together. From the one, self-existent, the other eternally draws its existence by participation and to the extent it reproduces the intelligible by imitation.[3]

Both statements represent united but distinguishable ideas. First, the perceived world is analogous to an eternal world that is intelligible, or, in the Christian version, is God. Then, beginning with the sensible world, one can achieve a sympathetic recognition of the qualities that are analogous to first principles or divine ideas.

Pursuing this second point, I propose to describe as 'recognition processes' all those procedures of thought, reflection, creation, discovery, and explanation which, considering objects and events in mundane experience, profess to attain by some stages of thought, to a clear apprehension of primary qualities in the universe, and sometimes even to a kind of knowledge of the eternal first principle itself.

It has been noted that traditional recognition processes before the Renaissance emphasized the looking-inward stages. By the seventeenth century recognition processes, often in the same Platonic tradition, involved the most intensive scrutiny of ideas that were developed from systematic studies of aspects of the material world. The student who is interested in the overt contrast between medieval recognition processes, and the later (which however still have a similar analogical assumption as a basis) need only compare some of Bonaventura's statements with the procedural recommendations of Francis Bacon in the *Novum Organum*. For example:

> Our soul has not been able to be raised perfectly from the things of sense to an intuition of itself and of the eternal Truth in itself unless the Truth, having assumed human form in Christ, should make itself into a ladder, repairing the first ladder which was broken in Adam.
>
> Therefore, however much anyone is illuminated only by the light of nature and of acquired science, he cannot enter into himself that he may delight in the Lord in himself, unless Christ be his mediator. ...[4]

Contrast this impeded path towards Truth with the following:

> There are and can be only two ways of searching into and dis-
> covering truth. The one flies from the senses and particulars to
> the most general axioms, and from these principles, the truth of
> which it takes for settled and immovable, proceeds to judgement
> and to the discovery of middle axioms. And this way is now in
> fashion. The other derives axioms from the senses and particu-
> lars, rising by a gradual and unbroken ascent, so that it arrives at
> the most general·axioms last of all. This is the true way, but as
> yet untried.[5]

This is a deliberate and rather stark contrast that needs
further analysis and explanation. These thoughts are allied
within historical and epistemological contexts that are both
related to each other as well as being different from each other.
Bacon scholars now have found that his attitude towards the fall
of man was one that emphasized a loss of natural knowledge in
the fall.[6] Here, I am suggesting that Bonaventura's ladder
broken in Adam makes a related point in their respective views
of the progress of knowledge. However, there is also an important distinction. Bacon thought that man lost and needed to
regain his knowledge of nature through philosophy, and his
knowledge of God through scripture. By contrast, Bonaventura
was a mystic who only stressed knowledge of nature in so far as
it participated in the exalted knowledge of God. This distinction also needs to be qualified. Bacon might have described the
loss of natural knowledge as a loss of awareness of God's power
in the universe. Even though the reality of God was understood
to be far greater than the expression of His power in the universe, there is no doubt about Bacon's own belief that knowing
the universe makes a kind of bridge between man and God.

> For our Saviour saith, *You err, not knowing the Scriptures, nor the
> power of God*; laying before us two books or volumes to study
> (Scripture and Nature), if we will be secured from error; first,
> the Scriptures revealing the Will of God; and then the creatures
> expressing his Power; whereof the latter is a key unto the
> former. . . .[7]

Here natural knowledge is a key to the moral and spiritual
knowledge contained in the scriptures. Both volumes are put
before men by God. Nature is not really only just a stepping
stone to the meanings of scripture. God gave both objects of
knowledge to men and men ought not to ignore the divine
purpose that contains a mandate to discover the world.[8] As
Bacon sees it:

> the knowledge of man is as the·waters, some descending from
> above and some springing from beneath; the one informed by
> the light of nature, the other inspired by divine revelation.[9]

What Bacon is suspicious of is cumulative knowledge, the knowledge conveyed by past teachings. Men must now go straight to the source in nature to build a more certain knowledge. Note that the first-hand character of this activity again moves Bacon close to St. Bonaventura and to the whole Augustinian tradition. For, this tradition also did not primarily recommend scholarly pursuits and also promoted the striving for a kind of first-hand knowledge. But the pattern of both similarities and radical distinctions continues; for, Bacon believes that it will be possible for future generations to build upon the first-hand knowledge that he and others using this method are establishing. A bad cumulative tradition will be replaced by a better one, with the understanding that direct reference to nature will always be necessary.

By contrast St. Bonaventura is both anti-historical and anti-empirical. The acquisition of knowledge is a personal spiritual experience. The human faculty for it and the divine source of it are available to all mankind. Even the stages of knowing can be mapped out. Still, the experience is entirely personal and individual. Hence, the guidance can be passed on to future generations but not the actual knowledge itself. Yet, at the same time, both systems reinforce the inspiration and, indeed, the intention of the divine creator. Here it is in Bacon:

> (The knowledge of nature is) not only opening our understanding to conceive the true sense of the Scriptures, by the general notions of reason and rules of speech; but (is) chiefly opening our belief, in drawing us into a due meditation of the omnipotency of God, which is chiefly signed and engraven upon His works.[10]

Then, at this point in time, discovery is not unrelated to contemplation.

Shortly below I will continue comparing and contrasting Bonaventura with Bacon because it offers a way of pinpointing conceptual changes and seeing just where historical pressures were felt most. The terms of the analogy between God as creator and man as thinker were altering while, at the same time, this model continued as a frame of reference.

For both Bonaventura and Bacon revealed knowledge before the fall was the direct gift of God to Adam. Apparently Bacon even thought that although man had understood nature while still in paradise, God had given moral laws together with this natural knowledge. These were laws that man was intended to accept rather than understand. Then, as Prometheus stole fire or light, man craved moral enlightenment, the right to understand and make his own laws. In consequence, he fell and lost his innocence and his knowledge of nature.[11] Thus, now men had to make efforts and work to recover first, the loss at the fall, and then one additional loss that Bacon saw as from ancient wise men, pre-socratic philosophers. Perhaps providence was responsible; but, providence also offered the possibility of the rediscovery of the knowledge of nature through the work of induction and experiment.

The knowledge before the fall was a knowledge outside of historical time. All of St. Bonaventura's recommendations are directed towards men's personal recovery of that state of apprehension outside of time. Nicholas of Cusa had also emphasized an a-temporal source; but, he did not think the soul had lost knowledge of nature by being embodied. The whole of temporal experience was for the perfecting of knowledge. However, Renaissance thinkers and, in his own way, even Francis Bacon posited another loss; this was the lost knowledge of the ancients. Therefore, the personal effort to see beyond time by faith was given a parallel and temporal stream. This was man's effort to recover a knowledge that he presumed he had once had. This did not contradict faith but complemented it while, at the same time, being far less ambitious.

The extraordinary a-temporal situation and the fall marks a grand ethical lapse. Adam lost his innocence. In the moral area innocence is the higher yet parallel gift to that of knowledge. Then Bacon sought a recovery of both natural and ethical knowledge through understanding the Creator's marks upon creation.

Bonaventura gave nature very little space in his scheme, a spark, a stepping stone. While, leaving aside faith, which we already know to be 'opened' by knowledge, Bacon gave nature vast territory. It is not a spark but a guiding light. And even in nature the mind seeks guiding principles. This is a progress from the complex and several to the simple and few, if not to the one. The character and direction of this movement is entirely traditional, while the distribution of territory is entirely Baconian. He writes:

> ....For knowledges are as pyramids, whereof history is the basis. So of natural philosophy, the basis is natural history: the stage next the basis is physique; the stage next the vertical point is metaphysique. As for the vertical point, *opus quod operatur Deus a principio usque ad finem*, the summary law of nature, we know not whether man's inquiry can attain unto it. But these three be the true stages of knowledge and are to them that are depraved no better than giant's hills. . . .

Bacon continues making the point that ethical goodness is a prerequisite for the investigator. He must be holy in the description of His works, holy in the connection of them, and holy in the union of them in a perpetual and uniform law. Bacon continues:

> And therefore the speculation was excellent in Parmenides and Plato, although but a speculation in them, that all things by scale did ascend to unity. So then always that knowledge is worthiest which is charged with the least multiplicity.[12]

His image of the pyramid gives the territorial distribution. The small region is the most important but the vast base region *must* be understood to make any sense of the small. Nature does more than stimulate man on his quest for knowledge. It informs him in every necessary and essential way. At the apex of Bacon's pyramid we arrive, or we just might arrive, at the summary principle of nature; so this whole pyramid below the point may be compared with Bonaventura's first stage, the way of God. Of course, Bacon does not separate his external and internal paths; as before in Cusanus, the notions in the mind are developed from experience. But undoubtedly the importance of the territory of nature has been vastly expanded within the vision of the whole process of knowing.

The thread with the older epistemological tradition is maintained, however, and this time it is in Bacon's point that only the ethically good can discover nature. We are still on a holy quest.

The feeling that a positive direction of the human will and an ethical purpose was necessary, in order to acquire knowledge of nature, or of super-nature, is most forceful within the whole tradition of thought that viewed physical reality as an image or model of The Ideas.

For example, Paracelsus did not believe that the unethical and uninspired physician would be able to find the antidotes and cures hidden in natural things. A related belief expressing the moral efficacy of discovery itself was expanded throughout the seventeenth century. For instance, consider the following thoughts about Robert Boyle:

> The message is clear: nature presents to the student a model of harmony with God's purpose that men would do well to emulate. Each creature functions in such a way as to conduce to the end of all. If 'The Very Brutes' can do this, how much better able should men be to do the same? The study of nature then is not an end in itself. Nor was Boyle interested here in science in a modern sense. He believed such study to contribute to man's moral, civic, and religious enterprise. All knowledge ultimately

becomes ethical knowledge, teaching men to live more virtuous-
ly, and the pursuit of knowledge an ethical pursuit...to the
extent that men put Boyle's formula into practice they tune their
lives to providence and so contribute to the universal harmony
just as 'The Very Brutes' do and teach them to. Thus, as the
indolent are reformed, the ranks of the virtuous swell; harmony
will then come to pervade human affairs as it does all else . . . .[13]

In the seventeenth century, most of medicine appears to have
been invested with similar moral purposes.[14] Yet none of this is
too distant from Alberti, who, we know, also believed that
knowledge of proportion in the beings was able to refine proportion within civic and family activities. He viewed this in
Pythagorean terms, but the symbols of balance and harmony
were also applied to purely physical areas.

In Bonaventura's system it was necessary to have the grace of
God to see. Later, this is conceived of with a comparable stress
upon piety, but a tremendous difference in the style of the
piety. Instead of meditating and praying men also saw that
they had to look, touch, test, and think.

Bacon actually places emphasis on, now not only the moral
sensibilities of the one who would know, but also upon his ability to do this in the right way, to deploy the proper style:

So if we should rest in contemplation of the exterior of them (of
divine works), as they first offer themselves to our senses, we
should do a like injury unto the majesty of God, as if we should
judge or construe of the store of some excellent jeweller, by that
only which is set out toward the street of his shop.[15]

Although this is a timely attitude, one necessary for the
development of empirical science, it still resembles earlier
attitudes, for instance, those of Leonardo. And although the
point of getting beyond the surface is here applied to physical
nature by both Leonardo and by Bacon, it had always been
there but not always there for physical nature. St Bonaventura
was just as anxious to get beyond the surface to the real truth;
while he saw the truth in wholly spiritual images. This peeling
off and getting beyond the surface then is traditional, but the
focus on physical nature is more modern. So, when Francis
Bacon and later Robert Boyle emphasized the distinction between a superficial appreciation of nature and a rational admiration of it they were taking up a traditional epistemological
point but focusing it on nature.

Bonaventura too had been offering a discipline, a practice
intended to refine and perfect knowledge from the superficial
and purely sensuous to the rational, intellectual and spiritual.

Both paths share the assumption that the universe is a model within which something of true reality is expressed. The first step on the approach to knowledge requires reverence for that greater reality. The following procedures involve methods intellectual and/or contemplative, with many unique combinations, as we have seen. Clearly, there are giant steps between Bonaventura's and Bacon's pathways; but, these are steps that apparently do not exclude some important and striking parallel assumptions.

The old within the new

Connecting Francis Bacon with an old tradition may seem wrong; for, he himself made much of the newness of what he had to say. He disavowed connections with the schools of ancient philosophy and especially with Pythagoras, Plato and Aristotle. But in fact, Bacon's system makes a contrast with the past which, though striking enough, is by no means as stark as he is commonly assumed to have tried to make it. Current research has brought out his association with and debt to others, especially to Renaissance thinkers. For example, his own idea as to the character of first principles, an idea that he changed over the years, was formed with the influence of alchemical sources, as well as by the atomist philosophy of Democritus.[16] Although Bacon criticized bad astrology, he also accepted the value of good astrology. What he despised was the proud and esoteric aspect of Renaissance magic. At the same time he was himself indebted to Ficino, Cornelius Agrippa, and others of this esoteric tradition.[17]

The crux of Bacon's reform was methodological. He did not really repudiate all of the achievements of the past. And, when it came to the grand assumptions, he even advanced the analogical image of nature. All he attempted (though it was a great deal) on this part of the ground was to make a complete reform of what I am here calling the 'recognition process'.[18] He did not deny objective and intuitive powers of mind, but he did reject the use of them as sure and certain methods of knowing nature. The grandeur of intuition is tainted by the human inability to completely distinguish it from imagination. Reason provides this power to distinguish when the method of induction and experiment is used. So, he writes:

> To God, truly, the Giver and Architect of Forms, and it may be to the Angels and higher intelligences, it belongs to have an affirmative knowledge of Forms immediately, and from the first

contemplation. But this assuredly is more than man can do, to whom it is granted only to proceed at first by negatives and at last to end in affirmatives after exclusion has been exhausted.[19]

Francis Bacon viewed nature as a divinely ordained system in which all the particulars manifest some portion of the laws of that system and the laws are further united in a summary principle or law. He adopts the common term *Forms* to describe natural laws with all their particulars (Bacon uses the word clauses).[20] Whosoever comprehends the forms sees that nature is essentially based upon a unified system of forms despite the apparent unrelatedness of things:

> The true form is such that it deduces the given nature from some source of being which is inherent in more natures, and which is better known in the natural order of things than the form itself. For a true and perfect axiom of knowledge then the direction and precept will be, *that another nature be discovered which is convertible with the given nature, and yet is a limitation of a more general nature, as of a true and real genus.*[21]

Knowledge can be reduced to a few primary axioms. There is an analogy between the whole and the parts, and the passage from 'Vulcan to Minerva' is the mind's refinement of its understanding of the details and the order of this scheme:

> The nearer it (the investigation) approach to simple natures, the easier and plainer everything will become . . . .[22]

The idea is one of a homogeneous system of nature and of natural law. The 'clauses' or particulars contain a general nature common to many of them. This ascends to the very simple axioms. J.M. Keynes identified this sort of notion as the assumption underlying all modern science.

Even so, Bacon was assuming rather more than that the character of nature is such that the sun will rise tomorrow. Nature is the expression of divine power and wisdom. Human knowledge ought to be made into a replica of the natural order, a mental image analogous to the whole and the parts of nature. This is ordained and it is man's destiny to discover that order in time. His prayer at the end of the *Great Instauration* distinguishes God the designer from man the appointed interpreter of nature. Human works can and must correspond to His work within creation. Bacon writes:

> . . . May He graciously grant to us to write an apocalypse or true vision of the footsteps of the Creator imprinted on his creatures.

Therefore do Thou, O Father who gavest the visible light as the first fruits of creation, and didst breathe into the face of man the intellectual light (mind, as the alchemical breath of God) as the crown and consummation thereof, guard and protect this work, which coming from Thy goodness returneth to Thy glory.[23]

If this seems a simply politic sort of prayer, consider the following passages from the *Novum Organum:*

For I am building in the human understanding a true model of the world, such as it is in fact, not such as man's own reason would have it to be: a thing which cannot be done without a very diligent dissection and anatomy of the world. But I say that these foolish and apish images of worlds which the fancys of men have created in philosophical systems, must be utterly scattered to the winds. Be it known then how vast a difference there is . . . between the idols of the human mind and the ideas of the divine. The former are nothing more than arbitrary abstractions: the latter are the creator's own stamp upon creation, impressed and defined in matter by true and exquisite lines. Truth therefore and utility are here the very same things: *and works themselves are of greater value as pledges of truth than as contributing to the comforts of life.*[24]

I am not raising a capitol or pyramid to the pride of man, but laying a foundation in the human understanding for a holy temple after the model of the world. That model therefore I follow. For whatever deserves to exist deserves to be known, *for knowledge is the image of existence* . . . .[25]

Bacon believed that man was divinely endowed to know nature and the age was at hand wherein that knowledge would be perfected.

Stripped to the barest essentials, I would say that the epistemological visions of St. Bonaventura and Francis Bacon differ most in their respective conceptions, firstly, of the recognition process, and secondly, of the style of divine involvement with man's attainment of knowledge. The calling on Christ and divine grace are the very personalized helps in Bonaventura's inward and upward road to knowledge. By contrast, providence applies to mankind *as a whole*; and Bacon makes his individual seeker responsible for his own morality and methods in the seeking. This is a less instantly miraculous, less personal, conception of the thing; although, in both cases, the receiving of the light certainly has transcendental shadings. Bonaventura's vision of spiritual progress involves traditional Aristotelian and Neo-Platonic distinctions within the natural order. There are qualitative differences between material manifestations of that natural order, cosmic ones, finite ones, purely intellectual ones, and spiritual ones, and a vision of the divine ideas. On the other hand, Bacon's model of the order of nature in the mind is achieved by a disciplined practice that directly addresses itself to experience. Certainly, the mind processes sensual information and even its own thoughts with inductive tests. If truths are expressed on other planes of reality, these are not the planes that are accessible to the disciplined application of the human mind. Bacon does not so much repudiate intuitive powers as he channels and systematizes them:

> I maintain a sort of suspension of the judgement, and bring it to what the Greeks call Acatalepsia, - a denial of the capacity of the mind to comprehend truth. But in reality that which I meditate and propound is not Acatalepsia, but Eucatalepsia, not denial of the capacity to understand, but provision for understanding truly; for I do not take away authority from the senses, but supply them with helps; I do not slight the understanding, but govern it.[26]

Bacon takes all experience into account, not only natural science, but political matters, emotions and passions, operations of the mind like memory and judgement, in fact the character of all natural things. He uses inductive methods of systematic observation, reasoning, experiments, tabulation, the comparison of tables and of results, and the mutual correction of errors in the results, all in order to test man's knowledge.

We can understand Bacon's analogy between the parts and the whole of nature on the simple basis of common axioms or laws that unite the 'clauses' or particulars. Ultimately all of these are further united in the divine concept of nature. Men understand this, but it is doubtful if they can achieve the summary axioms of history, natural theology, natural philosophy, etc., even less an understanding of His idea of nature. So even in Bacon (at the level of assumption) there is a curious non-knowledge, the supposition that the axioms are united in God's concept although the method does not aspire to take men to that concept. However, it can take men to a deep and significant understanding of the divine impression within nature.

The mystical views of St. Bonaventura and the modern ones of Francis Bacon alike confirm the real existence of the natural world and also of man's capacity to understand it. In Bonaventura's vision this even ascends to man's capacity to see beyond natural reality. Their stages of illumination are radically different. Both begin in the world; then, Bacon's ascent is a wholly intellectual process. Bacon offers us only the bare bones of Neo-Platonism: the ideas of the divine mind, His providence, the impression of His power in nature, and another impression, potential in the human mind while actual in providence. Certainly this is not an orthodox Platonist structure, but neither was Nicholas of Cusa's. However, we do have the essential analogy between the Creator's ideas and creation, between the Creator's wisdom or providence and the model perfected within the human mind and demonstrated in human works.

At times Bonaventura and Bacon even use the same language of symbols. In Hebraic, Christian, and Neo-Platonic traditions the image of King Solomon represents man's desire and capacity to attain both knowledge and wisdom. In the mythical and imaginary past of 'Solomon's House' in the *New Atlantis* there are symbols that are similar to some that Bonaventura used in his 'Stages in the Ascent to God'. For St. Bonaventura the number six in itself has spiritual meaning, whereas in Bacon it stands as the symbol of a partly mystical event, the temporal fruition of the divine will pertaining to the making of the mind's model of the order of nature. Bonaventura is steeped in the mystical meanings of number; yet, systems of knowledge described by the number symbols of the creation were also of sufficient appeal to Bacon for him to have repeated the creation symbols in his *New Atlantis*. Not only this, but St. Bonaventura's view of the loss of implanted knowledge by sin and the restoration by grace corresponds to Bacon's conception of loss at the fall and a providential recovery by ethical philosophers.

Then within a Christian and Neo-Platonic tradition of knowledge Bacon is unique in making the quest communal, the college is an institution; and he also has a different vision of the style of divine involvement insofar as providence is a continuous order, whereas grace (which can, of course, be part of providence) is also a personal and immediate act. Bacon's knowledge-aspired-to is a knowledge of nature and of man in all aspects, all knowledge of God's power in the universe; while, the mystical systems were more ambitious. Lastly, whereas Bonaventura uses his numbers both as symbols and, one feels, as modes expressing a spiritual reality, Bacon just uses them as symbols in a straightforward way. The College of the Six Days' Works is suitably named because it reminds men of the six days of the creation; but Bacon doesn't go so far as to suggest that this pattern of six should be reproduced in the step towards the solution of any problem.

The world is real

Throughout the Platonic tradition the finite world was given a real existence that could be perceived and, to some extent, be understood through recognizable analogies within nature, analogies with the eternal ideas. You will recall that even the most mystical of western systems gave a validity to men's sensory and conceptual experience that some oriental systems did not concede.[27] No matter how many hierarchical stages we have had to cope with, no system of consequence has told us to deny experience altogether and to deny the self. One cannot reasonably deny one's person if that person has an immortal soul and is made in the image of God. Hence Christian mysticism reinforced the Greco-Roman view that the world and the individuals in it were real. Then, western traditions established a close relation between conception and product, between God and his creation, and even possibly, between human works and nature; in short, between the ego and outside objects. Some oriental mystical systems not only deny this identification between ego and object but they even deny the most primitive inclination, the feeling that I am real. This is an extreme of mysticism that goes far beyond self-depreciation and denial.

By contrast the religious and Platonic currents that conveyed the analogy between the whole and the parts of nature to Renaissance men were, at least potentially, man-glorifying currents. For, in this line of thought, man was esteemed as one who - even in his base terrestrial condition - shared a part of the qualities of divine mind and spirit. Nature was intended to serve man, thus, by implication, man was the master of nature and he was set above all earthly creatures. Now although points like these had not always been used to stimulate the study of nature or validate human works they were implicit in culture, and they were increasingly called upon in the Renaissance and seventeenth century. Despite the displacement of the earth from the centre of the cosmos in the Copernican system, these points continued to be used both to confirm the study of nature and the value of the human intellect. As the conception of the physical universe expanded it looks like the ego also expanded, at least in the case of many leading thinkers, and man grew more ambitious in his knowledge. As creator after the divine creator men appear to have identified with the vast universe and its designer. Thus, Cassirer's observation was true when he said: 'The infinity of the cosmos threatens not only to limit the ego, but even to annihilate it completely; but the same infinity seems also to be the source of the ego's constant self-elevation, for the mind is like the world that it conceives.'[28]

Sceptics aside, the exalted view of man was not just the product of a humanistic determination to have it so. Varying sources appeared to justify it when looked at through the eyes of Renaissance culture. Implicit or explicit in traditional literature men singled out the view of themselves as the interpreters of God's works and as creators in His image. Aristotelian traditions may have attached little value to human works, but combined Platonic and Latin traditions contained elements that could be used to contradict that low value. Renaissance men, inspired by many diverse elements within their culture, called upon these favourable traditions to support them in their high evaluation of themselves and of their works. Of the Christian fathers, St. Augustine was especially esteemed. St. Augustine wrote about pleasurable effect of the knowledge that man is not only the object of divine grace, not only passive, but that man is also the carrier of the image of God within his own being. In this tradition both St. Bonaventura and Cusanus used the distinction between image and object to emphasize the active role of man in the acquisition of either spiritual or natural knowledge. Augustine had especially pointed to the fact that man had the capacity to recognize God both in himself and in the rest of nature.[29] Dante and others picked up and developed this point. Even as mystical a thinker as Thomas à Kempis supplied grounds for seeing human knowledge as divinely ordained. Certainly this needed to be abstracted from its wider context in Kempis, yet the selection of such points and their new placement in humanistic contexts was a major feature of Renaissance scholarship. Later I intend to say more about inspirations from classical Roman sources; for now I will discuss developments within Renaissance Neo-Platonism.

The cosmic position of man was given ecstatic praise in the *Corpus Hermeticum*.[31] This body of works, translated by Marsilio Ficino in 1465, formed an important part of the ideology of the Florentine Academy. The corpus is represented by several works written between the second and third centuries A.D. These contain Greek philosophy of the period together with mixtures of Platonism, Stoicism, Jewish, and possibly Persian ideas. In the fifteenth century these were believed to have been the work of a single author, Hermes Trismegistus. The corpus was seen as lost knowledge recovered, for Hermes was thought to have been an Egyptian philosopher either contemporary to Moses or to have lived shortly afterwards. A teacher-disciple genealogy traced his influence to Plato and to Pythagoras. In and above the mythical sources of the corpus, Platonists also drew upon the writings of Lactantius, one of the fathers of the church. Lactantius revered Hermes Trismegistus, together with the Sibyls, as a prophet who had foretold the coming of Christianity. Altogether the reputation of the corpus preceded its translation; and Cosimo de Medici asked Ficino to translate it first while the complete works of Plato were still awaiting translation. The rejoicing at the unique position of man is exemplified in the following passage that begins with the point that all creatures are in God:

> See what power, what swiftness you possess. It is so that you must conceive of God; all that is, he contains within himself like thoughts, the world, himself, the All. Therefore unless you make yourself equal to God, you cannot understand God: for the like is not intelligible save to the like. Make yourself grow to a greatness beyond measure, by a bound free yourself from the body; raise yourself above all time, become Eternity; and then you will understand God. Believe that nothing is impossible for you, think yourself immortal and capable of understanding all, all arts, all sciences, the nature of every living being. Mount higher than the highest height; descend lower than the lowest depth. Draw into yourself all sensations of everything created, fire and water, dry and moist, imagining that you are everywhere, on earth, in the sea, in the sky, that you are not yet born, in the maternal womb, adolescent, old, dead, beyond death. If you embrace in your thought all things at once, times, places, substances, qualities, quantities, you may understand God.
> Say no longer that God is invisible. Do not speak thus, for what is more manifest than God? He has created all only that you may see it through the beings. For that is the miraculous power of God, to show himself through all beings. For nothing is invisible, even of the incorporeals. The intellect makes itself visible in the act of thinking, God in the act of creating.[32]

The analogy reads, as God creates so man thinks. The human understanding, on a limited scale, parallels the act of creation. The analogy between God, man, and nature is quite specific:

> Man is united to the gods by what he has of the divine, his intellect; all other creatures are bound to him by the celestial plan and he attaches them to himself by knots of love. This union of gods with men is . . . only for those who have the faculty of intellection. Thus alone among creatures man is double, one part like God, the other formed of the elements.[33]

These man-glorifying themes were taken up with great fervour. Renaissance versions of the analogy between the whole and the parts of nature, and between microcosm and macrocosm, tended to lift man from a passive role, that of an embodiment of the germs of all things, to that of a user of this tremendous imaginative potential. In him are all things; so let him become all things, understand all things, and in this way become a god. No one put it better than Pico in his *Oration on the Dignity of Man*. Beasts have a specific and pre-ordained nature and intelligences also have a fixed spiritual nature. By contrast, man was given the power to alter his nature, to become all things.

The Neo-Platonists did not celebrate the ego by themselves. Humanists like Petrarch, Coluccio Salutati, Lorenzo Valla, Platina and Aurello Brandolini also found inspiration in Augustinian traditions. Their faith in the powers of man was largely expressed in the areas of politics and morals, of civic humanism. We have seen this in Alberti's *Della Famiglia*. The Platonic and humanist traditions were not always separate, and the humanist tradition of a *theologia poetica* was actually combined in the *theologia platonica*.[34] Thus the glorification of man was not the result of developments in only one particular stream or intellectual tradition. The broad direction of Renaissance society was such that men tended to see themselves in this way. They selected and formed ideas that confirmed and reinforced their views of nature, man, and God.

Up to this point I have selected examples from the thoughts of men who represent Neo-Platonism in some form or another. Panofsky has made it clear that we cannot view Leonardo as a Platonist in the way that we can Michelangelo.[35] Still, we have seen that Leonardo's assumptions about nature and human knowledge deeply resemble the ideas of the Christian Platonist, Nicholas of Cusa. Similarly, Alberti who had had sharp differences with the Florentine Academy was also a kind of Platonist; he believed the universe to be a model of the divine idea, and man to be a creator after the divine creator. The variety of expression belonging to Platonism should not be unexpected; for Professor P. O. Kristeller has frequently remarked that almost no idea that was considered characteristic of Platonism was held by a majority of Renaissance Platonists.[36] Clearly, questions about which men were real Neo-Platonists and about what body of beliefs made up the content of Renaissance Neo-Platonism are difficult to answer. Plato scholars accept the Neo-Platonism of the philosophy of Plotinus as a truly Platonic philosophy.[37] But, if the view shifts from whole integrated philosophical systems to frameworks of assumptions then the Platonic inspirations often show themselves, and this is true even if a basic principle has been altered. After all, Cusa rejected the Platonic *Ideas*, yet it would be all wrong to see him apart from Platonic traditions. In a similar vein, gnostic ideas like those of the *Corpus Hermeticum* were eclectic and came late in ancient Neo-Platonic traditions. These then became part of a historical tradition without owing all of the substance of their content to the philosophy of Plato. The eclectic character of the Neo-Platonic historical tradition continued throughout the

Middle Ages and the early modern era. As this is not a philosopher's attempt systematically to characterize a movement, we can even see that sometimes Aristotelianism was engulfed by the Platonic animal.

The many meanings and the importance of the idea of beauty

A consistent metaphor between beauty and enlightenment appears within the Platonic tradition. Certainly, beauty itself was an eclectic notion that came to include symmetry, proportion and harmony. The concept was applied to things like moral worth, to the order of the cosmos, to the relation between the universe and God, as well as to what is pleasing to the eye, the ear, and the mind. As we have seen with the notion of continuity, beauty was a concept that had little to do with the element or physical substance to which it was applied. It was a word that in the Renaissance came more and more to indicate a proper relationship, one between parts and the whole, or between wholes on different planes of existence. In the broadest sense, if continuity was connectedness, beauty was rightness. In any application, beauty could make the analogy between the beings or things under consideration. This is clear in Plotinus:

> But is there any similarity between loveliness here below and that of the intelligible realm? If there is, then the two orders will be in this alike. What can they have in common beauty here and beauty there? They have we suggest this in common: they are sharers of the same Idea.[38]

So the Idea can manifest itself within many ways and in many beings and things, and the substance of these will vary. Plotinus makes the point that if you cannot detect the beauty of your own soul, you must do as a sculptor does, perfecting the lines, and disengaging the beautiful form within the marble, or in the soul. For:

> ...To proceed from observing the symmetry of living things to the symmetry of all life is to exercise a part of that faculty which, even here below, knows and contemplates the perfect symmetry of the intelligible realm.[39]

This process of knowing is possible because of the actuality of the creator's intelligence, or, in Plotinus' words, The Intelligence:

> The Intelligence must be understood not as intelligence in potency or intelligence evolving (which would, in any case, require another prior intelligence) but as intelligence in actuality and for all eternity . . . .It thinks of itself and by itself, it is its thoughts. . . .[40]

Recall that Cusanus developed this concept as the actuality of everything within the Unity of God.

The philosophical ideal of beauty supported men's application of notions of beauty and harmony to many different fields or disciplines. Beauty came to be applied to both epistemological and aesthetic questions. Architecture, all the visual arts, music, and the formal aspects of literary and dramatic arts all implied this dual connotation, one, of informing the mind, the other, of pleasing the mind by means of proper decorum, style and symmetry. Thus, the long-term association between beauty and enlightenment was emphasized within early modern thinking, and it, in turn, tended to confirm man's desire to understand, imitate, and perhaps, even to control nature. This confirmation worked both for conceptual ambitions and for their expression within works, in Francis Bacon's language, for experiments of light and for experiments of fruit. And this seems to be true, that this ancient metaphor between beauty and light acted as the catalyst and support for the practices in the arts, in natural magic, and in natural philosophy. Metaphorically speaking, Abel and Cain were nurtured on the same mother's milk.

The medieval crystallization of this dynamic notion of beauty was accomplished in the thought of St. Augustine (354-430). Inspired by Augustinian ideas, Dante later mentions Bonaventura as a saint in the *Paradiso*. The *Convivio* also exhibits both pseudo-Dionysian and Augustinian hierarchical ideas. The spheres of the cosmos were associated with angelic hierarchies and with man's ascent to illumination.[41] The writings attributed to Dionysius the supposed Areopagite and contemporary of St. Paul were actually written in the early centuries of the Christian era. These writings mingle Platonism with Christianity. They contain the vision of the nine angelic hierarchies accepted by St. Thomas Aquinas. There are parallels between Dionysian mysticism and Hermetic gnosticism.[42] The blend was reinforced in the synthetic thinking of Ficino. Hence, a tradition that had its roots in Plato's *Timaeus* and Boethius' *Consolation* also included these highly mystical writings attributed to the

Pseudo-Dionysius.[43] All of these sources inspired St. Augustine, and directly and indirectly, through intermediaries like Dante and Cusanus, this tradition influenced many Renaissance men.

The synthesists of the Florentine Academy combined Augustinian Christian Platonism with other ideas that Augustine himself had not approved. Augustine did not like magic. Ficino evaded this, sheltering behind Lactantius, who, you will remember, praised Hermes Trismegistus. In this way Ficino confirmed his formulation of the belief that man was on the path to enlightenment with magical practices supporting the human ambition to understand and to manipulate nature. Man could use his knowledge to influence his destiny.[44] The earlier Leonardo-Faust image is one that encompasses this point.

Those who have concentrated on the rise of empiricism or the progress of the sciences have often tended to undervalue Ficino's mysticism. Essentially, this is because Ficino caused an effective and dramatic revival of hierarchies, of stages of illumination transcending the rational. This can be seen in contrast to Leonardo who felt he had to work empirically or through mathematics. Ficino primarily worked through sympathy and magic. Now in one respect, the redirection of the mind towards hierarchies must be seen not to have been progressive. However, refinements in interpreting the history of ideas do not come about in this way, with historians marking score cards, true or false, progressive or regressive. The values that develop from any specific culture or system of ideas can develop from many different parts of that system. In the case of the academy it was the tremendous affirmation of the potential of man for the attainment of real knowledge and power. In their system and later in several related systems, the human potential cannot be separated from the actual practice of magic. However, this is not necessarily how everyone received their optimism. Descartes could get equally excited about the spiritual reality of the mind, and Francis Bacon about his own non-magical method. Yet all contributed to many successive eras of optimism and sustained the ever-growing ambitions of the European intellectual world. Another positive feature of magic was that it was a practice and confirmed work, the manipulation of all sorts of materials, and sometimes, the systematic observation of natural things. For example, the sympathetic and herbalist medicine of Paracelsus. Although historians can mark down ideas, and even whole systems, they have got to respect the fact that the progressive potential of concepts does not happen according to the logic of these concepts but rather according to many subtle cultural parameters. Irrational systems, or aspects of them, can and did serve in the advancement of learning. Bacon's conviction that an age of knowledge was at hand holds an unacknowledged debt to Ficino, Bruno and to the whole mystico-magical tradition.

Traditions often mingled in varying ways to be formed into the assumption of the harmony of nature, the extended analogy between the divine plan, the heavens and the earth, human beings and even their arts, sciences and works. Many mingled associations inspired physicians, philosophers and different kinds of artists. An example might be Ficino's monodic Orphic hymns. These were supposed to have had health-giving effects and powers abetting practices of natural magic. But later these were developed in theory by the musical humanists. The hymns had promoted the idea that ancient music had been monodic and that this was the way to produce profound effects in the mind, spirit and soul of man. Even this very potent notion of the effects had had a varied background; for, it was developed from sources in sympathetic magic and also from humanists' interpretations of history and theory of education.

In painting often the hidden correspondences signified in the iconographic content were Hermetic and/or Cabalistic, while the naturalistic style of the painting, the perspective, formal harmony, and the decorum of the *istoria* were concurrently inspired by Greco-Roman and Arabic traditions and by humanists' interpretations of them.[45] Frances Yates cites the iconography of Botticelli's 'Primavera' as the expression of a Ficinian sort of magic and Dürer's 'Melancolia' of the Neo-Platonic and Cabalist magic of Cornelius Agrippa.[46] In an extension of this point recall the Saturnian melancholic mood colouring the disposition of Leonardo.[47] Dürer was definitely influenced by both Alberti and Leonardo. His quest for ideal proportions matched and sometimes exceeded that of Leonardo.[48] So, number and harmony were often uniting themes, linking the classical sense of order with a mysterious world of magical significance. Without expanding these suggestions, it should be clear that unqualified distinctions between magical, mathematical and humanistic traditions can be defective. The moral, decorous, and formal sense of proportion and beauty, nurtured by humanists, and the intermingled goals, 'back to antiquity', and 'back to nature', were frequently also overlaid and complemented by a sympathetic and correspondential schema between numbers, sounds, images, celestial bodies and/or ideal prototypes.[49]

Different types of universality

Two very general roles of major importance have been suggested for the analogy between the whole and the parts of nature and its mates; first, they confirmed the powers of the mind in both conceptual and expressive activity, and second, they advanced concepts of the homogeneity of nature and the universe, the parts could and did imply the whole.[50] In the present section the related themes of universality and of the bringing together of disciplines will be discussed in a wider historical context than before.

The desire for personal universality or for mankind's achievement of a universal corpus of knowledge was the natural complement to man's high confidence in the power of the human mind to discover and understand. As before in the section on Leonardo-Faust, the craving for effectiveness was actually associated with men's higher estimation of the destiny and the capacities of the human mind. Similarly, the so-phrased bringing together of disciplines was, in part, a conscious quest to deepen understanding, by bringing to light the generic similarities at the core of the different spheres of knowledge. To be sure, it was sometimes unconscious or, at least, only partly deliberate. Clearly, not every eclectic mind from the fifteenth to the seventeenth century was engaged with full deliberation in the pursuit of parallels between disciplines or in the resolution of apparent contradictions between, say, philosophy and religion. However, because of recent discoveries and the greater availability of material the assumed existence of such similarities was, more than ever, in the air. Renaissance men were often led naturally from involvement in one field of activity to another.

Vitruvius had noted that all the sciences and arts have theory in common despite great differences in practice and technique.[51] An analogical scheme of nature underlies this belief. On this basis Vitruvius recommended that the architect become a master of the theoretical background of many different disciplines:

> He should be a man of letters, a skilful draughtsman, a mathematician familiar with scientific inquiries, a diligent student of philosophy, acquainted with music; not ignorant of medicine, learned in the responses of juris consults, familiar with astronomy and astronomical calculations.[52]

It is common knowledge that this ideal of universality was taken up afresh by Renaissance men, and pursued by subsequent generations of thinkers. Few, however, are aware that the ideal of universality remained a consistent, and even a self-conscious, keynote in European society right to the encyclopaedic movement in the eighteenth century.

It is found in the thought of humanists, in the ideals of the Florentine Academy in the fifteenth century, and in the later exponents of the Magus image. Certainly, an individual might participate in rational, humanist and magical traditions all at once, and share different versions of the same ideal. Sir Isaac Newton may provide an example of this, and I shall say more about him shortly. In the sixteenth century universality had been the ideal of the 'Elizabethan man' and it was also revived in the French court and the academies. With many differences in stress, this ideal was expressed once more in the credo of the seventeenth-century scientific academies. But, in the course of time, conceptions of how to attain a universality of knowledge changed radically, while the desire to attain some form of it is usually detectable.

The Vitruvius example represents a personal ideal of universality. A man like this desires insight into the first principles of all knowledge, as well as great practical knowledge in a wide variety of fields, fields that related in some way to the business of the architect (i.e., mathematics, geography, the law pertaining to land and land ownership, etc.). However, even at the height of the revival of this ideal, in the fifteenth century, few men managed to approach personal universality. Although, I might add, right up to the early nineteenth century, to the generation of Alexander von Humboldt, various forms of personal universality were pursued by some European intellectuals.

There were, of course, also sceptics who doubted whether nature was so ordered that men could truly comprehend it. However, on the whole, extreme scepticism, like that of Pascal after 1645, did not inspire inquiry into natural philosophy. Mostly, it was those who believed in the tremendous potential of human intellectual endeavour who were inspired by some form or another of the universalist ideal.

The individuals or groups of men who wanted to devise a true method of discovery, or to compile a true philosophy of nature based upon definite principles or laws were also universalists. Like the personal universalist, these men wanted to discover the underlying principles for all natural things. This was the presumed corpus of knowledge upon which everything else depended. Similarly, in the late seventeenth and eighteenth centuries the collectors and systematizers of knowledge, those who took the anthropological approach examining the diverse cultures of the world, and the men who wanted to invent a kind of universal language were all some sort of universalist. They wished to bring about the following complementary ends: man's discovery and record of the true philosophy, by means of bringing all the facts, conditions, and theories together in one communicable body of knowledge. Also many of those who participated in universalist ideals saw themselves as participants in a new revival and restatement of a lost or almost-forgotten knowledge, perhaps devising a new method, and either redis-covering or actually uncovering the true and real corpus of human knowledge. Universalists frequently appear to have felt themselves to be on the threshold, at the brink of something newly significant that would greatly refine and/or speed man's progress in knowledge. This state of mind can be detected in thinkers who are otherwise far from each other in time, in cul-tural context, and in intellectual style. For example, both Ficino and Descartes can be said to have felt it. Ficino saw himself on the verge of a reformulation of the perennial 'true philosophy'; while Descartes felt that he had to make a personal discovery of at least one certain principle to further uncover the nature of things, before he could attain real knowledge of anything at all. Thus, no matter what the territory of knowledge was seen to be, be it learned ignorance or natural history, be it purely natural, metaphysical or theological, and no matter what the method, *the goal* or the motive is the part that relates to the true and universal. There is this persistent feeling of being at the crucial point of a new beginning, or at the necessary and final turn with the goal in sight.[53]

The sequence of these great but distinguishable themes, the universal man, the universal method, and the universal corpus of knowledge, cannot be made out in tiny chronological seg-ments. But it is possible to say that the style of the *uomo univer-sale* tended to give way to collective styles, to one person under-standing the basic principles of phenomena, the laws of nature, or to groups of men developing a knowledge of these princi-ples or laws. Magic was also quite important in this shift; for the magician could call upon agents to inform him and increase his powers. He could summon far more than he could possibly touch or conceive by himself.

The desire to comprehend the whole scope of being had been expressed by Marsilio Ficino, who believed that this goal was necessitated by the very nature of the intellect. Again this longing of the mind is a familiar theme from the works of Cusanus who characterized it as the spiritual analogue to phys-ical desire. Florentine Neo-Platonists thought that men had to attempt a comprehension of 'the whole breadth of being' because the natural object and end of the mind was 'universal truth and goodness'.[54] The following general assumptions were the necessary companions of universality. The universe was a moving replica of the divine concept, the parts of nature were integrated and interrelated in the whole order of the universe; and the human mind was so made that it either strove for or possessed the capacity to recognize that order. It could understand the order of being or, at the very least, of physical nature. All of these assumptions, comprised a loose framework for thinking, including thinking in natural philosophy, that for a very long period tended to confirm men, encouraging them to persist in the hope of fulfilling the ideal of universality.

Even the personal expression of this ideal remained popular in the seventeenth century. Here is an example concerning a musician. The inspiration of the previously cited Vitruvian image is clear. This is from an English version (1653) of Descartes' *Compendium of Musick* which was translated and prefaced by William Viscount Brouncker (1620?-1684). Brouncker was a founding fellow and the first president of the Royal Society of London. Here is the ideal musician:

> ...A complete Musitian (please you, to understand him to be such, as Hath not only Knibbled at, but swallowed the Whole Theory of Musick; i.e. having profoundly speculated the Pythagorean Scheme of the various Sounds arising from various Hammers beaten on an Anvill, respective of their different Weights, doth clearly and distinctly understand as well the Arithmetical, and Geometrical Proportions of Consonances and Dissonances: for, it is not the mere Practical Organist, that can deserve that Noble Attribute) is required a more than superficial insight into all kinds of Humane Learning. For, he must be a Physiologist: that he may demonstrate the Creation, Nature, Properties, and effects of a Natural Sound. A Philologer, to inquire into the first Invention, Institution, and succeding Propagation of an Artificial Sound, or Musick. An Arithmetician, to be able to explaine the Causes of Motions 'Harmonical' by Numbers, and declare the Mysteries of the new Algebraical Musick. A Geometrician, to evince, in great variety, the Original of Intervals Consono-dissonant, by the Geometrical, Algebraical, Mechanical Division of a Monochord. A poet; to conform his thoughts and Words to the laws of praecise Numbers, and distinguish the Euphonie of Vowells and Syllables. A Mechanique; to know the exquisite Structure or Fabrick of all Musical Instruments, Winde, Stringed or Tympanous ... A Metallist; to explore the different Contemperations of Barytonous and Oxytonous, or Grave and Acute toned Metalls, in order to the Casting of tunable Bells for Chimes, and etc. An Anatomist to satisfie concerning the Manner, and Organs of the Sense of Hearing. A Melothetick; to lay down a demonstrative method for the Composing, or Setting of all Tunes and Ayres. And lastly he must be so far a Magician, as to excite Wonder, with reducing into Practice the thaumaturgical, or admirable Secrets of Musick: I meane the Sympathies and Anitpathies betwixt Con-

sounds and Dissounds; the Medico Magical Virtues of Harmonious Notes (instanced in the cure of Saul's Melancholy fitts, and
of the prodigious Venome of the Tarantula, and etc...; and
finally the Cryptological Musick, whereby the Secret Conceptions of the Mind may be, by the language of inarticulate Sounds
communicated to a Friend, at good distance.

Certainly this is an idealization. However, contemporary lives
such as Christopher Wren's, Robert Boyle's, and John Dryden's
do testify to a definite though more limited style of universality, and certainly to many associations between the disciplines.
The business matter of the early sessions of the Royal Society
of London also exhibits the same wide range of interests and
pursuits.[56]

A century before this, in France, the founders of Baïf's
Academy for poetry and music had envisaged that body as a
kind of university wherein all the disciplines were taken seriously.[57] Powers of poetry and music arousing sympathy in the
hearers were intended to advance the educational process. Thus
the poetry and music represented the ultimate work, the
human expression in imitation of all nature and experience.
Because it was seen to have both moral and educational value
the poetry and music ought not to be understood as a limited
field, in the way that we would tend to see it now. The
academicians' world picture and, later, that of the seventeenth
century scientific academicians still retained a kind of Renaissance wholeness, if not quite the Renaissance style. The self-
image of the artist or philosopher and that of his circle of
learned friends or his institution still harks back to the *uomo
universale*.

The newness, the feeling of starting afresh, of being on the
brink of discovery frequently relates to method, as well as to
the goal attached to attaining the actual corpus of knowledge.
This is unmistakable in the ambitious statement of Francis
Bacon:

There was but one course left, therefore, to try the Whole thing
anew upon a better plan, and to commence a total reconstruction of sciences, arts, and all human knowledge, raised upon the
proper foundations.[58]

And following, here is an equally ambitious but far more personal statement by Descartes:

But I had observed that all the basic principles of all the sciences
were taken from philosophy which itself had no certain ones. It
therefore seemed that I should first attempt to establish

philosophic principles . . . This preparation would consist partly
in freeing my mind from the false opinions which I had previously acquired, partly in building up a fund of experiences
which should serve afterwards as the raw material of my reasoning, and partly in training myself in the method which I had
determined upon . . . [59]

Although it is couched, much more definitely, in the actual
context of a philosophy of science, a comparable desire for the
universal first principle is implicit in the Third Rule of the
Principia of Sir Isaac Newton.[60] Like the others, Newton also
sees himself at a crucial beginning point, the description of 'the
universal qualities of all bodies whatsoever'. The qualities,
extension, hardness, impenetrability, mobility, and *vis inertia*
of the whole are the result of these same qualities in the parts.
Thus, by analogy, Newton leads us to conclude that the smallest invisible bodies must also possess extension, hardness,
impenetrability, mobility, with their proper *vires inertiae*. Newton describes this point as the foundation of all philosophy. His
universalization of these qualities rests on the basis of Rule III,
which states:

> The qualities of bodies which admit neither intension or remission
> of degrees, and which are found to belong to all bodies within
> the reach of our experiments, are to be esteemed the universal
> qualities of all bodies whatsoever.[61]

In the three above citations Bacon and Descartes say that they
are on the brink of a *new method* of discovery, whereas Newton
uses an analogy to establish a *universal principle*. But clearly the
object and goal of the earlier methods was, also, the establish-
ment of universal axioms or principles. They were desiring what
Newton claimed to have exposed. In this broad tradition then,
Newton too can be seen to be a universalist. The justification of
his foundation of philosophy rests upon an analogy between
the primary qualities of bodies within reach of the experiments
and all other bodies, the macrocosmic bodies in space, and the
invisible primary units of matter. In this rule Newton places an
important weight upon this analogy and this is despite his own
statement to the effect that nothing can be known with certainty
without drawing all conclusions from observation and experiment.

Clearly, the disposition towards universality involves more
than the personal style of it inspired by Vitruvius. All who felt
the need to universalize their systems, methods, and to find
first principles common to many or to all the particulars were,
to some extent, relatives of the Renaissance *uomo universale*.

Behind this ideal lies their assumption of correspondences, sympathies, parallels, or analogies at the theoretical base of the human arts and sciences. Human knowledge was seen to be so because nature was made along analogical lines.

Learned societies also show the universal goals, and the inter-disciplinary approach is to be associated with the ideals of uni-versalists. While it is true that in the early modern period most of the European circles and academies were dedicated to the advancement of a particular discipline or a related field of dis-ciplines, almost all had more catholic interests as well. Ficino's Florentine Academy became the spiritual model for many sub-sequent academies. The goals of the Florentines were so wide as to wish to bring about the resolution of philosophy with religion. We have remarked that one of its spiritual descen-dants, Baïf's Académie de Poésie et de Musique (1571-3), provided for the institution of courses in all arts and sciences. The academy was too short-lived to profoundly influence the intellectual life of the era; but, at the same time, this academy by itself shows a compression and an extreme of the values of those times. Many of the preoccupations of Baïf's circle reap-pear in the later works of Mersenne and Descartes on music theory, and acoustics, and also in Descartes' theory of the pas-sions. Frances Yates uses Mersenne's impressions to give us an example of the breadth of intellectual interests evidenced in the sixteenth-century poetry and music circles in France. In *Quaestiones in Genesim* Mersenne discusses Copernican theory, and Galilean mechanics, as well as expounding Baïf's music theory.[62] The individuals in Baïf's circle show that they aimed at both personal and external goals of universality. Ronsard and Baïf studied together for five years (one working, one rest-ing, all round the clock) while they tried to master all of the disciplines.[63] A fellow and friend, Dorat, complemented their efforts with the study of Greek Letters. In 1557 Guy de Brues made a written sketch of Ronsard and Baïf at their studies. They appear as philosophers discussing Copernicus, and they also cite Neo-Platonic notions, and points of medieval philosophy and science. In using these examples, I am not try-ing to depict them as natural philosophers as well as poets and musicians. Indeed, this would be a serious distortion of Profes-sor Yates' point. Rather, they saw the arts (especially poetry and music), and the sciences forming a corpus of knowledge that could uplift and improve their whole society when gentle-men, artists, and scholars mastered the notions that linked the disciplines within the corpus. Later, Mersenne assumed this ideal. What it basically meant was that special powers like the powers of music, were to be used as the instruments of general education. The mind was to be awakened, charmed, made receptive to the universal body of knowledge. Here is a mingling of the educational ideals of Plato's *Republic* with a large range of goals that eventually came to be expressed in the Encyclopaedic movement, and sometimes in Freemasonry in the eighteenth century.

Changes in styles of the expression of universality involved not only the shift from the individual genius or magus to the academician; in addition they encompassed shifts in the social role of the universalist. In the early Renaissance architectonic scheme the *uomo universale* had served his prince or individual patron. Extreme changes, like the development of the European monarchies during the fifteenth and sixteenth centuries, were also reflected within styles of universality; for, gradually more actions and services came to be performed for king and country, for the public, for society, and, later, for mankind in general. Obviously, this was not an absolute shift; men of genius often still served individual patrons, Goethe, for example, and the services that had been performed for Renaissance patrons were not always exclusive. These services were frequently intended to serve a public function; for example, the statues commissioned by the guilds in the niches of the Or San Michele in Florence. In addition, in the Renaissance there was also a tendency for intellectual and artistic services to extend to something in and above social and philosophical value. A genius could actually lend his private patron some of the dignity of genius, the place of the gifted artist or thinker in the scheme of things. If the human mind was exalted, then so was the powerful man of taste who recognized and nurtured the genius and his works. This attitude is exemplified by the extraordinary deference which Pope Julius II or Duke Cosimo I of Florence showed towards Michelangelo, even though they both were perfectly willing, on occasion, to exploit and quarrel with him. By his very reality, and by the fact of his service the aura of the Renaissance genius included his patron, and, in the last analysis, it also included man in general, the power of the mind, the value of human works.

There has always been a tendency to assess the potential of the human mind and of the human being from an identification with the achievements of gifted and successful men (with the frequent and lamentable exclusion of women and of some men on racial grounds). The *uomo universale* not only possessed practical gifts, he both embodied and expressed the spiritual position of man in nature. Contemplation of his place within the scheme of things, gave many a satisfaction akin to aesthetic and mystical experience. And even now, many a man rejoices in his own manhood because Plato, Mozart, and Einstein were all men. This is mostly a positive form of confirmation. And, although presently this is a generalized and really rather vague thing, this assuming-of-the-aura was highly self-conscious and even political in Renaissance society.

The Renaissance style of taking satisfaction in great minds and great works gradually came to be overtaken by another kindred style.[64] The new style showed itself in the form of an increasing appreciation of the public functions of artists and intellectuals. These men came to see themselves as servants of king and country, and also, as the educators of, rather than as examples to, their fellows. Most essentially, they frequently thought of themselves as contributors to the developing model of the universe within the human mind. Thus, the satisfaction of making a personal identification with the genius that had been popular in the Renaissance, actually became a satisfaction with progress itself. The community of philosophers advance that progress; and in so doing, they benefit the larger community, the country, and ultimately, mankind.

The great monarchies of western Europe, consolidated about the beginning of the sixteenth century, encouraged the shift of the universalist scheme in this public and utilitarian direction - perhaps not least by improvements which they effected in communications, in an age when engraving and printing were revolutionizing the scope of available learned materials. Also, kings and governments tended to become patrons of learning, first, to satisfy specific needs, technological development, etc., and then, because ministers and kings are also creatures of their times and they tended to view progress in the way that the philosophers represented it. All of this promoted the development of collaborating efforts towards the achievement of universalist ideals. The most successful of the circles thus formed sometimes achieved the dignity of royal academies, and some of these circles, moreover, corresponded with other similar groups, or with learned individuals, in distant places. I also associate the schemes to create both a universal language and an international system of educational reform with this externalization of universal ideals. More than ever before, universality was intended to benefit society. It clothed itself in a progressive and rather mystical conception of the attainment of knowledge.

At all events, it is clear that seventeenth-century philosophers were mostly enthusiastic about directing all forms of knowledge and discovery outward for the appreciation and criticism of the learned world. Not far afterwards in time, esoteric philosophies, like Rosicrucianism, and later, the brotherhood of the Freemasons, actually contradicted this still-fresh openness of the learned world. Yet, at the same time, they did not contradict the ultimate social goals common to the dawning enlightenment. Secret systems of wisdom with hidden practitoners of various sorts wanted to uncover those universal first principles and benefit mankind with them.[65] If many of the outstanding minds of the seventeenth century and the enlightenment had not been interested in secret knowledge, if they had not formed esoteric circles and brotherhoods, there would be no apparent paradox. But often, the very people who promoted open means of expression and exchange were the same who privately cultivated esoteric knowledge. Undoubtedly there are political aspects to this but, I suggest that this is not the whole explanation for the pattern spreads from the time of Newton to that of Goethe. How can we evaluate, for example, Isaac Newton's exchange of scientific, mystical and even occult ideas with his small accepted circle of philosophers when, at the same time, the general tendency was for open expression, and he was himself persuaded to publish his scientific works? Even if the Master of the Mint thought it wise to keep alchemy, albeit high-level philosophical alchemy, quiet, historians would still have to explain the wider phenomenon. People as different as Mozart and Lavoisier became Freemasons. Some version of the universalist assumption may form their common background, but this will not explain the contrast between open and closed knowledge. This contrast appeared in both Catholic and Protestant countries over the space of two hundred years. So, there are not easy solutions to this problem, but I hope to bring forward suggestions in future.

On the public side the openly expressed style of universality is clearer. For example, in 1664, the astronomer Adrien Auzot wrote to Louis XIV to try to persuade him of the plan for a Compagnie des Sciences et des Arts. Auzot was an early member of the Académie des Sciences in 1666. All that has been said about externalization of universal ideals and their connection with public service is apparent in Auzot's plan. The Compagnie was intended to give the king technical advice, to seek knowledge for the greater comfort of France and of humanity, and to establish a bureau of standards and information. Inventions could be tested there, and unfair practices exposed. Practical projects were in navigation, farming, flood control, and the reclamation of exhausted lands. Idealistic universalist goals were crucial to Auzot's Compagnie; for the group was proposing to formulate a new natural history based upon the systematic investigation of natural phenomena. Auzot also foresaw the society continually widening its scope through correspondence with other learned bodies. The sorts of people selected for first admittance also indicate universalist aims. These were the most skilful and learned scientists, famous artists and sculptors, inventors and people capable of producing useful works. To these he added linguists and even travellers to help in the transmission and communication of ideas.[66]

Looking back at the kind of services that the Renaissance genius was likely to promise his prince and patron, it is clear that some overlap with the promises of seventeenth-century academicians. However, the new things are themselves a comment upon the new dynamics of seventeenth-century society, a world where standards have to be agreed upon for the testing of inventions, and so on. This contrast is clearer when a comparison is made between Auzot's plan addressed to Louis XIV, and Leonardo da Vinci's personal offering to Ludovico Sforza practically two hundred years earlier. Leonardo's appeal is largely personal; not, how we may be of service to the state, but, how I can serve you, and those who are your subjects. How I can accomplish works that will add 'to the glory of your illustrious ancestors, and to the honour of your family's name'. The actual services offered were practical, largely those of a military engineer. At the same time, Leonardo made limited recommendation of his artistic skills.[67] There are points of closeness, academicians still had to serve for the glory and majesty of the king. But the communal and progressive character of it all is truly modern. The academy thrived upon communication, upon an international set-up for information and criticism. Auzot's proposed academy, which became partly absorbed in the 1666 Académie des Sciences, saw itself on the brink of discovery. The true book of nature was about to be discovered in the 1660s. But we have already stood on that threshold.

Common assumptions about nature and art

Historians of science in the seventeenth century have always been anxious to distinguish the serious natural philosophers from contemporaries who were primarily amateurs, dabblers, or even just joiners. In some senses it has been important to do this because many men of general learning or men of social consequence tended to be swept into the scientific enthusiasms of the 1660s, in England and in France. Not all of these can be called natural philosophers; although, many of those who were marginal to thought or to invention were not insignificant when it came to publicity, finance, and communications. It was not necessary to be a scientist in order to be a universalist. For the most part, scientists and amateurs alike shared basic assumptions about the position of man in nature, about the orderly character of nature, and about the importance of the general advancement of learning. Notwithstanding regressive trends like the questioning of Copernican cosmology, the overall pattern, especially in northern Europe, was one of increasing dedication to the possibilities raised by the new science.

Consider the visit of the idealist J.A. Comenius (1592-1670) to England in 1641-2, and his enthusiastic reception by learned men, some of whom were later to become founding fellows of the Royal Society of London. It shows a close association between social and educational idealism, and enthusiasm over the future prospects of science. Comenius' scheme, *Pansophia*, was an outline of educational ideals in an enthusiastic and optimistic attitude. In the past, this tone had been set by works, such as Campanella's *City of the Sun*, and Francis Bacon's *New Atlantis*. To some extent, Erasmian educational ideas had been absorbed, but they were mingled with notions of the new science and of education from nature. Thus, educationalists saw themselves to be at a crucial hour of beginning. Clearly, the newly discovered corpus of knowledge needed to be properly taught, so that men could develop the appropriate standards for discovery. This dream relates to science too. For, while seventeenth-century methods and practices in science may have become more particularized, drawing less and less creative material from other disciplines, the philosophy of science was, more than ever, universalist both in its basic assumptions and in its goals. Progress in science was to bring about progress in learning, and, in its turn, the new generation would stimulate more progress in science within an increasingly enlightened society.

The learned world seems to have embraced complementary enthusiasms and common goals, and, in and above this, similar assumptions about nature also tended to influence persons of very different professions and pursuits. A not immediately obvious comparison of assumptions made by the poet, John Dryden, and the natural philosopher, Isaac Newton, can illustrate this.

For Newton, recall the previously cited case of his reliance upon the analogy between the whole and the parts of nature. Newton used his third rule of philosophizing to extend the primary qualities of matter known (by observation and experiment) to all matter. Thus, he reasoned from known instances to instances that could (it seemed) never conceivably be known because the primary particles of matter were transparent and invisible. It is clear that Newton was not content to establish his primary qualities as the qualities of *known* matter. He had to universalize them, for he saw them to be the primary qualities of *all* matter. His belief in the analogy between the whole and the parts of nature was sufficient to have provided him with grounds for doing this. Thus, the foundation of his philosophy rests upon this antique notion of analogy.[68]

This example shows that the vitality of the analogy had definitely not given out just because some sections of the learned world were not concerned with ideal numbers. Aspects of John Dryden's ideas about poetry and music can provide a complementary example. In Dryden, the other mode of expression of the analogy appears, the analogy between nature and art. And this parallel continued to provide a lively basis for aesthetic notions in the seventeenth century.

Like Newton, Dryden also saw his theory as resting on a foundation of natural law. Dryden's acceptance of a doctrine called *Rhythmus* was based upon his assumption of both physiological and psychological characteristics for man. These characteristics were seen to be entirely natural and as absolute in human nature as Newton's primary qualities were in physical nature. And in this case, the presumed truth about human nature relates to Dryden's theory of the power of poetry and music. In the tradition of musical humanism, Dryden assumed that, under certain conditions, poetry and music could imitate real experience by having the impact of experience. Presently some Dryden scholars see this as his belief in the powers of consonance and/or conventional musical harmony, and only in that particular and limited conception of harmony. Others do not agree. They feel that, at some point, Dryden rejected conventional notions of harmony and substituted *Rhythmus* in its place. Strong evidence is given for this second argument. However, I would like to point out that, as far as the analogy goes, Dryden's belief in either musical harmony or in *Rhythmus* must rest upon his assumption that poetry and music can reproduce the image of something very basic to human nature, be it musical harmony or rhythm. The image actually makes the experience because it lifts something from nature and brings it before an audience within the form of art. So, if we find Dryden expressing an enthusiastic belief in imitation, in either of these forms, this will illustrate either a continuance, or possibly a fresh revival, of belief in the analogy between nature and art.

Essentially, John Dryden appears to have thought that poetry composed in a certain way and set to music could affect human passions in highly specific and predictable ways.[68b] These effects (known from the effects that the ancients attributed to music) were to be produced by the correct complementarity between the subject matter expressed in the words, the sounds of the words, and the metre. All this was to be accompanied by appropriate rhythms in the music. In other words, the imitation of nature in poetry and music was to be based upon right numbers, now perhaps rhythmic and metre beats, and further, upon an assumption of sympathy between these right combinations and the human passions.

This theory of *Rhythmus* was formulated by Isaac Vossius, a continental scholar who had been popular at the court of Queen Christina of Sweden. In the 1670s he moved to Windsor, became canon of Windsor, and in 1673 published *De poematum cantu et viribus rhythmi*, containing the idea which Mace contends so influenced John Dryden.[69] The influence is illustrated in Dryden's preface to the opera *Albion and Albanius* (1685) and in his *St Cecilia Odes* (1687 and 1697).[70] This theory of *rhythmus* recalls earlier theories of sixteenth-century musical humanists. We know that the crucial elements, those that were combined in order to produce the effects, had been repeatedly argued. Opinions varied as to whether consonance and dissonance, harmony, modes, or rhythms were the most important musical factors, and, as to the method whereby any number of these things were to be complemented by literary content, syllables, sounds of words, classical poetic metre, and even intonation and histrionic style. But all through these variations theorists continued to agree that the educative value and power of the effects was real, even when they had different ideas about whether the effects were produced directly in the soul or merely in the passions of the audience. Even in Vossius' rather Cartesian mechanical theory, the movements of the passions also involved the ethical and spiritual resources of the affected.

I see rhythmus in connection with antecedent theories of the French musical humanists and I do not make as strong a distinction as Mace does, as to its newness.[71] At the same time rhythmus does present differences that distinguish it from the earlier theories. Poetry was meant to dominate the music. Dryden writes: ' . . . It is my part to invent, and the musicians' to humour that invention.'[72] However, this is not completely unlike a similar precedence given to the word by some in Ronsard's circle and Baïf's Academy. When set to music Dryden's poetry addressed the passions.[73] In contrast, earlier theories involving the effcts of music had the poetry and music directly addressing the mind. Or they were addressing the emotions: which were not quite the same thing as the mechanical Cartesian passions.[74]

The assumptions of Dryden and Newton are significantly comparable; yet, they are also different, in so far as they apply to different disciplines. These examples reveal the analogy between the whole and the parts of nature, and the idea that art should embody an imitation of nature, in some of the more modern guises of these notions.

In pointing to the continuing vitality of this network of assumptions, I do not wish to diminish our estimation of either the originality of seventeenth-century thinkers, or the validity of their awareness of the newness of their perspectives. It should be clear that, in their full context, these analogies were new. They were applied in a timely manner to material that would have been unthinkable in the past. Actually, the analogies provided an ordering, a way of seeing relationships, and the unusual historical vitality of this scheme rests upon its flexibility. By the seventeenth century, the scheme imposed fewer and fewer limits on the specific subject matter that was being ordered. This additional flexibility shows itself primarily after ideal numbers and Aristotelian hierarchical categories had become unimportant. So the serious nature of the historical role of the idea of harmony did not diminish when these features of its earlier formulations became unpopular.[75] But all the levels of distinction were not gone; many Christian and Platonic physio-psychical distinctions still remained. We are still in a world where the mental image, developing in one mind or in many, is second only to divine providence. It was still argued by some, that man was the best of God's works, the chosen lord of nature. Thus, the analogy between creator and creature was still dominated by this ontological distinction between His creature and His image. And the greater part of western thought supported this level of distinction until long after the end of the seventeenth century.

The doctrine of *rhythmus* departed from conventional musical humanism by giving rhythm precedence, making it more important than harmony, and by its association with Descartes' theory of the passions. Certainly, Baïf's circle had already seen rhythm as the instrument to bring about the effects when it was complemented by the appropriate metres. Mersenne and Descartes were aware of this. So, when historians write about the fall of harmony, as C. Palisca and D. P. Mace did, they are referring to a particular fall in the fortunes of counterpoint and consonance and dissonance as the principal means of bringing about the effects.

However, the whole notion of effects is associated with a wider idea of harmony. The art form imitates a natural pattern and awakens a similar one in the audience. This is a version of the idea

of natural harmony and, in the past, musical harmony had once
been the primary example of it, together with the rhythms of
nature, the seasons, the months and the year, birth, growth and
death, etc. Musicians did not give this imagery up. Haydn did not
write 'The Seasons' or 'The Creation' with anything else in mind.
Mozart's 'The Magic Flute' gave full grand operatic expression to
the ideal of harmony, the harmony of nature, with music and
drama combining to bring about a spiritual elevation in the
audience.[76] Examples could be endless.[77]

The point is that the words-and-music people and the rhythm-
and-metre theorists all relied on traditional concepts of natural
harmony and of its imitation in the arts. While there were periods
when the notion of imitation did not depend primarily on musical
harmony, it is still unthinkable to ignore the wider potency of the
association between musical harmony and natural harmony
before the early nineteenth century. Even after that time, many
composers continued to view their works in this tradition. Read
the theoretical comments of Stockhausen and you will find
thoughts resembling those of the Platonists, a belief that music
imitates and expresses something near to truth itself.

On the other hand, and in the smaller view, it is true that
Vincenzo Galilei and Girolamo Mei had wedged a space between
consonant ratios and the wider idea of harmony. It is also true
that the general outlook of the sixteenth century could be
characterized by some conception of the idea of harmony,
whereas afterwards these concepts never reigned supreme in
quite the same way. But ideas of harmony did not die or even
cease to be important in the conceptual framework of many
artists, scientists and thinkers. Galilei's point was not that music
could not imitate natural harmony and bring about the effects,
but that the imitation should not depend exclusively upon
numerical ratios between the tones. Sympathy, or the awakening
of the spirits, is also a form of harmony, and it is a more resilient
form than any that had been based upon prescribed formulae of
any kind. In the end, how many people living now have heard of
natural harmony and how many of *rhythmus*? It is not a bad way of
telling which idea has died and which has not.

Mechanical analogies can illustrate the long life of notions of
natural harmony just as well as numerical ones. In the
Renaissance, patterns like those of the seasons and the times were
easily associated with mechanical works. In their own way,
mechanical events can be seen as rhythmical. You will recall that
Leonardo da Vinci saw them so. His flying machine would have
combined the aerodynamics and physical structure of both bat
and bird. If he had succeeded in making it it would have been
built upon the natural model. Motion in air and in water were

analogous. There was an analogy between man and the earth, a birth, growth and death, structural and rhythmical parallel; there was an analogy between the whole and the parts of nature, the parts participated in the whole, which was an order prior to their ordering. The works of man were beautiful and useful also in so far as they imitated, and participated in the order of nature. This review of assumptions just goes to show that mechanical models were not images wholly apart from the rest.

Even before the Renaissance mechanical analogies were frequently used in branches of natural philosophy. Many of these are to be found in speculation about impetus and other physical problems. Their popularity increased and spread later to wider physical, biological, and chemical fields. I am in no way attempting to summarize this field. The example that follows is intended to show that the mechanical idea can be just one particular and intense form of the creature idea. Plato's universe was an animal, and by the seventeenth century many people tended to see the animal mechanically. However, this was not an age of computer robots. The mind was still placed apart, a designer after the divine creator, an operator of works.

Interesting examples of analogies expressing a form of the idea of harmony in mechanical terms were produced in the works of William Harvey. He adapted an analogy between the work of a watermill and the blood flow and valve action in human veins after having taken this model over from his teacher Fabricius of Aquapendente. Harvey visualized the blood as water and the heart as a machine. He also viewed the action of the auricles and ventricles in the heart in mechanical terms.[78]

In and above these very specific analogies that advanced Harvey's discovery of circulation there are related assumptions, perhaps no less important to him, assumptions about the general order of nature. These general assumptions involve a wider range of analogies that certainly are the complete relatives of the specific mechanical ones. The cosmos may not yet have been viewed largely as a machine. However, it was an harmonious order and that order could be expressed in mechanical ways. For instance, he drew a parallel between the human body, the body politic or the state, and the heavenly bodies in the cosmos. The heart was like a king in his kingdom and like the sun in the heavens. Therefore was the king being likened to a machine, or was the sun? Not really, but all three – heart, king, and sun – were the vital centres of the activities of all the rest. They all dominated the orderly activities of their parts. A machine is one form of the expression of this kind of relationship; and mechanical principles are one type of harmonious expression. In the seventeenth century this type became so much the dominant type in the models used by natural philosophers, that these models came to obscure the wider body of expression from which they originally developed.

Later in his career Harvey shifted the balance within his analogies from his original focus on the centre to the general dynamics of the whole. He then endowed the blood with central importance if not position. The shift has been associated with Harvey's acceptance of the theory that the soul resided in the blood and also with a possible political shift from Royalism to a secret Republicanism.[79] In any case, the blood and circular analogies with the cosmos had always been of great importance to Harvey.[80] In either view, Harvey retains his cosmological parallel. The soul's being active in the blood would square with the growing insistence that divine providence manifested itself in the laws of nature. This assumption falls somewhere between the Renaissance architectonic view of nature and a developing pantheistic one.

The increase in the use of specific mechanical analogies in the seventeenth century affected the learned world as a whole, and not only that part devoted to natural philosophy. Descartes saw the body as a machine-like entity; animals behaved in accordance with mechanical principles, and the function of the *esprits animaux* was entirely mechanical. As we have seen, these ideas had impact in artistic circles. And in natural philosophy, Robert Boyle's analogy between combustion and respiration is an outstanding example. Thus, once more, the potency of the idea of harmony should not be underestimated. Harmony must not be seen to die prematurely with the collapse of earlier interpretations of it. God's machine was just as harmonious as God's organ was once reputed to be, even though many of the interpretations of how harmony worked had changed.

Universality and change

By now the reader may have developed the impression that inter-disciplinary studies and all the academies devoted to them were similar from the fifteenth to the end of the seventeenth century. In an attempt to bring out continuity I may seem to be saying that differences of time and place, the culmulative progress in some fields, general changes in society and culture, and the shifting scheme of problems that captivated men's imaginations in successive generations were of little consequence. But nothing could be further from the truth. This is not what I am trying to convey about harmony, eclecticism and universality.

Historians mark shifts or differences and they sometimes underestimate flexibility in thinking as they describe the changes. More often novelty is an expression of flexibility

rather than a creation *de novo*. Thus, a sort of generic assumption of the harmony of nature seems to have caught much of
the western imagination during the early modern period. As in
Leonardo harmony did not rule out feelings of pessimism. At
times, however, some thinkers turned to scepticism. Then the
whole idea of harmony was rejected. However, the things that
have captured my attention appear to have been overwhelmingly expressed in accordance with harmonious views. Trends
that involved the bringing together of disciplines were substantially associated with high points in the popularity of notions of
harmony. In the fifteenth century, for example, many concepts in the theory of architecture had been associated with
ideas from medieval cosmology and from supposedly ancient
theories of music. By the late sixteenth and early seventeenth
centuries the composers and theorists of music were using similar associations and also different associations as well. For
example, they used the inspirations drawn from classical scholarship but also they used acoustical experiments. Their aesthetic ideals shifted from preoccupation with ideal numbers to
frequent combinations of music with poetry and/or drama. A
parallel illustration can be drawn from personalities. Despite
the very great differences between them, Leonardo and
Michelangelo were more similar to each other than Galileo to
his contemporary artists, for instance Scamozzi and Maderna -
not to mention Bernini. In other words, both universality, and
the trend towards inter-disciplinary association expressed itself
differently in different personalities with respect to the different circumstances they were in. However, each time there was
this basic association, the harmony of nature was affiliated to
the purpose or goal of bringing together knowledge in order to
form a universal man, a universal philosophy, or a universal
body of knowledge.

There seem to have been two principal social contexts of the
development of science during the Renaissance. I do not mean
traditions of ideas like Neo-Platonism, humanism and magic; I
am speaking about social and institutional forms that allowed
for the development and transmission of ideas in natural
philosophy. One was the artists' studios, the circles and
academies that became popular in fifteenth and sixteenth-century Italy. Later, academies that had often been inspired by
Italian examples spread all over Europe. Another much older
established source was in the universities, within faculties dealing with disciplines that were associated in the broad field of
natural philosophy. It was within the university tradition that
much of medieval science had developed. Universities, however, were not static. They also reflected and responded to

wider contemporary intellectual life. We may recall that Toscanelli, after a time at the university of Padua, taught mathematics in Florentine artists' studios. The varieties of inter-disciplinary association developing in circles and academies within the cities were often different from the long-established associations within the faculties of universities. For example, medicine and cosmology had a long history of association, but the cross-fertilization between painting, cartography and natural history was rather more expressive of the influence of the studios. New configurations were constantly developing, and university scholars were not impassive. The response of scholars was more often made in terms of the experience of individuals than it was reflected in the university curriculum. For instance, Galileo studied at Pisa and then taught at Padua. But, through his father Vincenzo, he was also involved from an early age with ideas that were being explored in the circles and academies. Galileo scholars are seeing increasing importance in this source of inspiration.[81]

The openness and eclecticism that had successfully served the disciplines of natural philosophy in early modern eras sometimes tended to provide diminishing returns as one approaches the eighteenth century. Either serious or, at times, pedantic academicians in the Royal Society were irritated by the participation of fellows who were simply interested amateurs. In spite of this annoyance, at least some of these general participants did perform vital services for finance, and for the communication and transmission of ideas. They may have even imposed a cross-fertilization of ideas that was both a distraction from the essential business of natural philosophy, while it was sometimes productive, keeping the business of natural philosophy in a real association with the business of the wider learned world. However, the disciplinary categories were becoming more distinct, and this did answer one of the real needs of the sciences at that time. Voltaire saw and expressed this timely attitude in his English Letters.[82]

By contrast, in the sixteenth century it had still been possible for many individuals to make substantial and original contributions to different fields, including natural philosophy. Certainly, Leonardo is the outstanding example. Less well known but, from my point of view, just as significant as Leonardo or Michelangelo, is Girolamo Fracastoro (1478?-1553). In chapter five I mentioned his discovery of the sympathetic vibration of strings.

However, acoustics were not Fracastoro's only interest. He was a physician, author of the famous Latin poem on syphilis and the first authoritative treatise on infectious diseases.[83]

Other natural philosophic interests were in botany, cosmography and astronomy. And Fracastoro was active and proficient in areas outside the sciences. A superb Latin poet, he was also a translator of classical poems and the author of original and interesting treatises, one on poetics, the others on the human mind and imagination.[84] The list of interests pertains to his overall view of nature; for Fracastoro saw nature as the expression of a system of sympathies, correspondences, and analogies that maintained the whole and that expressed the relations between the parts. In 1546 Fracastoro sent Bembo a treatise, entitled *De simpathia et antipathia rerum,* in which he discussed the attraction and repulsion of like for like and unlike. Every thing in nature manifests the power of sympathy between the elements. Fracastoro's model encompasses structure and behaviour. Although the atomists explained sympathy by the motions of the atoms, Fracastoro sees analogy as the principle of attraction; for example, in a magnet there must be some latent principle that resembles iron. Fracastoro applied this scheme in his work on contagious diseases. Just as pests attack one animal and not another according to whether or not there is some analogous principle between the particular pest and the attacked animal, so with contagious diseases and men. The principle may be in the parts, as, say, between a particular disease and a particular organ, or a particular disease and a man at a particular age. Analogies can exist between diseases and the condition of the humours or of the vital spirits.[85] All of Fracastoro's analogies were united in one universal principle of nature. In addition, he associated his own personality, his physical and spiritual make-up, with this scheme. His assumptions then, are intimate, they directly affect his vision, his universal commitment, and they also provide the usual supports and inspiration credited to like assumptions. He makes his general assumptions quite explicit, they appear everywhere. On the imagination, he develops one level of sympathy and antipathy.[86] And on poetry, he develops the wider principle, poets imitate the universal idea of the creator.

Here are two uses of the concept of imitation or sympathy, the mind's natural response to an analogous image, and the creator artist parallel; just as God created the universe, so man comprehends the principles at work in the universe and he devises works in imitation of them. This blend alone might be enough to discomfit the historian of traditions. For, it sits atop many traditions and combines them in ways that may have astounded and offended their philosophical originators. Fracastoro's notions of sympathy and antipathy were developed from a long line of Aristotelian inspirations in medicine,

alchemy, poetics and natural philosophy. But what has happened
to the low Aristotelian estimation of works? Poets imitate the
universal idea, they give men the images of the divine idea. Surely
this was developed from lines of thought that combined
Aristotelian with humanist-classical and Platonic traditions.
Fracastoro blends these with ease, not because he has a split
personality, a doctor Fracastoro, and a poet Fracastoro, but
because for him they blend. He was still a kind of Renaissance
universal man. He saw ecstasy and illumination as higher and
more complex forms of the fairly mechanical sympathy that
originated in sense preception. Once more, that sympathy of the
mind was a more advanced form of the basic sympathy and
antipathy in physical nature; if the magnet held a latent principle
resembling iron, the mind also held a higher latent principle
resembling the good.

Fracastoro's views about imitation in poetry evoke threads of
association with both past and future, with Leonardo's comparison of the arts, and again with Dryden's parallel between
painting and poetry. Yet, Fracastoro certainly was responding
to the problems of his own particular place and time; for
example, his views on contagion were original and important in
the history of medicine. It is said that Athanasius Kircher basically restated Fracastoro's ideas on contagion from what he
saw through a microscope. Fracastoro's views about the arts are
not separate or apart from his wider views of nature and reality. This is yet another example of continuity in change, of
thinkers who are not so much thinking in the same way, as they
are using the same or similar assumptions within their thinking. Fracastoro is not Leonardo; even his universality is enacted
in a different style and time, and yet they were both intimate
with a similar source. Not a document or a theory, not a
prescribed formula or a systematic philosophy; but rather, both
showed the tendency to self-consciously project and map their
own particular versions of the ideal of harmony on to nature
and on to human thought. This is a very amorphous and general, and yet, also a very basic and powerful thing for thinkers
to share in common.

The principal speaker of Fracastoro's poetic dialogue is
Navagero. And it is he who identifes the poet with the supreme
painter, both imitate nature; and not merely the surface of
nature, but the universal and beautiful idea of the creator.[87]
The mind's perfected idea is what is imitated, and the work
will, in its turn, strike the mind and affect the audience. The
poet is gifted first, in his capacity to represent it. This is a
towering role. The artist projects his experience on to the
audience, the audience can be persuaded to accept the artist's

experience as real, as a statement of truth, and in successfully accomplishing this, the artist introjects his own experience and confirms it. Thus, his belief that truth will 'strike the mind' is reinforced whenever he achieves the 'effects'. The 'effects' then confirm the ideal which is itself bound to the prior assumption that the artist can go to the essence of experience. Here art and philosophy, and this includes natural philosophy, are close to each other. These are the grounds upon which Navagero places the poet's insight above the philosopher's:

> If some philosopher, using unadorned language, should teach that some mind pervade the universe, I should fall in love with this idea as being a noble idea. But if this same philosopher should tell me the same thing in poetic fashion . . . [here Fracastoro quotes Virgil's *Aeneid*, VI, 724-7, which expresses a similar idea] . . . I shall not only love, but be struck with wonder, and I shall feel that a divine something has entered into my soul. *Therefore, my friends, if the poets teach more things, if these are beautiful and more pleasing, we ought not to think. . .that music and divine song elevate but are not useful.* [88]

During present times being scientific is frequently equated with knowing the truth. The claims to objectivity that have been made over centuries have established the scientific disciplines as those most likely to express the truth. Artists, poets and theologians supposedly put forward subjective points, points based on insight or on faith. As we cannot refer their knowledge to tests and experiments, we cannot easily judge what we know or do not know. Of course, the issue has been raised, that our systems of validation may themselves be limited. This is not my point here. Our values and the problems of knowing brought about by them simply are not the values of a Fracastoro. His philosopher's truth and his poet's truth do not belong to different spheres of evaluation. He is a Renaissance scientist, who, at the same time, thought that it was possible to argue that the vision of the poet was a more comprehensive vision of truth than any other. It is not that the philosopher's vision or the poet's vision is more objective, as against the other. Both have capacities to recognize the truth, but further, the poet is moved by it and, in turn, he makes it moving:

> . . .the poet by nature is one who can be seized and moved by the true beauties of things. . .Some beauties are real, some apparent. The poet is he who is moved by the real . . .[89]

Fracastoro even makes the imagination the primary intellectual tool, above reason, in the recognition of his primary, or real, qualities. The poet can be so affected by his own first-hand

experience, that the imagination can induce a state of Platonic
frenzy, a heightened seeing. It happens to Navagero on Mt
Baldo:

> Navagero looked around him in all directions and then, as if
> touched by the muse, or inspired by Apollo, first began to sing.
> Then, catching up a copy of Virgil...he began to recite with
> such vehemence and yet with such harmony...that it seemed to
> us we had never heard anything sweeter.[90]

The impact of the truth of experience is used to dramatize
truth itself. Such motives and aims resemble those of Baïf's circle; and Renaissance natural philosophy was often significantly
associated with this belief in using the effects for both conceptual and educative purposes.

In *Turrius sive de intellectione*, Fracastoro identifies imagination as the highest mental faculty. In itself, this is an extraordinary departure from conventional faculty systems in which
the imagination was a mechanical bearer of images. Fracastoro
has it take over some of the role of judgement and combine this
with an intellectual feeling for the real truths within the apparent images. Here emotion is placed on the high plane of the
baroque cultural world. Feeling could be intellectual and/or
spiritual. Rapture and ecstasy were seen, once more, as consequences of real knowledge, the light of truth. Plato's divine
madness was again to be the ally of philosophy and, in addition, now of art and science too. Fracastoro's imagination held
the power to understand the relations between the parts, and
of the parts to the whole; it received many impressions from
the senses, compared them, saw the respects in which they were
associated and how each individual was also related to the
whole. The artist became a philosopher when first, he saw
experience with wonder and awe, and then, on the basis of this
inspiration, applied himself to discovering the causes of
things. This is why many philosophers are poets, and many
poets, great philosophers.[91] After insight and discovery, the art
of poetic expression follows. Fracastoro certainly applied this to
himself when in 1530 he published his scientific work on
syphilis, in verse.[92] Because it could affect the reader, poetry
could bring the direct experience of truth to men. The poet is
not directly touched by God or by muses, but *by the divine work
in nature*. His poetic gift is, in fact, an extreme of natural
human imagination. The poetic art, however, is contrived. It is
an expression beyond the normal that is formed to convey the
poet's vision. Frenzy can make men think that poets are
touched by God, but it is really the music that causes this, either
the poet's own vision and/or his works; music spurs the poet on

to invent a speech that can convey divine oracles to men.[93]

Fracastoro's self-image also expresses his assumptions about nature and art. His eclecticism was entirely self-conscious. His favourite divinity, Apollo, was the patron of medicine, poetry, and enlightenment. This figure was given prominent parts in the myths of all his longer poems and frequently appears in the shorter.[94] Fracastoro's self-chosen emblem was an altar dedicated to Aesculapius, Minerva and Apollo.[95] These things are not just conventional. Fracastoro was taking the attributes to himself in a deeply personal way. Indications of his attitudes are expressed in the poetic dialogue. Navagero's friendly antagonist, Bardulone, asserts that poets write 'open and shameless falsehoods'. The reply shows Fracastoro's evaluation of allegory, myth and fable as sources of truth. He makes a sophisticated distinction between particular and apparent truths on the one hand, and other truths that might be called common psychological truths, truths about the traditional ways that men experience both natural and spiritual things. These are not just subjective truths. They express common human experience and this is why they ought to be seen to be valid and real. Fracastoro is quite definite about this:

> Indeed, everything which may be allowed to invention is true either because it has the appearance of truth, or because it has allegorical significance, or because it is a common belief, either of all or many, or because it accords with the universal, the simply beautiful idea, and not with the particular. Things are true because of their appearance, as for example: 'Three times we see the broken heavens and the dripping stars.' And because of allegorical significance, as fables, especially old ones, some of which signify certain mysteries of sacrifices and religious observances, some hidden in the nature of things which is not to be known by everybody, others the histories of kings, their vices and virtues. The old idea was that forms were metamorphosized, that groves were sacred, that rivers and fountains had their protecting spirits, that certain gods had the care of us. . . All this was not beyond the beliefs of mortals . . .These are very similar to what poets invent. But everything that is added to the particular subject is drawn from the nature of the subject, either by metaphor, epithet, or other means that are inherent in nature itself, causes and effects, and other devices of that sort.[96]
> Therefore none of these ought to be called untrue, for that is untrue which has no existence at all. These do exist in a way; either through appearance, or through significance, or in the belief of men, or in accordance with the universal idea.

It is unjust to call poets liars; as their name indicates, they are, rather, perfectors.[97]

The poet's process of knowledge is not exclusively one of scientific validation. Yet, in some ways, Fracastoro's poet
appreciates the traditional beliefs of men in something of the
way of the anthropologist or psychologist. They are truths
about belief. It will not do to separate the poet from the natural
philosopher too much in this. Even Francis Bacon placed
unusual value upon ancient myths and fables as the recepta-
cles of knowledge. They were the esoteric expression of knowledge of nature. Newton too believed in such an ancient knowledge, couched in myth. Clearly, I am mentioning different
thinkers working in different immediate cultural settings. Yet,
in the wider cultural picture, it looks like the ideal of harmony.
or some version of it, and the goal of universality, or some version of that goal, were frequently united.

Notes to Chapter Six

1. St Bonaventura, *The Mind's Road to God*, trans. George Boas,
   The Liberal Arts Press (New York, 1953), p. 8, para. 2.
2. C. J. De Vogel, 'On the Neo-Platonic Character of Platonism
   and the Platonic Character of Neo-Platonism', *Mind* (Jan.
   1953), lxii, 245, p. 50.
3. Plotinus, *Enneads* (IV, 8 [6], trans. in *The Essential Plotinus*,
   Elmer O'Brien, S.J. Mentor Books (New York, 1964), p. 68 (6).
4. Bonaventura, *Mind's Road to God*, p. 28, para.2.
5. Francis Bacon, *Novum Organum*, Book I, xix; cf. Mary Horton,
   'In Defence of Francis Bacon: A Criticism of the Critics of the
   Inductive Method', Stud. Hist. Phil. Sci., 4 (1973), no. 3, pp.
   241-278.
6. B. C. Garner, 'Francis Bacon, Natalis Comes and the Mythologi-
   cal Tradition', J. *Warburg and Courtauld Institutes*, 33, 1970, pp.
   264-291; also cf. R. McRae, *The Problem of the Unity of the Sciences:
   Bacon to Kant* (Toronto, 1961), pp. 24-45.
7. Francis Bacon, *The Advancement of Learning*, Book 1, vi, 16, his
   ital.
8. B. Garner, 'Francis Bacon', p. 290.
9. Bacon, *Advancement*, Book II, v, 1.
10. *Ibid.* Book I, vi, 16.
11. B. Garner, Francis Bacon, p. 291.
12. Bacon, *Advancement*, Book II, vii, 6.
13. J. R. Jacob, 'The Ideological Origins of Robert Boyle's Natural
    Philosophy', J. *European Studies*, (1971), 2, pp. 1-21, quote p. 7.
14. Walter Pagel, 'Religious Motives in the Medical Biology of the
    XVII Century', *Bull. of the Institute of the Hist. of Medicine*, vol.
    III 1935, nos. 2, pp 97-128, 3, 213-231, 4, 265-312, *passim*.

15. Bacon, *Advancement*, Book II, vi, 16.
16. Paolo Rossi, *Francis Bacon: From Magic To Science*, trans. S. Rabinovitch, (Chicago, 1968), pp. 12-15, 122-125. Also see, Francis Yates, 'Bacon From Magic to Science by Paolo Rossi,' *N.Y. Review of Books*, Feb. 29, 1968. Some work by Graham Rees, will, I think, shed light on this point. Unfortunately my book was finished before I could make a detailed examination of his articles; these are, 'Matter Theory: a Unifying Factor in Bacon's Natural Philosophy' (July 1977), pp.110-125; and for transmission of his ideas see 'The Fate of Bacon's Cosmology in the Seventeenth Century', (March 1977), *passim*, both in *Ambix*, vol. XXIV, nos. 1 and 2.
17. D. P. Walker, *Spiritual and Demonic Magic from Ficino to Campanella*, (London, 1958), pp. 199-202.
18. Bacon, *Novum Organum*, Book I, xxxii, and *The Great Instauration*, Library of Liberal Arts, (N.Y., 1960), pp. 3-17.
19. Bacon, *Novum Organum*, Book I, xli-lxviii, Book II, xv. (the quotation).
20. *Ibid.* Book II, ii, iii, xiii.
21. *Ibid.* Book II, iv. Italics are Bacon's.
22. Bacon, *Novum Organum*, Book II, viii.
23. Bacon, *The Great Instauration*, p. 23.
24. Bacon, *Novum Organum*, Book I, cxxiv., my italics.
25. Bacon, *Novum Organum*, Book I, cxx., my italics.
26. Bacon, *Novum Organum.*, Book I, cxxvi.
27. A. O. Lovejoy, *The Great Chain of Being*, pp. 93-4.
28. E. Cassirer, *The Individual and the Cosmos in Ren. Philo.*, p.191.
29. J. A. Mazzeo, 'The Augustinian Conception of Beauty and Dante's Convivio', *J. Aesthetics and Art Criticism*, vol. 15, no. 4, p.436.
30. Thomas à Kempis, *The Imitation of Christ*, tr. L. Sherley-Price (Penguin Books, 1952), chapter 3., p.31.
31. Frances Yates, *Giordano Bruno and the Hermetic Tradition* (London, 1964), chapt. 1.
32. Yates, *Bruno.*, p.31. *The Mind to Hermes Corpus Hermeticum* XI, optimist gnosis.
33. *Ibid.* pp. 35, 36., *The Asclepius or The Perfect Word* . . .; optimist gnosis.
34. Charles Trinkaus, *In Our Image and Likeness*, (Chicago University Press, 1970), pp. 500-517.
35. E. Panofsky, *Studies in Iconology*, (New York, Harper Torchbook, 1962) ch. IV, p. 182.
36. P. O. Kristeller, *Facets of the Renaissance*, (New York, 1959), pp. 104-5, 109.
37. C.J. De Vogel, 'On the Neo-Platonic Character of Platonism and the Platonic Character of Neo-Platonism,' *cit.* pp. 43-64 and especially p. 53.

38. Plotinus, *Enneads*, (I, 6, (1)).
39. *Ibid*. (V, 9 (5)).
40. *Ibid*. (V, 9 (5)).
41. A.O. Lovejoy, *Chain of Being*, pp. 85-86. A significant difference between Augustinian thoughts and those of Dante was that Augustine, like Aristotle, felt that the Creator's work in nature could not be significantly imitated. However, Dante emphasized the analogy between creative work of the artist and the divine office of creation.
42. F. Yates, *Bruno*., p.118.
43. P.O. Kristeller, 'Renaissance Platonism', p.105.
44. Jean Seznec, *The Survival of the Pagan Gods* (New York, 1953), pp. 58-60.
45. E.H. Gombrich, 'Icones Symbolicae: The Visual Image in Neo-Platonic Thought', J. *Warburg and Courtauld Inst.*, vol. II (1948), pp. 163-192; and also R.W. Lee, 'Ut Pictura Poesis: The Humanistic Theory of Painting', *The Art Bulletin*, vol. 22 (1940), p. 268, Appendix 6, and pp. 228-235.
46. F. Yates, *Bruno*, p. 146.
47. For a discussion of Melancolia and painting cf. P. Askew, 'Giovanni Serodine, A Melancholy Astronomer', *Art Bulletin*, vol. LXVII, no. 1 (March, 1965) pp. 121-128.
48. E. Panofsky, *Dürer* (Princeton, N.J., 1943).
49. E. Panofsky, *Ren. and Renascences*, p.30.
50. This second feature could only fully develop when Aristotelian cosmology was rejected. Before this, the beings and things of nature gave only diminished reflections, not partial or limited models of greater wholes.
51. Vitruvius, *Ten Books on Architecture*, Loeb Library, Book 1, chapt. 1, 15, 16.
52. *Ibid*. p.9.
53. Cf. Marsilio Ficino, *Five Questions concerning the Mind*, tr. J. Burroughs in Cassirer *et al.*, *The Renaissance Philosophy of Man*, (Chicago, 1948), pp. 193-212. René Descartes, *Discours de la méthode*, Pt. 1, (Manchester, 1949) pp. 3-11.
54. Ficino, *Five Questions, passim*.
55. Renatus Descartes, Excellent *Conpendium of Musick* with necessary and judicious Animadversions Thereupon, by a Person of Honour (London, 1653).
56. Meetings of what eventually became the Royal Society of London began in the 1640s and took place in London and in Oxford. The charter was granted in 1662, but formal meetings had begun in Nov. 1660.
57. D.P. Walker, 'The Aims of Baïf's Académie de Poésie et de Musique,' J. *Renaissance and Baroque Music*, vol. 1, no. 2., June 1946.

58. Francis Bacon, *Proemium to the Great Instauration*, ed. Fulton H. Anderson, (New York, 1960), p.4.
59. Descartes, *Discourse on Method*, pt. 2. tr. L. Lafleur, (New York, 1956), (22), p.14.
60. This passage and the accompanying interpretations of Newton below were all brought out by J.E. McGuire when a guest lecturer at Cornell University, September 1966-February 1967, cf. 'Newton and the Pipes of Pan' by J.E. McGuire and P.M. Rattansi, in *Notes and Records of the Royal Society of London*, vol. 21, no. 2, December 1966. My only point is to associate Newton with the ideal of universality on the basis of what McGuire and Rattansi have argued.
61. Isaac Newton, *Principia*, Book 6, Rule III.
62. Frances Yates, *French Academies*, p.103.
63. *Ibid.* pp. 14, 15.
64. Kindred, because in both situations the universalist represents man within nature. In the earlier version he represents man in a rather static and architectonic scheme. Later, he still represents man, but within a moving picture. Men of genius can further progress and enable men to control and conquer nature.
65. Cf. Dorothy Koenigsberger, 'A New Metaphor for Mozart's Magic Flute', *European Studies Review*. vol. 5, no.3, (July, 1975). In future work I intend to clarify this apparent historical contradiction between the self-conscious opening of knowledge and the almost simultaneous and fairly widespread treasuring of secret knowledge.
66. Albert J. George, 'The Genesis of the Académie des Sciences', *Annales des Sciences*, vol. 3, no. 4 (Oct. 15, 1938), pp. 372-401, Auzot's plan, pp. 378-80.
67. Kenneth Clark, *Leonardo da Vinci*, pp. 45-46.
68. McGuire and Rattansi, 'Pipes of Pan'. p. 121.
68b. As I have suggested, many aspects of Dryden's thoughts on these matters are still open to scholarly discussion. The original article by D.T. Mace, 'Musical Humanism, The Doctrine of Rhythmus and the St. Cecilia odes of Dryden,' *J. Warburg and Courtauld Institutes*, vol. 27, 1964, pp. 251-292, was adversely criticized in a reply to Mace by H. Neville Davies, 'Dryden and Vossius a Reconsideration.' *Ibid.*, vol. 29, 1966, pp. 282-295. A reply by Mace is printed in the same vol. pp. 296-310. My reading of Dryden's parallel between painting and poetry, prefixed to *De arte grafica* by C.A. Du Fresnoy, gives a general kind of support for Mace's view. In this parallel Dryden says that both painting and poetry contain images of the passions and can produce the effects. If he believed this for poetry and painting it seems reasonable to interpret similar remarks about poetry and music as

the expression of a similar belief. Cf. Notes to Chapter 7, n. 10.
69. Mace, 'Musical Humanism,' p. 261.
70. John Dryden, *Works*, 'Preface to Albion and Albanius', ed. Sir
    Walter Scott (Edinburgh, 1883); cf. pp. 236 and 237. 'The chief
    secret is in the choice of words; and by this choice I do not here
    mean elegancy of expression, but propriety of sound, to be var-
    ied according to the subject. Perhaps a time may come when I
    may treat of this more largely out of some observation which I
    have made from Homer and Virgil, who amongst all the poets,
    only understood the art of numbers, and that which was prop-
    erly called *rhythmus* by the ancients.'
71. Mace, 'Musical Humanism', p. 267.
72. Dryden, *Works*, Preface to *Albion and Albanius*, p. 237.
73. The opera *Albion and Albanius* was set to music by Grabut.
74. Mace, 'Musical Humanism', p. 287. The actual feelings, for
    example anger or joy, are the same, but the theory of the pas-
    sions expresses a specific physiological mechanism for their
    operation.
75. By the seventeenth century it is often necessary to separate
    harmony from its associates beauty, and, in a way, even good-
    ness. Harmony could mean just the truth and reliability of
    nature. The concept did not always serve optimists, and many,
    like Thomas Hobbes, saw this order as brutal and savage.
76. D. Koenigsberger. 'A New Metaphor for Mozart's Magic Flute',
    passim.
77. For some particularly amusing examples cf. H.G. Koenigs-
    berger, 'Music and Religion in Modern European History', *The
    Diversity of History*, ed. J.H. Elliott and H.G. Koenigsberger,
    (London and Ithaca, 1970), pp. 35-38.
78. William Harvey, *The Movement of the Heart and Blood in Animals*,
    trans. K. Franklin, (Oxford, Blackwell Scientific Publications
    1957) chapts. 6,8,9, see also H. Butterfield, *The Origins of Mod-
    ern Science 1300-1800* (London, 1949) pp. 42-47; and M. Boas,
    The Scientific Renaissance 1450-1630 (London, 1962), pp. 282-5.
79. Christopher Hill, 'William Harvey and the idea of a Monarchy',
    Past and Present (April 1964), no. 27, pp. 54-72.
80. Walter Pagel, *William Harvey's Biological Ideas*, (New York, 1967),
    pp. 89-122.
81. E. Cochrane, *Tradition and Enlightenment in the Tuscan Academies
    1690-1800*, (Rome, 1961), ch. 1.
82. Voltaire, *Oeuvres Complètes*. 'Letters Philosophiques sur les
    Académies, l'édition de 1734, lettre XXIV (Paris, 1879),
    Mélanges 1, pp. 182-183, note 7.
83. Hieronymi Fracastorii, *Syphilis*, cf. translation of H. Wynne-
    Finch, (London, 1935); *De Contagione et Contagiosis Morbis et Eorum
    Curatione* (Lyons in 1550), there is a N.Y. ed. 1950, also both in

Opera omnia, Venice, 1575.

84. Fracastoro, *Naugerius, sive de poetica; Turrius, sive de intellectione; Fracastorius, sive di Anima* in *Opera Omnia;* there is a translation of the treatise on poetry, cf. R. Kelso, *University of Illinois Studies in Language and Literature,* vol. IX, no. 3, (Urbana, 1924), pp. 9-74.
85. Fracastoro, *De Contagione,* Book i, chapt. xiii, 'The analogy of Contagions,' pp. 38-39 in the N.Y. ed.
86. M.W. Bundy, 'Fracastoro and the Imagination', *Ren. Studies in Honour of Hardin Craig,* reprint of the *Philological Quarterly,* xx. iii (July, 1941), p. 48. This level is to be found in his concept of sub-notions. The mind reacts to the presentation of objects to the senses one after another. By its essential character the mind will be attracted to the species of the good and repelled from the bad.
87. Fracastoro, *Navagero,* tr. Kelso, *passim.,* and cf. p. 60.
88. *Ibid.* p.71.
89. Fracastoro, *Navagero,* tr. Kelso, p.71.
90. M. Bundy, 'Fracastoro and Imagination', pp. 50-52.
91. M. Bundy, 'Fracastoro and Imagination', p. 52., cf. also E. Garin, *La Filosofia: Storia dei generi letterari italiani* (Milan, 1947), vol 2., p.106.
92. *Syphilis sive morbus Gallicus.*
93. Fracastoro, *Navagero,* tr. Kelso, p. 65.
94. Fracastoro, *Contagione,* p. viii, note 1, ed. W. C. Wright.
95. E. Panofsky, 'Artist, Scientist, Genius notes on the Renaissance– Dämmerung,' in *The Renaissance* (Harpers, New York, 1953), p. 139.
96. Fracastoro, *Navagero,* tr. Kelso, pp. 69, 70.
97. *Ibid.*

7
CONCLUSION: THE RENAISSANCE ANALOGY OF NATURE

> You smile? why, there's my picture ready made,
> There's what we painters call our harmony!
>
> Robert Browning

Numerous examples have shown the notion of analogy between the whole and the parts of nature, and/or between one of the arts and nature, or even betwixt and between the various arts, in so far as they were seen to embody or employ natural principles - all of these correspondences have shown a surprising vitality in western culture. Although such general notions might easily be relegated to relatively unimportant places in cultural history, precisely because they are very general ideas, and because they cannot easily be evaluated, the examples that have been brought forward have revealed the opposite; that, in fact, this family of assumptions was frequently essential, either in the formation of specific and innovative ideas, or in the psychology of thinking and the creative outlook of the learned world within the many eras between the Renaissance and the end of the seventeenth century and, sometimes, even beyond.

The flexibility of this set of assumptions was probably the element that most insured their long-term influence. For instance, natural law and the developing model in the mind for Francis Bacon was not quite the same as nature's order and the universal ideas formed in the poet's mind for Girolamo Fracastoro. Yet it was possible, and indeed necessary, to show how these assumptions were related to each other.

A weakness of contemporary scholarship is the *gut* reaction of thinkers of all sorts to words like flexible. If an idea is flexible is it not vague? And if it is vague, will it not entangle us in the ever-present menace of 'cotton wool'? Better let's not talk about it. Still, suppose it is there?

Somehow and in some ways historians have got to attempt the scholarly appreciation, not simply of the specific content of various systems of ideas, but also, of the assumptions, beliefs, attitudes and feelings, and the cultural prospect of the men who were doing the thinking. If there is danger of woolliness in these attempts, just imagine the lack of discernment involved in not making them, in ignoring what is not easily brought forward because it is not easily brought forward.

The reason I have gone in for known examples and have used the work of many excellent scholars is, first, to establish the role of the analogy within an admittedly important set of cases. Second, I wanted to concentrate my efforts on uncovering the many forms of expression of this set of assumptions, and relating the examples to the wider history of these concepts. Thus, this study is not a new analysis of the thought of Leonardo or of Mersenne or of any other of the leading thinkers that have provided examples. It is an attempt to expose something of their mentalities by looking at their assumptions about nature and/or about human works. It is also an attempt to appreciate both continuity and change in this set of assumptions over a wide period of time. I anticipate and hope for refinements of my suggestions from experts in the various fields that have been drawn from in this essay.

The pictures drawn with examples from Cusanus, Alberti and Leonardo, from Italian and French musical humanists, from Fracastoro, Bacon, Newton and Dryden, and others with varying central interests, are pictures of the continuing intellectual and psychological impact of assumptions of harmony. These common assumptions appear in many different guises, and their details vary with the cultural fashions of three centuries. Yet, some psychological habits remain remarkably stable. Harmony was undoubtedly a reassuring starting point, the insurance of a rational reality not only within providence, but even in nature, in human nature, and in the very least of God's beings. Some form of the idea of harmony might be popular at any stage of culture that encouraged an holistic appraisal of nature. Just as long as the overall model of reality and physical nature had priority, and all the existing individual examples were seen to appear from that prior order, the notion of harmony was naturally secure because it promised at least some possibility of intellectual and/or artistic advancement. This point only indicates how general concepts of harmony might have served in any number of human quests for knowledge. The actual ways that the analogies did serve are brought forward from the examples. However, this point does indicate one very basic thing about the vigour of Platonism in the west. The Ideas, or God's Concept, or His Word, and the act of creation were prior to all else. All that followed bore the reflection or the stamp of this priority, not only of the act, of the idea itself. Thus things and beings bore in themselves traces or marks of their ordering. Essentially Platonism, be it good or bad, pure or bastard, secured man's path to knowledge. It would take an age of numerous and impassioned sceptics to let this one go entirely.

Many examples have dealt with proportion as it was visualized in mathematical terms. In and above decorum, the emphasis was upon number. In addition to natural philosophy, and theory of architecture and music, this Pythagorean emphasis was found in the medieval science of perspective.[1] From the twelfth century the divisions of philosophy came to include perspective within the system of the sciences. Interest in this science was revived in the early fifteenth century when it came to be applied in the theory and practice of painting.[2] Although perspective does not actually show how human beings see, at that time it was thought that perspective not only made the image appear like the object, but that it described how objects appeared in man's vision.[3] Paolo Toscanelli returned from Padua to Florence with a copy of Biagio Pelacani's (Biagio de Parma) *Quaestiones perspectivos*, written in 1390.[4] The likelihood is that Toscanelli did not just see this science as a technique but actually as the explanation of how reality presented itself to the human eye. Thus, the presumed scientific importance of perspective was undoubted, and this enabled Renaissance painters to make the claim that painting was also a science. It was based on geometry, it provided examples of how the real world appeared to the eye. It ought, Leonardo argued, to be regarded, just as number was regarded, as a scientific statement of reality.

Now this kind of argument was especially characteristic of the fifteenth century when artists were still actively engaged in developing perspective, while they were still involved in solving technical problems and developing a theory of the naturalistic style. But when the techniques for putting a three-dimensional image on a two-dimensional surface had largely been mastered, the ensuing questions tended to become rather more aesthetic than scientific.[5] After about 1550 theoreticians were primarily interested in forming the definition of painting, of its content and its ends. The terms of analogy between painting and nature shifted from parallels based on mathematics to parallels based upon the power of painting to reproduce experience and to affect the viewer. The painter like the poet and, just as we've seen before, the musician like the poet can evoke the reality of experience itself and produce the renowned 'effects' by his art.[6]

Humanists couched this in the vocabulary of classical revival. It was the classical *ars poetica* that was applied to painting. Dante contributed to this new tradition by drawing a parallel between two poets and two painters. And the same can be detected much later in the language of Fracastoro.[7]

The principal sources for the parallel between painting and poetry were the *Poetics* of Aristotle and the *Ars Poetica* of Horace.

Other complementary sources were the writings of Cicero and Quintilian.[8] The central nature of these arguments revolved around the theme of art as the imitation of human nature in action. Art is moving as experience is moving, perhaps even more so, in so far as art can abstract and raise experience. However, even in the classical sources the theory of imitation was not entirely separate from more idealistic Platonic notions. Cicero had himself talked of ideal notions in the mind of the sculptor.[9] If the notions were not seen as essentially number then they had another, even more mysterious, essence. The point is that analogies based on *imitazione* ought not to be classed as entirely separate from analogies based on the embodiment of ideal qualities. It will help to keep John Dryden in mind and his theories of harmony and/or rhythmus and his detailed comparison of poetry with painting.[10] Dryden shows himself quite capable of blending the humanist idea of imitation with Platonic ideas based on appropriate number combinations.[11] French and Italian musical humanists have also shown that they were not so neat about dividing their sources of inspiration. Although the shift from number was definite and marked in painting and in poetry, it was not absolute, nor was it wholly divided from earlier Pythagorean and Neo-Platonic models of analogy. Remember how Alberti managed to combine notions of decorum with notions of right-number. As historians we definitely run the danger of slicing our pie more cleanly than it, the real pie, was ever actually sliced.

The English dramatist Ben Jonson can provide a closing example of this mingling of traditions, blending analogies based on notions of magical or alchemical sympathy with those based on numbers or on other presumed ideal qualities, together with those in which the structure of the specific work was seen to instigate special effects in its audience. This was a presumed affinity between the aesthetic character of the art-form and human nature.

Jonson was a universal man, a humanist who translated Horace's *The Art of Poetry*, and, surprisingly, also a bricklayer with a deep interest in architectural theory. He knew Vitruvius and possibly Alberti and Palladio.[12] As a poet and dramatist he was also cognizant of sympathy and antipathy in medicine, alchemy and magic. My point is that although Jonson's career shows evidence of his susceptibility to a number of distinguishable currents forming the ideal of harmony, his treatment of them is entirely synthetic. He happily combined Pythagorean and Platonic inspirations with magic and further with painting-rhetoric-poetry parallels. I am suggesting moreover that this kind of synthesis was at least as normal for thinkers of the Renaissance and seventeenth century as the more single minded assimilation of mathematical, humanist or magical traditions. Just for a few, Alberti, Leonardo, V. Galilei, Fracastoro, Mersenne, Newton, Dryden, and now Jonson have produced synthesis in their notions of harmony; although, naturally, there is an individual element in each synthetic ideal. Here is an example from Jonson:

> Picture took her feigning from poetry; from geometry her rule, compass, lines, proportion and the whole symmetry. Parrhasius was the first won reputation, by adding symmetry to picture . . . Eurompus gave it splendour by numbers and other elegancies. From the optics it drew reasons, by which it was considered how things placed at a distance and afar off, should appear less: how above or beneath the head should deceive the eye and etc. So from thence it took shadows, recessor, light and heightenings. From moral philosophy it took the soul, the expression of senses, perturbations and manners . . .[13]

When Jonson commented on the triumphal arches erected for the entry of James I in 1604 he used mingled Aristotelian and Vitruvian ideas of harmony.[14] Late in his life *The Discoveries* also express any number of analogies that blend past traditions. Perhaps the most compressed might be the following:

> . . . that which happens to the eyes when we behold a body, the same happens in the memory when we contemplate an action.[15]

The mingling of analogies does not preclude a still definite shift of stress from number formulae to wider aesthetic correlations. Of all the arts, architecture and music did not exhibit this shift in quite the same way as the more literary art forms. In fact it is possible to distinguish between two complementary but separate sets of activities in music theory. One is largely aesthetic, and this tradition has been illustrated in the earlier chapter on French and Italian musical humanism. The other activity involved solving problems about the acoustical qualities of music. Here, the ancient association between meaning in music and mathematics still tended to prevail although the specific formulae changed. Certainly, I do not intend to work through both this philosophical and scientific acoustical tradition. But, by way of illustration, I will mention Leibniz's theory of consonance.

Leibniz attempted to explain the pleasing experience of consonance by giving a new twist to Boethian inspirations. As before, music addressed the human soul, but now by a process of unconscious counting. The soul was apparently more numerate than the mind; for, the mind did not realize the counting but only the pleasing sensations arising from it. In Leibniz's theory the sense element in artistic pleasure was of a basically intellectual kind because it depended upon an unrecognized awareness of either proportion, measure or rhythm.[16] This view can be contrasted with that of Descartes in which the number combinations directly stirred the passions not the soul.

The acoustical tradition continued and never without philosophical aspects. The experience of pleasure in music was consistently thought to have a basis in physical nature and not to be purely cultural. Explanations could go on to Helmholtz and beyond; however, the continuance of a specific mathematical tradition has been indicated.

The analogy of nature might be represented as essential to the fertility of the environment in which the expression and transmission of ideas took place in the Renaissance and seventeenth century. As developing science was an important part of this environment, questions have arisen about this set of assumptions. Were they helpful or harmful to the progress of science? Examples in this work have indicated that they could be helpful, especially when constricting hierarchical formulae broke down. So I am not really addressing myself to that problem, but rather, to the problem of historical interpretation, to the proper use of hindsight. (An example will clarify my point.) A distinguished historian of Renaissance science made the remark that it might be impossible to regard the activities of Ficino's Academy as providing the philosophical background from which men might ultimately come to look out upon nature and the universe.[17] In the most straightforward way this is correct; the Platonic Academy did not go in for the observation of nature, the recording of detail, or measurement, or even for mathematics. Yet, at the same time, the academy, like Alberti and Leonardo, participated in a wider cultural environment in which there was an atmosphere of enthusiasm and optimism about the future prospects for human understanding. The academy actively contributed to this atmosphere even though the academicians mostly viewed the universe as an object of philosophy and wisdom, and this is not quite the same thing as the study of nature. But the question ought to be raised, why must the historical contribution of the academy, or any similar group, be confined only to an assessment of the self-conscious goals or activities of that group? Ficino would not know that some French academicians, inspired by his group, would shift the emphasis from wisdom and magic to the universality of knowledge that was becoming the style in the late sixteenth and seventeenth centuries. This shift of emphasis was first expressed in terms of seeking the 'effects' by poetry and music, but it was also later expressed in terms of the universalist goals of the Académie des Sciences.[18] Of course, the Académie did not come into being as an inevitable consequence of Florentine Neo-Platonism, but the mentality expressed in the Académie, and in other seventeenth-century groups, was not completely unrelated to the mentality of the earlier group. The desire for universality in one form or another, the desire to manipulate and control, the confirmation of ambition, the essential belief in the powers of the mind and in a knowable order of nature, and perhaps, even in some measure, of greater reality, were all common. These are not marginal things to have in common.

Thus, on the basis of this example drawn from the content of this essay, I recommend an appropriate use of hindsight in cultural history. This is not meant to displace the necessary internalist approaches to history of ideas, approaches hastily shown in the previously cited observation of the impact of the Florentine Academy. It is meant, however, to modify and influence the wider conclusions that are drawn from such approaches. The role of the ideal of harmony was played out in giant steps in our cultural history. As neither ourselves nor our predecessors are giants, historians must use the long view to assess the path and meaning of such grand assumptions.

Notes to Conclusion

1. Robert Klein, 'Pomponius Gauricus on Perspective,' *Art Bulletin*, 1961, XLIII, pp. 211-230. Also, R.W. Lee, 'Ut Pictura Poesis: The Humanistic Theory of Painting', *Art Bulletin*, 1940, XXII, pp. 197-263. Erwin Panofsky, *Renaissance and Renascences in Western Art* (Stockholm, 1965), pp. 1-41.
2. John White, 'Developments in Renaissance Perspective', *J. of the Warburg and Courtald Institute*, Vol. 12, 1949, *passim;* and *The Birth and Re-birth of Pictorial Space* (London, 1957), p. 123.
3. E. H. Gombrich, *Art and Illusion*, p. 257.
4. R. Klein, 'Pomponius Gauricus', p. 211.
5. Lee, 'Ut Pictura Poesis,' p. 200.
6. See above, 'Harmony and Naturalism in Music' pp. 188-193.
7. Fracastoro, *Navagero or a Dialogue on the Art of Poetry*, p.60 (36).
8. Lee, 'Ut Pictura Poesis,' pp. 197, 199, 219. P.O. Kristeller, 'The Modern System of the Arts: a study in the history of aesthetics', *J. Hist. Ideas*, Vols. 12 and 13, (1951-2), p.515.

9. Kristeller, op. cit., p.503.
10. J. Dryden, Preface, *De Arte Graphica:* The Art of Painting by C.A. Du Fresnoy, in *Of Dramatic Poetry*, Vol. II (London, 1962).
11. See above, 'University and the Bringing Together of Disciplines', pp. 247-250.
12. Per Palme, 'Ut Architectura Poesis:' *Idea and Form by* A. Bengtsson *et.al.*, Uppsala Studies in the History of Art, New Series, 1, ed. N.G. Sandblad (Uppsala, 1959), pp.96-107.
13. Ben Jonson, 'De progres pictura', *Works* (Boston, 1860), p.879. Further quotations to this point can also be found in 'Timber, or Discoveries made upon Man and Matter', from 'Poesis and Pictura': 'Poetry and picture are arts of a like nature, and both are busy about imitation...'*ibid;* and from 'De Pictura': 'Whosoever loves not picture is injurious to truth, and all the wisdom of poetry. Picture is the invention of heaven, the most ancient, and most akin to nature.' *Ibid.*
14. Palme, 'Ut Architectura Poesis,' *passim.*
15. Jonson, 'Discoveries'; 'Of the Magnitude and Compass of any fable, epic or dramatic,' *Works*, p.890.
16. E. Bugg, 'A Criticism of Leibniz's Theory of Consonance', *J. of Aesthetics and Art Criticism*, 21, No.4, pp. 467-472 for explanation of perception and awareness see: R.W. Meyer, *Leibniz and the Seventeenth Century Revolution*, tr. J.P. Stern (Cambridge 1952), (1st. pub. 1948), pp. 120-123.
17. W. P. D. Wightman, *Science and the Renaissance*, pp. 20, 26-8.
18. See above, 'University and the Bringing Together of Disciplines', pp. 244-246.

BIBLIOGRAPHICAL NOTES

The field of reference for this work is extremely large, covering over two hundred years of early modern European cultural and intellectual history. The character of the work, however, is highly selective. It touches upon various points within this wider field in order to bring forward a view of the changing role of the analogy of nature, as I have stated in the *Preface*. Any comprehensive bibliography would have to be half the length of the book again while, at the same time, it would not be completely appropriate for this sort of book. The notes, in fact, show what I have used in my arguments and a good deal of their background as well. These additional bibliographical notes are also relevant to my discussions and their background in so far as they provide a list of principal primary sources and some comment on diverse secondary works in the field. These have been selected, both because they are leading works or even classics in one or another aspect of Renaissance and seventeenth-century arts, music, philosophy and science; and also because they pertain to my discussions. Several recent publications are also mentioned, sometimes with comment, because they relate my material to the developing field. But here too, I make no claim to be exhaustive.

Principal Primary Sources

Alberti, Leon Battista. *Of Statues*, trans. Leoni and Bartoli (London, 1739).
    On Painting, trans. J.R. Spencer (New Haven, 1966).
    Ten Books on Architecture, trans. J. Leoni (London, 1955), 1st. ed., 1726.
    I Libri Della Famiglia, trans. R. Watkins (Columbia, South Carolina, 1969).
    On Painting and On Sculpture, ed. and trans. C. Grayson (London 1972).
D'Alembert. *L'Encyclopédie*, 'discours préliminaire', ed. F. Picavet (Paris, 1919).
Aristotle. 'On the Art of Poetry', *On Poetry and Music* (New York, Liberal Arts Press, 1956).
Augustine, Saint. *The City of God Against the Pagans*, trans. W.C. Greene, Loeb Classical Library (London and Cambridge, Mass., 1960).

Bacon, Francis. *Novum Organum*. (New York, 1960)
'The Great Instauration', Prooemium, Preface, and Plan, *The English Philosophers from Bacon to Mill*, The Modern Library (New York, 1939).
'The New Atlantis', *Selections*, ed. P.E. and E.F. Matheson (Oxford, 1922).

Bonaventura, Saint. *The Mind's Road to God*, trans. George Boas (New York, 1953).
Brouncker, William Viscount, trans. Renatus Descartes, Excellent *Compendium of Musick* with necessary and judicious Animadversions Thereupon, by a Person of Honour (London, 1653).

Chambray, Roland Fréart Sieur de. *A Parallel of Ancient and Modern Architecture* (London, 1723).
Cusanus, Nicholas, *De docta ignorantia*, ed. E. Hoffman and R. Klibansky (Leipzig, 1932).
Of Learned Ignorance, (New Haven, Yale University Press, 1954).
Idiota, books I/IV, (London, 1650), Sutro Branch of Calif. State Library, reprint series 19. San Francisco, (May 1940).

Descartes, René. *Discours de la Méthode* (Manchester, 1949).
Discourse on Method, trans. L. Lafleur, (New York, 1956).
Oeuvres et Lettres, présentés par André Bridoux (Bruges, 1953).
Doni, G.B. *Lyra Barberina* (Florence, 1763).
Dryden, John. Preface to *De Arte Graphica;* The Art of Painting, by C.A. Du Fresnoy, in *Of Dramatic Poetry*, vol. II (London, 1962).
The Prologues and Epilogues of, ed. W. Gardner (New York, 1951).
Works, 'Preface Albion and Albanius', ed. Sir Walter Scott (Edinburgh, 1883).

Epictetus. *The Enchiridon* (New York, 1955).

Ficino, Marsilio. *Five Questions Concerning the Mind*, trans. J.L. Burroughs, in Cassirer, Kristeller, Randall, *The Renaissance Philosophy of Man* (Chicago, 1948).
Fracastorii, Hieronymi. *De Contagione et contagiosis Morbis et Eorum Curatione*, Libri 111 (New York, 1930).

Fracastoro, Girolamo. *Opera omnia,* (Venice, 1575).
   Navagerius sive de poetica dialogus, trans. R. Kelso, *University of Illinois Studies in Language and Literature,* Vol. 1X, No. 3 (Urbana, 1924).

Harvey, William. *On the Movement of the Heart and Blood in Animals,* trans. Kenneth Franklin (Oxford, Blackwell Scientific Publications, 1957).
Hedderwick, T., trans. *Dr. Faust* (London, 1887).
Helmholtz, H.L.F. von. *On the Sensations of Tone,* trans. A.J. Ellis (London, 1875).

Jonson, Ben, trans. "Horace, Of the Art of Poetry", *Works* (London, 1860).

Marlowe, Christopher. *The tragical history of the life and death of Doctor Faustus,* reconstructed by W.W. Grey (Oxford, 1950).
Mirandola, Pico della. *On the Dignity of Man,* trans. P.J.W. Miller (New York, 1965).

Newton, Isaac. *Philosophiae Naturalis Principia Mathematica,* 3rd. ed. (1726) facsimile 2 vols. (Cambridge, 1972).

Ornithoparchus. *Micrologus* (Leipzig, 1517), trans. into English by John Dowland in 1609.

Plato. *Timaeus,* ed. R.D. Archer-Hind (London, 1888).
   The Essential Plotinus, trans. Elmer O'Brien S.J. (New York, 1964).
Porcacchi, T. *Lettere di XIII Huomini Illustri,* (Venice, 1565).
Poussin, Nicholas. *Correspondance,* pub. by C.H. Jouanny (Paris, 1911).

Vinci, Leonardo da. *Literary Works,* ed. J.P. Richter (Oxford, 1939).
   Notebooks, ed. E. MacCurdy (London, 1956).
   Codex Madrid, ed. Ladislao Reti, *The Burlington Magazine* pt. 1 (Jan. 1968), pt. 2 (Feb. 1968).

Vitruvius. *Ten Books on Architecture,* Loeb Library, 2 vols., 1931-4.
Voltaire. *Oeuvres Complètes,* 'Lettres Philosophiques' 'Sur les Académies', l'édition de 1734, lettre XXIV (Paris, 1879), Mélanges I, pp. 182-183.

Zarlino, Gioseffo. *Le istitutioni harmoniche* (Venice, 1558).

Select Secondary Works

Students seeking an introduction to topics such as Renaissance universality and relations between the disciplines might begin with: Eugenio Garin, *Science and Civic Life in the Italian Renaissance*, tr. P. Munz (New York, 1969); Paolo Rossi, *Philosophy, Technology, and the Arts in the Early Modern Era*, tr. S. Attunasio (New York, 1970); P.O. Kristeller, *Renaissance Thought, the Classic, Scholastic and Humanist Strains*, (New York, 1961); and K. Clark, *Leonardo da Vinci*, (Penguin Books, 1958).

Joan Gadol's *Leon Battista Alberti: Universal Man of the Early Renaissance*, (Chicago and London, 1969), presents a searching and deep appraisal of the mind of this universal genius. His particularly aesthetic view of things is also appreciated in L.M.M. Baussola's *L'Ideale Estetico del Trattato 'Della Famiglia' di Leon Battista Alberti* (Rapallo, 1956), and P. H. Michel, *La Pensée de Léon Battista Alberti*, (Paris, 1930). Whereas C.W. Westfall, 'Society, beauty and the humanist architect', in Alberti's *De re aedificatoria, Studies in the Renaissance*, vol. XVI, 1969, questions the real relations between his ideals and his practice.

Leonardo studies that I have found particularly helpful are: Pierre Duhem, *Etudes Sur Léonard de Vinci*, 3 vols. (Paris, 1906-1913). The following papers presented in, *Léonard de Vinci et l'Expérience Scientifique au Seizième Siécle*, Centre National de la Recherche Scientifique, Presses Universitaires de France (Paris, 1952), were extremely helpful: A. Chastel, 'Léonard et la Culture', P.H. Michel, 'Léonard de Vinci et le problème de la pluralité des mondes', R. Klibansky, 'Copernic et Nicolas de Cues', and R. Dugas, 'Léonard de Vinci dans l'histoire de la mécanique; also, K.D. Keele's book *Leonardo da Vinci: On movement of the Heart and Blood* (London, 1952). Martin Kemp in 'Il concetto dell'anima in Leonardo's early skull studies', *J. Warburg and Courtauld Institutes*, vol. XXXIV, 1971, makes a very important point about Leonardo's view of the relations between the senses and the mind. J.H.R. Randall jr. looks at Leonardo and his work from the point of view of the successful progress of science, in 'Leonardo da Vinci and the emergence of modern science', *The School of Padua and The Emergence of Modern Science* (Padua, 1951); whereas Karl Jaspers' essay in *Three Essays: Leonardo, Descartes, Max Weber*, tr. R. Mannheim (New York, 1964), presents a philosopher's portrait. Connections with Cusan type concepts and with Toscanelli and Pacioli are suggested in Giorgio de Santillana, 'Paolo Toscanelli and His Friends', *Reflections On Men and Ideas* (Cambridge, Mass., 1968); B. Rackusin, 'The Architectural Theory of Luca Pacioli, *De divina Proportione* chapter 54', Bibliothèque d'Humanisme et

Renaissance, tome Librairie Droz S.A. Geneva 1977; Giuseppe
Saitta, *Nicolo Cusano e l'Umanesimo Italiano* (Bologna, 1957); K.
Hujer, 'Astronomy of the Early Renaissance and Leonardo da
Vinci', *Leonardo nella Scienza e nella Technica* (Florence 1969).
Parallels between disciplines are explored in R.W. Lee, 'Ut
Pictura Poesis: The Humanistic Theory of Painting', *The Art
Bulletin*, vol. 22, 1940; and Per Palme, 'Ut Architectura Poesis',
Idea and Form, A. Bengtsson *et. al.*, Uppsala Studies in the
History of Art, New Series, (Uppsala, 1959); G.D. Mras 'Ut Pic-
tura Musica: A Study of Delacroix's Paragone', *Art Bulletin*, vol.
XLV, no.3 (Sept. 1963); M. Johnson, *Art and Scientific Thought*
(London, 1956); and R. Wittkower, *Architectural Principles in the
Age of Humanism*, (London, 1949).

E.H. Gombrich discusses the meanings attached to images in
'Icones Symbolicae: The Visual Image in Neo-Platonic
Thought,' *J. Warburg and Courtauld Institutes*, vol. II, 1948, while
Sir Anthony Blunt still provides a clear general introduction to
artistic theory in this period, *Artistic Theory in Italy 1450-1600*
(Oxford, 1962). 1st pub. 1940. P.O. Kristeller's 'The Modern
System of the Arts: A Study in the History of Aesthetics', *J.
Hist. of Ideas*, vols. 12, 13, 1951 and 1952, describes the origins
of the science of aesthetics. Some recent studies explore
models and the structure of analogies and examples of them
in Renaissance literature; these are S. K. Heninger jr.'s two
books, *Touches of Sweet harmony: Pythagorean Cosmology and
Renaissance Poetics*, (San Marino, Calif. 1974), and *The Cosmo-
graphical Glass* (San Marino, Calif. 1977); L. Barkan, *Nature's
Work of Art: The Human Body as Image of The World*, (New
Haven 1975).

Several works by Erwin Panofsky have influenced me in writing this essay. These are: *Idea*, (Columbia, South Carolina,
1968) tr. J. Peake; and *Galileo as a Critic of the Arts* (The Hague,
1954; *The Codex Huygens and Leonardo da Vinci's Art Theory*
(London, 1940); *Studies in Iconology: Humanistic Themes in the Art
of the Renaissance*, (New York, 1962); *Renaissance and Renascences
in Western Art*, (Stockholm, 1960), 'The History of the Theory of
Human Proportion as a Reflection of the History of Styles',
Meaning in The Visual Arts, (New York, 1957), 1st pub. 1955;
and 'Artist, Scientist, Genius: Notes On The Renaissance
Dämmerung', *The Renaissance* (New York, 1953).

Concepts of Space, Time and Nothing are treated in: Max
Jammer, *Concepts of Space*, (Cambridge, Mass. 1969); John White
The Birth and Rebirth of Pictorial Space (London, 1957); G. W.
Whitrow, *The Natural Philosophy of Time*, (London, 1961); P. J.
Zwart, *About Time* (Amsterdam and Oxford, 1976); and
Rosalie L. Colie, *Paradoxia Epidemica: The Renaissance Tradition
of Paradox*, (Princeton, N. J., 1966).

I have found D.P. Walker's 'Musical Humanism in the 16th and Early 17th Centuries', *Music Review* (Cambridge, 1941-2) invaluable. Other works to be singled out in this field are: E. Lowinsky's 'Music in the Culture of the Renaissance, *J. Hist. of Ideas*, vol. XV, 1954; and H. G. Koenigsberger, 'Music and Religion in Modern European History', *The Diversity of History*, ed. J.H. Elliott and H.G. Koenigsberger (London, 1970). On various aspects of the academies: A.J. George's 'The Genesis of the Académie des Sciences', *Annales des Sciences*, vol. 3, 1938; D.P. Walker, 'The Aim of Baïf's Académie de Poésie et de Musique,' *J. Ren. and Baroque Music* (Rome, 1946-7); and Frances Yates, *The French Academies of The Sixteenth Century* (London, 1947) were extremely valuable.

The literature on the philosophical background of the Renaissance, on Renaissance thought, and physical, medical, and mechanical traditions in the seventeenth century is so vast that to mention anything at all is only a drop in the bucket; still I have found the following works particularly useful: E. Cassirer, *The Individual and the Cosmos in Renaissance Philosophy* (New York, 1963), 1st. pub. 1927; E. Garin, *La Cultura Filosofica del Rinascimento Italiano* (Florence, 1961); and *Ritratti de Umanisti* (Florence, 1967). Also: A.O. Lovejoy, *The Great Chain of Being* (New York, 1960, 1st. pub 1936; and R. Klibansky, *The Continuity of the Platonic Tradition* (London, 1939); C. Trinkaus, *In Our Image and Likeness* (Chicago, 1970) and T.K. Seung, *Cultural Thematics: The Formation of the Faustian Ethos* (New Haven and London, 1976). Some leading works in history of science are A. Koyre, *Etudes Galiléennes* (Paris, 1939); Pierre Duhem, *To Save The Phenomena: An Essay on the Idea of Physical Theory from Plato to Galileo* (Chicago, 1969); C. Webster, *The Great Instauration: Science Medicine and Reform, 1626-1660* (London, 1975); In 'The Changing World of The Newtonian Industry', *J. Hist. of Ideas*, vol. XXXVII, 1976, R.S. Westfall appraises continuing Newtonian studies. Finally, R. McRae, *The Problem of The Unity of The Sciences: Bacon to Kant* (Toronto, 1961) amplifies the notion of universality.

INDEX